Shutting Down the Streets

Shutting Down the Streets

Political Violence and
Social Control in the Global Era

Amory Starr, Luis Fernandez,
and Christian Scholl

NEW YORK UNIVERSITY PRESS
New York and London

NEW YORK UNIVERSITY PRESS
New York and London
www.nyupress.org

References to Internet websites (URLs) were accurate at the time of writing.
Neither the author nor New York University Press is responsible for URLs
that may have expired or changed since the manuscript was prepared.

Library of Congress Cataloging-in-Publication Data

Starr, Amory, 1968–
Shutting down the streets : political violence and social control in the global era /
Amory Starr, Luis Fernandez, and Christian Scholl.
p. cm.
Includes bibliographical references and index.
ISBN 978–0–8147–4099–6 (cl : alk. paper)
ISBN 978–0–8147–4100–9 (pb : alk. paper)
ISBN 978–0–8147–0873–6 (ebook)
1. Social control. 2. Political violence. 3. Globalization—Political aspects.
4. Anti-globalization movement. I. Fernandez, Luis A., 1969–
II. Scholl, Christian, 1980– III. Title.
HM661.S83   2011
306.209'0511—dc23   2011017987

New York University Press books are printed on acid-free paper,
and their binding materials are chosen for strength and durability.
We strive to use environmentally responsible suppliers and materials
to the greatest extent possible in publishing our books.

Manufactured in the United States of America

c   10 9 8 7 6 5 4 3 2 1
p   10 9 8 7 6 5 4 3 2 1

To our wounds, and the creativity and courage it took
      to get them
To our healing, and those who protect the space for it
To the silence of fear, in compassion and combustion
To the global we have made
To the dream we demand with our eyes open
To another security
To affinity and trust and affection
To difference and dialogue, late into the night, and
      enough time for it
To the abundance that is ours.

Contents

1

What Is Going On?

We began writing this book as a wall was built in East Germany. Two and a half meters high, it was composed of metal fencing with concrete foundations and was designed to cradle a curlicue of razor and barbed wire. Each bolt and hinge of the wall was soldered in place. It looked like a fence around a prison or a military base, and, indeed, it sported motion detectors and video cameras. But this fence wound its twelve kilometers, at €1 million per kilometer, through forest surrounding a small seaport town. It protected the three-day meeting of the Group of Eight (G8), expected to issue its annual proclamations about intentions to "Make Poverty History," except in Africa, or to stop global warming. The fence (a "technical barrier") was employed to keep out terrorists and, coincidentally, those who had expressed their desire to participate in the meeting, point out its hypocrisy, or draw attention to the failures of similar economic strategies in their home countries, whether in Europe, Africa, or other regions of the postcolonial Global South. It was guarded by no fewer than eighteen thousand police, as well as contingents from the German military.

The fence imposed an exclusionary geography—castle, moat, hinterlands—on a purportedly democratic nation and landscape. This security was funded mostly by provincial taxes paid by German citizens, whose willingness for such public expenditure was, in turn, purchased with a currency the sociologist Barry Glassner has called "the culture of fear." Terrorists are over there, over here, around the corner. Immigrants are invading occupations and culture. The youth are increasingly and irrationally violent. The anxiety evoked by these probabilities somehow overwhelms the quieter world in which our jobs (or hopes of them) become increasingly "precarious."[1] Media images and public policy bring violent *persons* into sharp focus and offer grand, comforting solutions, while the glacial melt of our economies is portrayed as natural or at least inevitable, and surviving is left to our own cleverness.

This is the era of what we call "alterglobalization"—the multilingual term that refers to the diverse yet synchronous solidarity movements that not only oppose globalization in its current form but also propose alternatives, or *alter globalizations*, to it. Alterglobalization is yet another phase of the centuries-long struggle between imperial powers and their targets. In this era, much is old, and little is new. As during colonialism, global elites use military force, political institutions, culture and ideology, rearrangements of the social order, and economic trickery to grasp the resources, labor, and markets of the parts of the world with natural wealth and the productive parts of their home countries—the farms, the small shops, and, lately, the creativity of their digitized teenagers. As throughout the era of colonialism, the apparent damages and dehumanizations delivered by this process are justified, even celebrated, as long-term improvements in the lives of the victims. As with colonialism, resistance takes every possible form and then some.

But today the world is supposed to be a democratic one, with human rights. And the vast majority of people expect it to be so. Now colonial processes take place in a global social fabric in which the invisible ink connecting the points of violence, theft, and destruction is painstakingly revealed by a resilient network of scholars and activists. Under the fierce protection of a web of geeks and expert communities, widespread access to new communication technologies enables instant circulation of reports of suffering and struggle, often with pictures and video. Critical interpretation of events gets faster, and political parties are cast aside in favor of direct solidarity among movements and peoples of every social position. In other words, it is getting harder to hide massacres.

This book is about the social control of dissent in the contemporary era. Global, preemptive, and violent social control demarcates dissent as criminal. The charge is insurrection. The accused have no weapons. We must conclude that protesters are not the ones who are "out of order." Democracies are not supposed to criminalize dissent.

A number of scholars have studied the policing of protest and the interactions between police and protesters, defining models of interaction, and showing how they are changing historically. Our concerns are quite different. First, we see policing as just one tactic of a system of social control far more subtle, indirect, and significant than civil management of protest. Second, we do not limit our definition of dissent to protesters. We are concerned with a much larger group—those people who *would* dissent. And we shift the unit of analysis from individual (would-be) dissenters to the social movements that give life, sustenance, and strategy to dissent.

Because we are making a drastic and significant shift from the familiar territory of the *policing* of *protest* to the *social control* of *dissent*, the remainder of this introductory chapter provides a review of social control and dissent as they have been conceptualized and studied previously and outlines the conceptual and methodological bases of our study.

Understanding Social Control

There are two conceptions of social control. The first, running from Thomas Hobbes through George Herbert Mead to today's criminal justice literature, conceptualizes social control as a set of mechanisms intended to protect the health of society by enforcing (even eliciting) normative social behavior. The second, running from Karl Marx through Noam Chomsky, sees social control as a tool of class struggle, in which mechanisms ranging from the state's use of force to ideological reproduction are used to protect elite power. Both approaches recognize both formal and informal mechanisms, but Michel Foucault connected the two approaches and, further, showed how power is pervasive in control *and* resistance—even showing how those polarities interpenetrate.

Political theorists such as Thomas Hobbes, Jean-Jacques Rousseau, and John Locke grappled with how governments could rule (or control) their citizens while still protecting their "natural" rights and liberties as citizens. For Hobbes, social control meant the ability of the state to maintain stability so that society remains civilized (counterposed to what he viewed as a "brutal" state of nature). According to Morris Janowitz,[2] social control was a concept used by American sociologists to describe a "common endeavor"[3] aimed "toward an ideal."[4] As developed by the liberal discipline, social control came to be thought of as the means by which a humane society reduces coercion, eliminates misery, and increases rationality. It was originally considered to be antithetical neither to pluralism nor to social transformation. Indeed, social control was understood to be the outcome of evolving social organization. In the 1920s, social problems were understood as failures of social self-regulation (social control). During the 1930s, this perspective spread to Europe and influenced the philosopher Karl Mannheim to conceptualize freedom as the social control (via parliamentarianism) necessary to protect society from authoritarian rule threatened by social planning.[5]

What Janowitz calls an "alternate formulation of social control as a process of socialization leading to conformity" was proposed by social psychologists in the 1940s. By the 1960s, sociologists reimagined what was going on. Instead of being seen as a benign process, they suggested that social control was wielded by the nation-state to incorporate the "mass of the population" ("the periphery") into the society's central institutions and value systems. The mechanisms of social control? "Civility,"[6] "self-control," and "disciplined cultural appreciation"[7]—what Foucault calls "disciplinary power," internalized and reproduced by the objects of power. Janowitz concludes that force and coercion have been restricted to ever "narrower limits in relations both within and between industrial societies."[8] Meanwhile, as parliamentary participation declined, social inequality has divided the population into interest groups, and social movements have emerged as a method of shaping society. As elite political structures suffer crises of legitimacy, they are less able to dictate moral and social value systems. It is here that we see the shift to what Foucault calls "biopower." Rather than influencing social relations through values and morality, power operates in the realm of desire. Consent is "manufactured" not only through mass mediated ideology but also through the production of insecurity, distraction, and consumership.[9]

While scholars in various other subfields were understanding social control in new ways, the disciplinary field of social control itself shrunk to a narrow concern with management of deviance and crime. What Jack P. Gibbs describes as the functionalist approach of the 1960s continued to see conformity to consensual norms as delivering reciprocal social relations. The conflicting Marxist perspective recognized social control operating in a context of antagonistic inequity, viewing criminal law as a means of enforcement and reproduction of class relations. The Marxist perspective was perhaps a little overzealous, ignoring crimes like murder, which are usually punished even in noncapitalist societies, and laws such as traffic regulations, which benefit all classes (of automobile users, although still discriminating against bicyclists).

The functionalist emphasis on norms helps us see how social control is enacted in subtle and indirect ways by *all* members of society, not only elites—a revelation that would make Foucault in/famous. At the same time, some actors have more capacity than others for agency in shaping social control.[10] In 1977, Gibbs announced that social control studies had been "in the doldrums for several decades," and hence there was no clear definition of social control. In 1982, he rejected social control as a general, collective process and insisted that it must have actors. The "social" dimension of social control refers to that process through which parties manipulate others through "means other than a chain of command." As normative consensus declined, Gibbs expected social control to shift to law and to positive incentives. In 1989, he argued that control should be the central object of sociological investigation.[11] Simultaneously, Dorothy E. Chunn and Shelley A. M. Gavigan urged critical scholars to abandon the "liberal" and "instrumental" concept of social control "in favor of one attentive to the dynamic complexity of history, struggle, and change."[12]

Meanwhile, almost all U.S. social control literature hurtled down one trajectory, criminal deterrence. Robert F. Meier and Weldon T. Johnson defined deterrence as "concerned with a particular *source* (the legal sanction), a signal (a threat) and a target (violators)." After one rigorous test, they concluded that extralegal factors are as powerful in producing compliance as legal ones.[13] Other scholars have sharply criticized criminology for failing to take a broad, systems perspective on the function of law, imprisonment, social control, and criminology itself in the context of capitalist social relations.[14]

American sociology, devoted to the idea of a liberal/liberatory democratic state and still in the main exceptionally reluctant to acknowledge class struggle, fetters social control to deviance. Critical criminologists concerned with such matters as the discrepancy between law enforcement of working-class and capitalist-class crimes remain marginal in their attempt to bring attention to white-collar and corporate crime, let alone the larger issue of criminalization as a dimension of class relations and capitalism. In contrast, European-style political studies conceptualize social control as the maintenance of existing class relations through private property and force. The state participates, taking the side of capital. In P. A. J. Waddington's words:

Patrolling the boundaries of respectability—and thus reproducing patterns of domination and subordination, and inclusion and exclusion—is the exercise of largely invisible state power. Individual officers selectively exercise their discretion on the street under the guise of neutrally enforcing the law and keeping the peace. But the police "keep people in their place" in quite another, and much more visible, manner when they suppress overt dissent against prevailing social, political and economic conditions. Here the notion of the police as neutral and impartial enforcers of the law is exposed for the myth that it is; since their first duty becomes transparent—to protect the state, whose coercive arm they are. The exposure of the fundamental role of the police as custodians of the state's monopoly of legitimate coercion can be revelatory. . . . [P]olicing of public order exposes the tensions between state power on the one hand, and citizenship on the other.[15]

Nicos Ar Poulantzas rejects the simplistic assumption that the state is an instrument in the hand of capitalists, stressing the relative autonomy of state institutions. Regardless of its degree of autonomy, it is clear that today the state contributes to the smooth functioning of capitalism by reproducing its hegemony, defending its property rights, and eliciting consent of lower-class groups through strategic alliances.[16]

Social control can be understood as the central preoccupation of the Frankfurt School and other Marxists, who undertook a systematic analysis of the subtle ways that political consciousness and criticism are preempted through culture, ideology, and institutions.[17] In the United States, similar analysis has flourished in specialized fields, such as education and media studies. Both European and American scholars have developed an analysis of education as a social control strategy that reproduces social inequality.[18] More recently, American scholars have traced how media institutions function to "manufacture consent" and reproduce politically expedient "illusions."[19]

Forged by fascism's popularity in place of socialism and by socialist parties' own limitations, the sophisticated analysis of what came to be known as the Frankfurt School scholars was matched by social movements that expanded the terms of social struggle to "de-colonize the lifeworld."[20] While movements proliferated to challenge noneconomic aspects of oppression, new concepts of power and struggle theorized how the most subtle and internalized dynamics of social control could be resisted. Perhaps the leading example is queer theory, which proposed that individuals' gender performances could be subversive to the gender binary and heteronormativity.[21]

The Frankfurt School built a set of theories of what Erich Goode calls "informal" social control.[22] Foucault's typology of "technologies of control" is one of the most popular and sophisticated of these. In this theory, technologies of production aim at controlling, transforming, and manipulating objects and raw materials; technologies of sign systems involve the production of symbols and signification; technologies of power determine the conduct of individuals and of flows and submit them to certain ends or dominations; and technologies of the self are techniques that individuals use on themselves to modify their souls, thoughts, conduct, and way of being. According to Foucault, these four technologies hardly ever function separately. For Foucault, the interesting interactions are those between the technologies of power and those of the self, termed "governmentality." By this he means that government not only legislates and rules; it is also implicated in shaping, guiding, and affecting the conduct of people. Indeed, government constitutes people—and does so in such a way that they become governable. Foucault recognizes a distinct difference between a mode of social control that depends on the threat of death and a mode of social control that manages to produce a certain form of life.[23]

One aspect of governmentality is "disciplinary power." This concept grasps the exercise of control over the human body, specifically at the anatomical and biological levels. Disciplinary power can emanate from national policies (e.g., abortion policies, capital punishment). Technologies of power control by classifying and objectifying bodies, particularly in institutions like prisons, hospitals, and schools. The benefit of this form of social control, according to Foucault, is the reduced need for coercion or force. These technologies teach us to produce docile bodies (and subjects) ourselves; we internalize what it means to be a citizen in a democracy and then police our own behavior. Biopower, on the other hand, aims not only at controlling individual behavior but also at producing populations. Shifting its attention from the individual body to the flow of bodies and goods through time and space, it aims at reducing the probability of an undesired event. Foucault connects the emergence of biopower to the ability of the state to use statistical technologies to understand and study its citizenry. On the basis of these technologies, the state implements policies that produce a productive population to fit its economic agenda. Moreover, where coercive power uses a hierarchical relation of force or domination to achieve its ends, disciplinary power circulates through discourse and is internalized and exercised by the dominated, who also participate in its reproduction and recirculation horizontally through society.

Understanding social control means understanding how various forms of repression encourage and discourage the transformation of dissent into participation in social movements. But scholars concerned with the control of social movements have generally not positioned their studies in the context of social theory of social control. Instead, they have worked within the concepts provided by criminology and social movements. Charles Tilly defined repression as "any action by another group which raises the contender's cost of collective action."[24] Frances Fox Piven and Richard A. Cloward argue that protest is "structured" not only by repression but also by channeling, cooptation, and direct and indirect pressure on movements to assert institutional legitimacy and conform to behavioral decorum.[25] Waddington et al. propose a synthetic analysis of social movements and social control, conceptualized together as integrated, relational dynamics of "public disorder."[26] Pamela Oliver defines repression as "ways of reducing protest without giving people what they want" but recognizes that "anything which suppresses or disrupts . . . communication and social networks through which collective action could diffuse and people could organize . . . can repress protest."[27]

The bulk of literature on the repression of social movements has focused on the policing of protest, which is only one dimension of social control. (We review this particular literature alongside our analysis of policing in chapter 4.) Compounding this limitation, social movements literature has paid little attention to operationalizing and measuring impacts of social control on dissenters who have not yet entered the realm of collective action. An exception is John Wilson, who analyzes the social control interactions among government agents, protesters, and "observers or potential joiners" and asserts that police action has its most direct impact on the mobilization of potential joiners ("whether by marching or licking stamps"), noting that it may encourage as well as discourage them. His definition of social control emphasizes criminalization as a policy and discursive tactic:

> Social control is exerted in the face of an apparent norm infraction and aims at revenge, restitution and/or deterrence. In the context of protest action, social control is the process of labeling and treating dissenters as deviants. This process will be referred to as *criminalization . . .* a denial of the political status of acts and affirmation of their deviant character.[28]

Oliver's recent work provides another rare focus on the repression of *would-be* dissenters. Reviewing the outrageous criminalization of African American people over the past three decades, she argues that crime and dissent share the properties that they involve challenging the dominant social order and that they are subject to social control. Authorities decide which things to define as crimes, authorities decide how much effort to put into the control of the different kinds of crimes, and authorities decide what kinds of tactics and strategies to adopt in crime control. Authorities decide which kinds of dissent to criminalize and they also decide which categories of dissenters are most dangerous. . . . What to criminalize and whom to target are the crucial elements of a social control system. The minute we recognize that it is possible to target people who are dissenters for control, whether or not they commit specific illegal acts of dissent, we are ready to see that "crime control" and "dissent control" can never be disentangled.[29]

Oliver sees the significance of this recognition as a failure of the sub-disciplinary boundary-making of social movements scholarship:

Part of a theoretical and political agenda among social scientists in the late 1960s was to reject older treatments of social movements that lumped them together with other forms of "deviance." As part of the debates about the meaning of the Black riots, many social scientists argued that they needed to be understood not as mere criminality nor as mindless emotional expression, but as extreme expressions of political grievance. But along with these political concerns, a generation of sociologists was engaged in a sub-disciplinary movement to create and legitimate a specialty in the study of collective behavior and social movements. . . . The sharp distinction between political collective action and common crime that was important in the foundation of the sub-discipline was never revisited.[30]

Riots were included as constituents of social movement study, but no systematic analysis was lavished on other criminalized transgressions by oppressed groups in order to determine which ones should be treated as part of the study of social movements.

A striking 2004 book by David Cunningham documents that the "normal" intelligence activities of the FBI, before, during, and after the official COINTELPRO, or Counter Intelligence Program, of 1956–1972, which targeted mainly supporters of the Black Power movement, also amounted to a kind of *counterinsurgency*, a concept that has been strikingly absent from the literature on social control and social movements and one that we believe must be introduced to this discourse.[31] Counterinsurgency actions of the state identify social movements as direct threats to the existing political authority; as such, they are targeted for elimination through the use of force. Thus, advocates of Black Power were targeted, monitored, and arrested. But we need to ask what are the criteria for classifying dissenters as counterinsurgents in a democratic society?

From this review, we take several concepts that we will refer to throughout the book. First is the concern of Marxists, critical criminologists, and a few social movements scholars with the political motivations for criminalization. Second is the social theorists' attention to forms of control that are interiorized in "technologies of the self" to "manufacture consent." Third is the historical record of domestic policing as counterinsurgency.

Understanding Dissent

Ever since corporations claimed rights to free speech protections under the U.S. Constitution in the 1970s,[32] it has been difficult to get a word in edgewise. Since dissenters now include the embattled tobacco lobby, racists, and violent anti-abortion groups, much of the scholarly discourse on dissent has focused on its "social costs" and on interesting questions such as how it relates to legislation like that prohibiting hate crimes.[33] More dramatically, in these years of urgent "wars on terrorism," dissent is portrayed as a self-indulgent and treasonous risk to fellow citizens.

Thoroughly out of fashion, the idea that nonelites might deserve some say-so in their societies has been rebranded as something called "civil society."[34] "Civil society" is a strange term. One might take it to mean a society that is civil—inclusive, respectful. Instead, its recent usage is an odd euphemism for "the rest of us," those outside the circuits of decision making. Civil society is a pretrivialized agglomeration of those who seek, meekly, some consideration—never mind that these are the majority of global citizens. Note that civil society does not dare to dissent; it merely seeks a vague and nonthreatening "participation."

The right to dissent has degenerated into the last word of those condemned, if only by the unfortunate circumstances of impoverishment. But this is a dispirited definition. The legal scholar Cass Sunstein proposes that dissent ensures the flow of information that an organization or society needs to make sound analyses and decisions.[35] Dissent is protected in democracies because of the basic idea that the majoritarian, popular, or hegemonic view might be factually or morally wrong, dangerous, or unwise. Dissent needs to be a *valued* registration of discontent or disagreement within a political community or contract.

Under what conditions is discontent translated into dissent? William Gamson's 1968 *Power and Discontent* emphasized the importance of feelings of trust (in one's government), personal efficacy, and access to organizations that encourage opposition.[36] David Schwartz suggested that "salience"[37] is important, and Stephen Craig and Michael Maggiotto added "entitlement," which they operationalize as "a belief that democratic governments should be responsive to the demands of citizens generally," and "a high sense of internal efficacy" to the conditions that foster the expression of discontent.[38] Henry Giroux has argued that dissent depends on hope.[39] Dissent also relies on "discursive space," a complex and subtle concept that means that there is some realm of openness, flexibility, and visibility in which discussions and dissent can flourish. Sunstein argues that dissent is endangered not only by laws but by any conformity pressures.[40] Neoliberalism also undermines citizenship, attempting to replace it with much more entertaining consumership.[41] Possible dissenters, then, may be preemptively silenced by tactics that influence their sense of entitlement, efficacy, organizational networks, trust in government, sense of hopefulness, and space. Moreover, John Gaventa has pointed out that powerlessness (or the failure to dissent) must be analyzed directly and distinctly from the operation of power.[42]

Dissent is usually conceptualized as a speech act, a discrete event with an individual speaker, a space, and a speech. This concept is based in the legal articulation of the individual's right to free speech. But how did the speaker arrive at this moment of dissent? Was he alone? What were his fears and risks? How did he have the courage to be there? How did he learn about the topic to be discussed? How much time did he spend in meetings in advance of the speech? Who developed the plan and prepared the infrastructure for the event at which he spoke?

The archetypal image of an isolated act of political speech is both rare and distracting. Significant political speech almost always takes place in an institutional, social, and cultural context. Dissenting speech depends on a social network of resistance and/or an external environment that provides at least a little (just enough?) encouragement to create a sense of entitlement, salience, and efficacy. A more accurate image of dissent places the dissenter in the context of some kind of mobilization or manifestation. These noninstitutional forms of contentious interaction are protected by law as "assemblies" in the United States[43] and as "protest events" in Europe. Assemblies are organized by a legal entity known and protected as an "association." Archon Fung points out that every major democratic theory promotes associations as both enhancement and evidence of democratic society, although different kinds of associations, operating in different political contexts, exert influence in uneven (and sometimes unexpected) ways.[44] Recognizing the importance of networks of resistance to meaningful dissent, we believe that the unit of analysis for dissent must be collective. But associations, too, are manifestations arising from and depending on a larger network of meaning and solidarity—a social movement. We believe that social movements are the appropriate unit of analysis both for studying dissent and for defending it.

What, then, is a social movement? This turns out to be a difficult question, about which scholars do not agree.[45] For our purposes, some of the most basic points shall suffice. First, social movements are *contentious*.[46] This means that they are engaged in conflict (disagreeableness, at least) to advance their ideas for social change. Second, social movements are *collective*, participatory activities. Third, social movements are *processes* through which ideas and organizations evolve in a changing context.[47]

Much social movements scholarship seeks to explain *how* social movements do what they do. This work is important to this study because social control seeks to interrupt that "how," reducing (or reducing the impacts of) movement action. A minority of scholars have concerned themselves with *what* social movements do with and to their societies. This work is also important because it reveals what is at stake for elites in the contentious projects of social movements and might help us understand *why* expensive, illegal, or unusual social control is implemented. It also reveals the larger social costs of social control, which delays or deprives society of social movements' insights and challenges.

The first approach to social movements, *in an effort to make sense of collective behavior* (at first concerned with crowds and panics in the context of American exceptionalism) *and to predict its impacts*, has focused on individual participants' motivations and on movement mechanics:

* Why do people participate in movements? The histories, motivations, and psychology of activists who dare to take part in social movements are understood as the matter of *political consciousness*.[48]
* How do social movements mobilize *resources* effectively (or ineffectively) to win their struggles? Resources include bank accounts, meeting rooms, underemployeds unfilled hours, abandoned buildings, satellite time, paint, celebrities, and organizations[49] with tax-free status or staff.[50]
* When and where do social movements act? Social movements operate in a political context that may provide more or less physical, discursive, and social space, manipulable signs and symbols, historical irony, compassion or information overload, shifting power relations between elites, or moments when the authorities are looking the other way. This context, with all of its various contents, is called the *political opportunity structure*.[51]
* How do social movements communicate with the larger society? They must conceptualize what they are about, simply and effectively *framing* their problem or project for public campaigns.[52]

The second approach, forged by scholars who recognize class struggle, sees social movements "as carriers of political projects." Thus there is more concern with the *content* of social movements, their "themes and logics."[53]

* Social movements' ideologies are their beliefs, including their analyses of social problems and futuristic visions. Ideologies enable participants to have an empowered understanding of the problems they are facing, to envision a different future, and to invest in a vector of struggle. Much more than a frame, ideologies' "systems of meaning" are "learned" through social structures and social networks.[54] A movement's ideology takes a position in a historic struggle and dialogue about society.
* Refracting the impacts of modernity and urbanization on the self, experience, culture, and social life, social movements may give rise to new social "interests"[55]—identities[56] and ideas, "themes and

logics,"[57] cultures of resistance,[58] and networks.[59] They may also rely upon afflictions of modernity, such as charismatic leadership, professionalization, and bureaucracy.[60]

✦ In the past few decades, this approach has identified an increasing focus on individual subjectivities,[61] including bodies[62] and emotions[63] as sites of resistance and politics.

The diagram in Figure 1 contextualizes our use of the concept of dissent. Dissent (and its social movement/s) develops into collective and public contestations through a series of zones of political involvement. Each zone provides an increase of intimacy, intensity, and resources (organizations, networks, culture, and social space). Dissent is a large and diffuse arena of contemplation, talk, and action. Although it may take many forms, from furtively writing graffiti to placing oneself as a human shield, *resistance* is dissent that involves some kind of transgressive action. When that action becomes collective (when it has, as Alberto Melucci proposes, established a "we")[64] and acquires some process, it has become a *social movement*. As social movements become organized, they learn how to sustain contentious action, launch campaigns, and/or assemble networks. *Protest*, the focus of most social movement analysis, is that subset of dissent in which it becomes public and visible. Protest may emerge as part of contentious campaigns and projects or spontaneously and independently. Protest events are nurtured by "submerged"[65] resources, cultures of resistance and networks that imbue and sustain perceptions of entitlement, outrage, and possibility. In both cases, protests should be seen as the most public, visible, yet rare manifestation of a continuum of social phenomena of dissent, many of which exist in often invisible "structures of abeyance."[66]

Our point is that an exclusive focus on protest is static and decontextualized. Understanding (and protecting) protest requires attention to its development and sustenance. Most significantly, we believe that protest cannot be protected without protecting social movements, which are ever-changing networks of discursive spaces and disruptions, not always coherent organizations and ideological polarities.[67] Among other things, this means that there are many opportunities to interrupt and redirect them. At the same time, movements' network forms are in some ways more robust than hierarchical ones and may have more elastic responses to control.

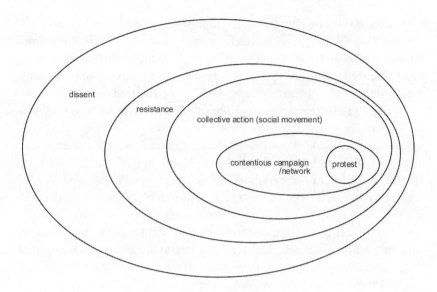

Dissent in the Era of Alterglobalization

What is alterglobalization, and what is special about its social movements? Alterglobalization is old. It is a continuation of cross-class anticolonial struggles, incensed by cultural and economic invasion. It reignites socialist revolutionary re-imaging of power. It draws on the best of labor movements' increasing solidarity and their threat of large-scale, perhaps international, simultaneous disruption. Alterglobalization is new, if only as a matter of degree, in the extent to which the battle is transnational, involving networks and tactics that operate in global space;[68] discursive, competing for hegemony over economic concepts and possibilities;[69] and creatively unruly, persistently breaking the "routine" of ignorable dissent and protest.[70]

It may also have novel kind of activist. Michael Hardt and Antonio Negri, looking to find a population that can challenge postmodern capitalism, find "the multitude," replacing concepts like "the people" or the "proletariat," which rely on a centralized conception of power and distinct classes. "The multitude . . . is legion; it is composed of innumerable elements that remain different, one from the other, and yet communicate, collaborate, and act in common."[71] What is "common" arises not out of some unifying material situation but instead out of the information society, which shapes subjectivities that recognize both singularity and collaboration.

Action within the alterglobalization movement is inspired by two traditions. One of them is characterized by the concept of "civil disobedience." As early as 1552, Étienne de la Boétie elaborated the importance of disobedience by demonstrating how ruling is based on consent and why consenting means ultimately being obedient.[72] The tradition of civil disobedience was further influenced by Thoreau in 1849, when he refused to pay taxes because that would mean supporting slavery and the U.S. war against México.[73] It was developed into a strategy by activist theorists, including Mohandas Karamchand Gandhi and Martin Luther King Jr. Civil disobedience is based on the refusal to obey a law seen by dissenters as illegitimate. It amounts to an intentional trespassing of the law, without, however, questioning the general legitimacy of sovereign politics. In fact, being arrested or prosecuted for the trespassing is often an integral part of civil disobedience. In this way, activists can show that they were consciously violating a law because of a particular injustice and not because they challenge the system as such.

Stemming from radical syndicalist struggles at the end of the nineteenth century (especially in France and the United States), "direct action" intends to prevent the implementation of undesired policies and to create autonomous social structures. Voltairine de Cleyre's 1912 account of direct action methods describes autonomous political action that rejects representation and mediation.[74] Direct action is employed by people who want to act on their own terms to resolve a situation. In this respect, direct-action forms are interconnected with the Do-It-Yourself (DIY) concept popular in the alterglobalization movements.[75] As a general cultural form, DIY refuses mediation by representatives or anointed officials. Instead, people organize themselves autonomously to produce and exchange. They authorize themselves and encourage others to do likewise.[76] Tilly and Tarrow view direct action tactics as premodern action forms that have vanished from the "modern repertoire."[77] Their conclusion is based on the common assumption that collective action within a nation-state is inevitably mediated and aims to create change only by influencing governmental practices.

During the 1990s, however, Europe witnessed a notable emergence and circulation of direct action tactics by environmental, animal-rights, and antiglobalization activists who revived the experience of the direct-action campaigns of the antinuclear and antimilitaristic movements of the 1970s.[78] Since the Seattle 1999 World Trade Organization (WTO) Ministerial, at which participating nations' intention to negotiate global

trade agreements for the new millennium was frustrated by street blockades, the repertoire of direct action has been a hallmark of the alterglobalization movement.[79] (See Appendix B for a discussion of the "violence"
of which the alterglobalization movement is sometimes accused.) Why
this shift to premodern action repertoires? Civil disobedience and direct-
action tactics point to a different mode of practicing resistance, one that
relies on the necessity of disruption.

Both civil disobedience and direct action contain an important tension
between legitimacy and legality. From the point of view of those engaged
in civil disobedience, when a law is experienced as illegitimate, illegal
actions to combat it are considered to be legitimate. In the tradition of
direct action, laws are seen as part of a regime that is itself illegitimate
insofar as it prevents people from organizing autonomously. Both civil
disobedience and direct action, therefore, accept illegal forms of acting,
seeing them as legitimate, even necessary, methods of expressing dissent
effectively. This is significant because, as Max Weber notes, the legal-
rational form of rule relies heavily on the perceived inherent legitimacy of
the formal rules themselves, backed up by the state's monopoly on the use
of force.[80]

What is also central to both traditions is the use of the body for challenging power structures and bringing about social change. This is not a
new concept; the Greek philosophy of sovereignty included the body.[81]
James Scott's history of resistance emphasizes the use of masquerade to
increase the power of the body.[82] Franz Fanon understood decolonization
as requiring the experience of bringing one's whole being to the point of
violence against the colonizer.[83] Hardt and Negri argue that alterglobalization insurrections have a peculiar dimension of embodiment, echoing
Foucault's theory of biopower (the production of "docile" bodies and ways
of living daily life).[84] Many forms of action visible in alterglobalization
mobilizations use the body as a political weapon.

The civil disobedience tradition and some forms of the direct-action
tradition recognize the importance of disruption to effective dissent.
Disruption functions as a costly intervention to the enactment of illegitimate laws and to the reproduction of the current scenario and its hegemonic norms. Piven and Cloward conclude that social movements win
only when, by using disruption, they raise the costs of an elite project to a
point at which it becomes in the interests of elites to obey dissenters.[85]

Most forms of protest rely on the notion of representation. People
complain about what their representatives are doing or not doing and

ask them to change their policies, or they try to build power to get their own representatives included in the decision-making structure. Disruption goes further, challenging the project of representation that is at the heart of liberal democracies. In fact, those taking disruptive action see representation itself as part of the problem, since it robs people of direct control over their social environment and contributes to the pacification of conflicts. Acts of disruption spurn appeal to or dependence on a third party, a representative, to take on the demands and find solutions. Rather, they constitute a direct and autonomous collective entrance into and grasp of the institutionalized political sphere. The methods of civil disobedience or direct action/disruption attempt to prevent policies from being implemented. In the alterglobalization movement, what is disrupted is the flow of official discourse that legitimizes new policies.

From this review of the literatures relevant to dissent, we will use several key concepts throughout the book. The first is that dissent is a process and that it has collective dimensions. Second, dissent depends for its development and articulation on a series of different kinds of social spaces. Melucci best describes the needs of these social spaces for secure experimentation. Third, dissent in the era of alterglobalization is direct and personal. It is carried out by activists, not by representatives. Thus, we need to be concerned with how social control affects the capacities of would-be dissenters to participate bodily. Fourth, effective dissent requires access to disruptive possibilities.

Methods

This book is based on multimethod research by three sociologists during the period 1999–2009. We have performed participant observation research at a collective total of twenty international protests in North America and Europe, beginning with the WTO meetings in Seattle in 1999 and including the NATO protests in Strasbourg, France, in 2009. (See Appendix A for a complete list.) In addition, the authors have performed participant observation at a collective total of more than fifty domestic events, often relevant to the international movement. Two of the authors conducted a research project that examined the effects of surveillance on activists in the United States.[86] Each author has conducted several interview-based studies on related aspects of social control, on which we draw. We analyzed relevant policy and legal documents to capture the shifting control tactics of authorities. Finally, in preparing this volume, we examined relevant archival material on alterglobalization, the antiwar/peace movement, and other current movements.

For reasons discussed earlier, our unit of analysis is the social movement (including its resources, spaces, cultures, and identities). We approach our analysis of social control of dissent by considering its impacts on the formation of social movements, not individual dissenters.

An important point to understand about our methods is why, if we seek to understand the social control of dissent—not just protest—most broadly, we take as our sampling frame protests of summit meetings. First, let us point out that each episode of summit-centered social control encloses not only the multiday protest itself, but activities that begin months or even years prior to the days of action and continue for years afterward. Summit meetings are laboratories for examining how institutions act to reduce the risk of undesired discourse. But this still doesn't explain why these events are a particularly important or valuable source of data. We believe that summits are especially useful because they are a snapshot of an entire social movement and its diverse participants and activities. These diverse participants and their experiences with social control are extraordinarily well documented throughout the event, before, during, and after. We can study the effects of social control on diverse groups for which the effect of that control on operations throughout the year would not normally be documented. Moreover, the activities of more pacific sectors of these social movements do not ordinarily conflict with the police, nor are they generally saturated with journalists asking about their satisfaction with the expression of their political rights. For consistency and brevity we refer to the summits using the following style: City Year Organization, for example Seattle 1999 WTO.

We have studied social control with our own bodies. This method produces a richness of detail that complements aggregate data. Wherever in this book you find data reported without a citation to another author's work, they are from our primary data. In addition, throughout the text you will find excerpts from our field notes. These are in italics.

Toward a New Framework for Studying the Social Control of Dissent

Contemporary empirical research on the social control of social movements, which is focused on policing of protest, reduces social movements to "protesters"; any impacts on the broader group of dissenters are left unstudied. A more thorough approach requires awareness of the developmental dimensions of social movements and their various forms and levels of participation. Different kinds of social control affect developmental sites and stages in the life of a social movement. This book proposes a framework for examining both the tactics and the effects of social control. We identify three sites of study: the geography of control, the political economy of control, and violence.

We begin with the crystallized image of dissent today—the fence. In an era in which ideological hegemony is a serious front in a purportedly democratic world, the struggle for legitimacy is serious and brittle. In 1998, alterglobalization movements reconceptualized protest marches. They proposed that the marches take as a goal entering the meetings or, if dissenters are not allowed in, blockading them. This was a brilliant addition to the existing repertoire of dissenting public speech and birthed a whole repertoire of technologies for blockading—educational fora, conferences, human chains, unarmed but armored citizens, and public art.[87] Protesters' lumbering and diverse physical assaults on global-governance meetings have been met with increasing expenditures on police and a remapping of the social space around each meeting of the International Monetary Fund, the World Bank, the WTO, the G8, and each free trade agreement negotiation. Geographic intervention has made visible and palpable the collaboration among states, corporations, and institutions that is behind economic globalization. The summer meetings have become a fragile symbol of its contested hegemony. Stronger walls are built to intimidate would-be dissenters, yet the strength of the walls indicates clearly the loss of legitimacy of the institutions huddled inside. This is obvious to every newspaper columnist.

Chapter 2 advances a systematic approach for the analysis of the governance of space. After introducing central concepts for the study of spatial interactions, drawing on recent innovations in social geography, political theory, and philosophy, we advance a systematic approach for the analysis of the governance of space. The control of the flow of bodies and the incapacitation of movement are revealed as the central objectives of the governance of space. Various tools are available for the spatial control of dissent: the selection of the location and the remapping of the spatial surrounding; tools for dividing space; tools for controlling movement; and tools for separating protesters from one another. We highlight the preemptive character of control which deflects, redirects, and interrupts assembly and the transnationalization of tools for governing space.

A public contemptuous of dissent and dissenters is easily made fearful of them and is willing to pay for "protection" (although whether security expenditures indeed protect citizenship is questionable). Chapter 3 examines the political economy of social control. We follow the traces of dramatic civil repression in the national economies, as well as in the state institutions of social control. Over the past decade, the cost of policing transnational protest has skyrocketed. Preparing for a summit, local and national law enforcement engage in extensive planning, training, and construction projects. Security for each protest costs governments millions, placing a contentious burden on the city or region hosting the meeting.

The operations of police are diverse and complex. They include the definition of the maintenance of vigilance over, and the prosecution of, crimes, the militarization of events and interactions, and even public relations activities with the media. All of these activities refer to the violent entitlements of the police and prison system. In chapter 4, we inventory these tactics. In chapter 5, we analyze the interrelationships among activist bodies, dissenting minds, social spaces that nurture dissent, and policing. We find that police tactics are in effect mass and individual psychological operations, serving to marginalize, isolate, delegitimize, and demonize dissenters and dissent. We argue that these effects ought to be considered political violence. Historical studies of totalitarian regimes' use of terror to maintain social control document the social fact that physical violence (disappearance, assassination, torture) directed against some individuals has a social control effect, as it uses terror to influence other individuals' minds and psychology, and to affect the social fabric of associational activity (suppressing dissent). This social fact has been analytically applied only to totalitarian societies and has not been conceptualized as part of a continuum, with applications in democratic societies. As a result, police tactics in democratic societies have not been considered in the multiplicity of their effects (on bodies, minds, and social space) or in their indirect effects on persons other than the immediate victims of policing, surveillance, and similar behaviors. We begin this consideration.

Much of what is known about social control at the moment was first tracked through activists' own work to protect and defend themselves. Methods range from legal collectives that work to teach people their rights and help people with criminal charges, to art projects intended to draw attention to surveillance, to creative ways of interacting with fences, to media projects focused on these issues. In chapter 6, we draw on this work for further insights into the social control of dissent.

Our concluding chapter does not recapitulate the book but instead goes beyond the analysis in the chapters to offer further theoretical proposals. In Appendix C, we provide ideas for future relevant research.

We do believe—and, as activists, we know—that hegemony is a struggle.[88] Although this book is focused on the mechanisms of social control in the Global North, we write it suffused with the struggles of the Global South and surrounded by tactics and interpretations of our wins, however momentary, partial, and insecure.

The Geography of Global Governance

Spatial Dynamics of Controlling Dissent

Standing on a balcony above the sixth floor I am trying not to look suspicious. The road down there is empty, although it is still early, about 10 p.m. Only a small group of men are standing at the crossroad. I am sure they are undercover cops. I try not to look in their direction, although it is hard to find something else worthwhile to look at. We are only a few meters away from the red zone. Tomorrow, the official celebration of NATO's sixtieth anniversary will take place. After a few years without major summits being held in cities, NATO decided to hold its anniversary in Strasbourg. Instead of the usual perimeter fences, dissenters were confronted with a "flexible security zone concept": zones in three colors indicating security status which could be readjusted at any moment. As usual, the red zone covering most of Strasbourg's historical center would remain a prohibited area. Since only a few bridges offer access to the center of Strasbourg from the protest camp at the outskirts, protesters reckoned that all the bridges would be cordoned by police from the early morning hours onward. Therefore, several groups had arranged sleeping places at houses in the centre. Retreating from the balcony, I entered a living room where about twenty persons tried to make themselves comfortable for a short night next to drums, costumes, and backpacks. At 5 a.m. we would get up to hit the road at 5:45 and be at the meeting place at 6 a.m. We hoped to be able to cross a few streets without being noticed. Given the instruments and the pink and silver dresses we would wear, not the most realistic plan. And we hoped others would make it as well.

(April 2009)

In 1975, few people took notice when the G8 (at the time it was only the G6) first met to promote economic stability and expansion in member countries. Even fewer people saw the meeting as problematic or worthy of protest. Global summit meetings went virtually unnoticed for several years, until movements in the Global South (especially in Latin America) confronted the International Monetary Fund (IMF) and the World Bank.[1] In the early 1980s, "food riots" (sometimes called "IMF riots") emerged in many developing countries, and Global South scholars and activists developed a critical analysis of the role of these institutions in the continued dependent development of the postcolonial world.[2] In 1985, a G8 meeting attracted its first mass protest; twenty thousand people took to the streets of Bonn, accompanied by ten thousand policemen. At the time, these European protests were so unthreatening that the then U.S. president, Ronald Reagan, traveled with only two personal bodyguards. Fourteen years later, in 1999, Bill Clinton visited a much more fortified city of Cologne. However, he was still able to sneak out of the meetings to have a beer and a steak in a local bar. Eight years after Clinton's visit, in June 2007, the G8 meeting was held in a tiny and isolated village in northeast Germany. This time, the geography of the hosting town was transformed into a mobile fortress, including a twelve-mile-long fence costing approximately €12 million. In addition, the national authorities declared a concentric three kilometer wide "no-protest zone" around the fenced area. This was reinforced with eighteen thousand police officers stationed in the region, along with three thousand army soldiers, two U.S. Marine boats, and several "observation" tanks.

This chapter focuses on the spatial transformations that occur around global governance. To understand these spatial dynamics, we draw on the discipline of geography. Henri Lefebvre argues that space is always political and ideological. Space is not something fixed, given, or even obvious. Rather, it is produced through social relationships and intricately connected to social stratification.[3] David Harvey takes this insight further, examining the role of space in social arrangements in late capitalist societies. Like other locations of social production (e.g., factories, schools), the rearrangement of space can produce conflict between different social groups.[4] Social conflicts have a spatial dimension; there is constant interaction and struggle between competing forces seeking to define and control use of space. Edward Soja makes a similar claim, suggesting that injustice and space are inseparable.[5] That is, the reproduction of class differences involves spatial configuration and arrangements. As a result, this spatial arrangement can develop into contentious politics that help uncover the dialectic of control and resistance.[6] Charles Tilly argues that spatial relations are important for a contextual perspective on processes of contention, since space, like political opportunities, constitutes and structures social relationships and networks.[7]

The social dynamics of space, however, also have a temporal dimension. Doreen Massey even proposes a break from the analytical dualism between time and space; in her perspective, they are necessarily intertwined. Therefore, she introduces the concept "tetradimensionality of space," constituted through its verticality, horizontality, deepness, and temporality.[8] This is an important concept for analyzing the production of legitimacy and the social control of dissent through the manipulation of space, since it means that the control of time is also a spatial practice. For example, summits not only are held in remote locations but also are timed to occur during the work week, limiting the mobilization of workers and students, who would need several days' holiday to express their dissent.

Space, Legitimacy, and the Contestation of Global Governance

In order to make clear why space became such a central aspect of the social control of global dissent, we first want to explain how dissent takes a spatial form in challenging global governance. The first important note is that manifestations of dissent do not just use physical space but also engage social relations.

International meetings of the World Trade Organization (WTO), the International Monetary Fund (IMF), the World Bank, the G8 and G20, the European Union (EU), the Free Trade Area of the Americas (FTAA), and the World Economic Forum have become crystallization points of global power relations.[9] However, these meetings are certainly not the only possible crystallization points for global conflicts. That they are now widely perceived in this way, as sites where hegemonic power structures can be revealed, is a result of activists' choice to *confront* summit meetings and to do so *spatially* (as opposed to doing so through media discourse, popular education, or other means).

In 1999, something happened that fundamentally changed the struggle around the legitimacy of global governance. On November 30, tens of thousands of dissenters blocked intersections around the convention center in Seattle that was the site of the WTO ministerial. What was later referred to as "the Battle of Seattle" was the coming-out party of the (Northern) alterglobalization movement. While protest outside meetings and ministerials had occurred in other parts of the world in previous years, this one managed to produce a global broadcast of resonant grievances against globalization. When the WTO meeting had to be suspended because few delegates could reach the convention center, this protest unmasked global governance and did so primarily through the disruption of space. The protesters in Seattle reappropriated the public functions of space and used space to question the very foundation and legitimacy of global governance.

The spaces surrounding summits are normally ordinary multiuse spaces of the city. While not all of this space is legally "public," a large part of it is generally accessible and used anonymously and freely, even as surveillance technologies are already encroaching on that reality. Urban space is not only a space of rights but also an infrastructure of commerce and a fabric of social life of the city. During summits, this space is abruptly and severely changed, curtailed, militarized, and made impenetrable. This affects not only the free and semianonymous use of the space for dissent but also the formal and informal exchanges and circulations of the city. The normal spatial functions of the social geography of the hosting area are suspended, affecting not only participants and dissenters of the meetings but also ordinary citizens and activities.

Lefebvre makes a threefold distinction that helps to explain the relations between dissent and space: perceived space, conceived space, and lived space. *Perceived space* (or spatial practice) relates to the social (re) production of space in daily life. *Conceived space* concerns the (dominant) representations of space, for example a map, related to the production of discourses and meaning. *Lived space*, finally, is the product of the interaction of the first two categories. It is in lived space that dissent makes its engagement, establishing space on its own terms (sometimes called "counter spaces" or "space of resistance"). As summits attempted to use the conceived space of world cities as a proper setting for their authority, social movements usurped the summits' entitlement by disrupting the normal reproduction of flows in those spaces. Movements violated the flow of traffic and commerce, replacing normalized hegemony with unfamiliar uses such as the presence of puppets, dancing in the streets, and surprising punctures of the purportedly inviolable boundaries of institutions such as banks. Attempting to reassert control, summits asserted special maps over the city, maps that asserted their need for "security" while purporting to "respect" democracy by demarcating special space for it. Again, movements refused to participate in this reproduction and flooded the map with creative contradictions of boundaries, transforming the summits' conceived space into a network of spaces of resistance.

Since the first mass protests during the 1980s, the G8 countries have needed to show that their talks are a legitimate part of "responsible governance." As dissent intensifies each year, the G8 countries have to prove ever more convincingly that they take seriously the concerns of the protesters and that they are working on solutions to global problems, such as poverty, AIDS, climate change, and poor countries' debts. The embrace of these social problems by the G8 is a diversion from the economic and financial concerns that originally dominated its gatherings. Of course, the social agenda resulted primarily from the demands that civil society and social movements placed on the organizations. For these meetings to appear legitimate and beneficial for the entire globe, the G8 countries must keep one eye on their own economic objectives and another on seemingly humanitarian endeavors. Without this balance, the group risks losing its legitimacy to direct global development. This balancing act worked relatively well until 1999.

The visibility of social conflicts has to do with the capacity of social movements to appropriate spaces of hegemonic production of visibility. John Agnew calls this the "global visualization of space."[10] Beginning with Seattle 1999 WTO, protesters ensured that global meetings would always be connected to imagery of mass protests in the streets, including blockades, tear gas, skirmishes, and police violence. This tactic was so effective that these global institutions were left with a serious dilemma: how to simultaneously defend the legitimacy of their agenda and their own legitimate place as part of democratic societies. That is, global institutions have to control challenges to their legitimacy and at the same time tolerate protest in order to appear to meet the basic ideals of liberal democracy. Governing forces, then, need to allow protesters access to the streets. We argue that, to solve this dilemma, global institutions use space as one of the primary locations for control. In order for global meetings to continue, these institutions have to simultaneously repress dissent and appear open and democratic. Severe repression could reinforce protesters' claims that the WTO, the IMF, the World Bank, the G8, and other institutions are undemocratic and harmful. Yet, welcoming the very protests that have proved so effective at disrupting meetings puts at risk the institutions' appearance of authority.

The G8 does not constitute an official institution with any kind of central office or commission. The group started as an informal meeting of the leaders of the six (now eight) most prosperous industrialized countries. Its ambitions for influence and visibility require it increasingly to follow the rules of legitimacy. Each year, meetings are prepared, hosted, and chaired by one of the eight countries, placing a certain logic and restriction on the choice of location. Wherever the meeting is held, the place becomes a space for contesting global power relations. The G8 members cannot admit that they would be better off meeting in an undemocratic nonmember nation (such as Qatar, where the WTO met in 2001) or returning to the remote mountains of Canada each year (the G8 met in Kananaskis in 2002). This spatial decision would mean losing the struggle for legitimacy. No, every year the meeting has to take place in one of the member countries. Since it is clear that the members do not dare to meet in a major city anymore and since there is no really remote countryside available in Europe (at least not remote enough to prevent thousands of activists from gathering nearby and blocking the summit), the G8 is confronted with a challenge.

The geographical moves of the G8 summits mirror the struggle over the legitimacy of the G8 itself and of global governance in general. It tells us how the struggle over legitimacy is organized spatially. And it shows how global governance needs to manifest itself geographically. Despite the immense effort and cost involved in securing those meetings, despite the media attention paid to the protesters' arguments, whether sympathetic or dismissive, and despite the fact that the summit meetings are unnecessary for achieving practical results for the countries involved, not having summit meetings is not an option. For the G8 countries, it would be equivalent to admitting that their meetings and policies are not legitimate.

This weakness of global governance institutions (the geography of legitimacy) is rarely mentioned in either the literature on globalization, or debates about the possible decline of the nation-state, or commentary on summit protests. These analyses tend to focus on the way protesters can *influence* the content of global governance rather than to the vulnerabilities of global governance.

So it seems that a very practical and seemingly effective way to confront global governance institutions is to leave them no space for actually manifesting their legitimacy. The streets of Seattle, Genoa, Calgary, or a little island in Italy become contested spaces of global governance. For the authorities, in turn, one question has become crucial: how can police govern space more effectively?

The remainder of this chapter explores empirically how dissent is spatially controlled to produce legitimate global governance. We identify four mechanisms of control: deciding on locations, dividing the space, imposing regulatory controls on individuals, and militarizing the chosen location. These four mechanisms cover the spatial operations before and during summit protests. As we examine these mechanisms, we do not suggest that they are about the total suppression of dissent. Instead, we propose to think of each mechanism as a way of *channeling* confrontations into predictable, and thereby controllable, flows of people, ideas, and events.

Selecting a Location

The selection of a summit location is an important aspect of the geography of global governance and mirrors the contestation of global power relations. This tactic first became apparent shortly after Genoa 2001 G8. The Canadian prime minister announced that next G8 summit would take place in a small mountain resort, Kananaskis. This was also the case when the European Union Ministerial Council decided to stick with Brussels as a permanent meeting place instead of rotating the meetings to the presiding member country. At the same time, neither the WTO nor the IMF nor the World Bank has held a major gathering in Europe since 2000, instead holding meetings either in the United States (where protest has become less robust in the aftermath of 9/11, 2001) or in places difficult for protesters to access, such as Qatar or Hong Kong. However, moving summit meetings from cities in favor of remote, rural, authoritarian, or island sites is just one of the rather broad spatial considerations reviewed by the authorities when selecting a location for a summit.

Already at Genoa 2001 G8, the delegations were hosted not in a royal building in the city center but on a boat in the port. The authorities justified this location by referring to the contested presence of President George W. Bush, whose security they would not be able to guarantee in the city center. While there are no reasons to doubt this official account, one should keep in mind that alterglobalization movements around the world had by this point demonstrated both the capacity to come very close to the meeting sites of summits and a total lack of interest in endangering heads of state. The careful selection of locations within cities thus can be related to the alterglobalization movement's ability to pose a visible challenge to and to have a disruptive effect on summit meetings themselves and the spatial flows involved in their organization.

The attempts of authorities to avoid disruption through careful choice of venue can be understood as a struggle to define and control territory. Deleuze and Guattari[11] introduce the concepts of deterritorialization and reterritorialization to explain the mechanisms behind the opening and the closure of a political field. Whereas states try to control territory through rigid segmentarity, social movements challenge these rigid boundaries by favoring connectivity. Deleuze and Guattari call these rigid segmentation "striated spaces" and the deterritorialized areas with open and decentralized connections "smooth spaces."

The networked and decentralized character of alterglobalization movements[12] provides a good example of the challenge of territorial boundaries and hierarchies. The alterglobalization movement has spirited representative opponents through borders to form a loud encircling apparition, conjuring a dispersed global movement all in one place. Suddenly peasant Korean farmers were beating drums in downtown Seattle. The territory of hegemony has been permeated; as Deleuze and Guattari put it, "the enemy's territory has been shattered from within"[13]—and would continue to be, no matter how it sought to isolate itself. The "striated space" of global governance has had to face the "smooth space" of global solidarity and cooperation.

Moreover, the action repertoire of blockading explicitly aims at disrupting the material flows necessary for a smooth summit meeting. The extensive spatial preparations, then, can be seen as a way to reterritorialize social control through segmentation of space into functional units. The selection of the location is a first step in this. In order to avoid disruption through decentralized blockades, authorities choose sites that are difficult to access and easy to protect.

After Seattle 1999, the next WTO Ministerial was Qatar 2001. A Muslim nation ruled by a monarchical family established in the mid-1800s, Qatar has a constitutional ban on mass demonstrations and open dissent. Thus, protest was preemptively limited through selection of a country both far from the networks of organized protest and totally hostile to protest itself. Protesters created other political territories for confrontation, such as blockading European airports to prevent delegations from leaving their countries for the Ministerial. In this way, they deterritorialized the spaces of a summit meeting of the WTO, which had tried to reterritorial-ize it—at least for one Ministerial—in isolation from any possible dissent.

While the selection of Qatar for the 2001 Ministerial produced the desired effect of reducing disruption, it also validated claims that the WTO was undemocratic and illegitimate. As stated previously, these global institutions need to balance two kinds of legitimacy. While they need to ensure undisrupted meetings, they also require that populations across the globe view them as legitimate forms of governance. If the insti-tutions are viewed as undemocratic, their claims to beneficent authority over the global regulation of markets are weakened. The decision to hide in Qatar was another strike against the WTO's by-then shaky credibility as a democratic institution.

Two years after the Qatar meeting, the WTO met in Cancún, México. While presenting a more open national climate than Qatar, the loca-tion presented significant obstacles for protesters. Unlike in Seattle, there is little history of political organizing in Cancún, so there were few local resources for mobilization. Cancún is also relatively isolated, reached only after days of road travel for Mexican protesters and expensive air travel for those living outside the country. Finally, it offered a geographically easy place to defend. The Cancún hotel zone is a narrow strip of land thirty-one kilometers long, with water on both sides, connected to the mainland by two bridges, one at each end. During the protest dates, the local authori-ties closed down the bridge nearest to the city, requiring dissidents to travel thirty-three kilometers if they wanted to protest close to the WTO meeting location. In addition, police established a series of security checkpoints on roads leading to the open bridge. Vehicles were inspected, and suspected activists were denied entry to the entire hotel zone.

Besides the political history of the locality and the ease of physically isolating the meeting location, the symbolic dimension of the locality also played an important role. The area around Cancún is supposed to be one of the beneficiaries of the free trade regime, delivered, in this case, by NAFTA. During the WTO meeting, the Mexican government sought to showcase its modernity and development, including advances in civil liberties since the infamous slaughter of university students in 1968. The isolation of the event, partly by the use of high fences, and the restrained police, who mostly stayed behind the fences, were intended to reinforce the perception of a well-organized state that tolerates dissent. To put it in Lefebvre's terms, the Mexican government was engaged in the reproduc-tion of conceived space, seeking to reify México as modern state.

We witnessed a masked group of people entering a Pizza Hut and demolishing it. Shortly after, the riot police showed up and surrounded the building but did not attack the protesters. Later, we learned that the Mexican government had given the order to police the event lightly, since officials wished to present México as a developing democracy. México was busy reterritorializing its own political image, so it left international franchises unprotected from anticorporate activists.

Without appearing to enact political closure, the state accomplished a nearly complete spatial closure of the summit's venue. By using the fence to separate weary police from energetic and lively protesters, the Mexican state nearly avoided a militarized image. (Two battleships stationed off-shore did not go unnoticed.)

In contrast, a few years earlier, at Québec City 2001 FTAA (Free Trade Area of the Americas), the Canadian authorities could not afford the luxury of geographical distance to keep protesters away from the Summit of the Americas meeting. Canada immediately lost its claim that it was hosting a democratic event when it erected a perimeter fence around the meeting, dividing the city.[14] The fence was promptly dubbed "Canada's wall of shame" by protesters, press, and the local population. Once the protests began, the not very strong fence was quickly breached by protesters. The police then spent days bombarding approaching protesters (and neighborhood residents) with tear gas, concussion grenades, and rubber bullets, losing any hope of presenting a democratic narrative and instead producing an image of lumbering soldiers defending a stone citadel from the rabble. Conveniently, the location of the battle in Québec was strategic on a symbolic level because the region already has an image of militant conflict. Images of police and protesters hurling tear gas back and forth at each over a fence over several days could be dismissed as ordinary regional culture but also as un-Canadian.

One year after the protest in Québec City, Canada hosted the 2002 G8 meeting. This time, the gathering was in Kananaskis, an isolated mountain resort. To ensure that the meeting would be held in isolation, the government territorialized a security area of radius of 6.5 kilometers, restricting travel along the nearest highway and establishing a no-fly zone with a radius of 148 kilometers; it also deterritorialized the organization of the wilderness by closing camping facilities in the area.[15] The rural location and the large perimeters made it difficult for protesters to organize a mass presence. The isolation was so successful that protesters were unable to get within viewing distance of the world leaders' meeting site.

Instead, activists had to territorialize Calgary, some 112 kilometers from the meeting, as the political location.

A similar tactic was employed for Georgia 2004 G8. The leaders of the eight most developed nations gathered at a resort on Sea Island, located ninety-six kilometers south of Savannah, Georgia. The location was selected for its seclusion, which facilitated the tight security measures. No protesters were allowed on the island, and even journalists were confined to Savannah.

Another criterion for selection becomes clear when we examine Gleneagles 2005 G8 and Heiligendamm 2007 G8. For both of these summits, police publicly admitted that they were looking not only for a remote location difficult to reach from major cities but also for an area where the population was not likely to be very supportive of the alterglobalization movements' activities. This admission is an important one, implying not only that police investigated the local political scene and population but also that they studied the sociopolitical history of that area. In the case of Gleneagles 2005 G8, officials noted that Scotland has fewer activist structures and a weaker tradition of summit protest than England. The hotel in Gleneagles is situated in a hilly area and is difficult to reach, being accessed by one highway and a few roads that pass through small towns. The nearest protest camp could be located only on the other side of a hill, about twenty-four kilometers from the summit's venue.

Heiligendamm 2007 G8 offered a chance to the German chancellor, Angela Merkel, to present to the world the region where she grew up. The little sea resort of Heiligendamm is situated in the poorest region of the former East Germany. At the same time, the seashore location was geographically desirable because police forces had to secure the meetings from only three sides and always had a backup route for getting delegates in and out by using the sea for transport (which they finally had to do, because activists blockaded all the land roads).

The luxury sea resort hotel chosen as the summit's venue stands in sharp contrast to the poverty and high unemployment of that region. Like Cancún and Gleneagles, this region offered to summit organizers the benefit of having very few left-wing activist structures and a history and a substantial presence of right-wing and fascist groups. For movement activists, this required putting a lot of energy into establishing contacts with the local population and creating the infrastructure that would be necessary for the week of protest. For a moment, it looked as if the symbolic dimension could be reterritorialized by activists when they presented the fact that the avenue leading to the conference hotel had once been declared the most beautiful parkway in Germany by Adolf Hitler, who was also still mentioned as citizen of honor in the register of a nearby town. These historical details were picked up by the world press and initiated a little scandal about German history and the political symbolism of the summit's venue.

We have seen that isolated social geography is as important as physical isolation. While Genoa is close to many Italian cities and even close to other countries, Heiligendamm was quite far from any major metropolis in Germany and fairly distant from other Western European countries. Gleneagles was far enough away from the two major Scottish cities of Edinburgh and Glasgow to dampen protests. This is the conceptual map of Europe that is now used for ensuring summit security. Officials planning Cancún 2003 WTO, Kananaskis 2002 G8, and Georgia 2004 G8 followed this pattern. From the perspective of governing space, the distance from cities is beneficial for controlling and restricting arrivals of activists from elsewhere, for minimizing access to activist infrastructure and sympathy, and for reducing the possibilities of and targets for disruptive actions at places near the summit.

In sum, geographical selection of secluded places for summit meetings can set the stage for controlling space. Selecting the right location can, from the outset, subdue the level of protest, making it more difficult for activists to travel, gather, organize, and disrupt the meetings. Over the past few years, there has been an increasing trend toward holding summit meetings at isolated, easily defensible locations. In this way, summit planners have politically deterritorialized the political space of oppositional political cultures and institutions that are active and networked in major cities and territorialized politically naïve or at least disorganized areas, taking advantage of their very different political territory. Summit meetings have more and more become striated spaces that easily defy the challenges of smooth spaces of global resistance from below.

Dividing Space

After the alterglobalization movement's success in challenging the space of global governance through the penetration of summit meetings, the authorities' tactics for controlling movement can be best understood as an attempt to reterritorialize dissent into striated and anticipated spaces. Deleuze and Guattari's analysis of how dominant power structures rely on a tactic of closing off spaces that have been opened through decentralized organized processes of deterritorialization can be very helpful for understanding the functioning of the tools for controlling movement. The tactics of controlling movement reveal how authorities focus on the regulation of flows. They try to disrupt the capacity of decentralized movements by reterritorializing their flows before and during protest events. The central objective here is the channeling of dissent into preestablished zones and the incapacitation of spontaneity.

Once a location is selected, authorities start to reorganize the surrounding area by rating spaces on a "danger scale." This process has the explicit intent of channeling dissent into preestablished zones, far away from the actual gatherings, in order to secure the operational flows involved in a summit meeting and to control dangerous objects identified beforehand. This process is primarily about space. That is, it is about the temporary reorganization of Lefebvre's "conceived space." It involves changing the social relations that exist within a specific city or location from a "normal" stratification of daily life to a new social existence where users of the city are divided into new categories (e.g., dissenter, local businessperson, summit personnel). Thus, the division of space involves the transformation of the locale before a protest occurs.

Again, it should be clear how important the time preceding the actual summit has become for the governance of space. While control over space is still an important part of the actual policing during protest events (as will be discussed in the next section of this chapter), authorities attempt to prestructure the space in such a way that disruptions of the summit meetings become unlikely, if not impossible.

The general logic of the operations involved in controlling space by dividing it can be captured clearly from the framework provided by Foucault. The techniques of enclosure, segmentation, subdivision of function-related units, and ranking, which Foucault describes as part of the emergence of a new type of social control taking place in hospitals, jails, and schools, are used in a similar way for the governance of public space around summits. Foucault's ideas are instructive in examining this process. Specifically, his notion of disciplinary diagrams helps to explain how space is divided for the purpose of control. In his inquiry into the control mechanism deployed against the plague, for example, Foucault showed how disciplinary diagrams emerged that required the strict division and careful supervision of space, reinforced by inspection and maintenance of order.[16] These basic ideas of containment are also used to control protest.

The most sensitive and highly controlled zone is the "red zone," marked by ever-longer fences, a no-go area (meaning that no one can go in without displaying credentials that grant access, which are sometimes issued to residents whose homes are within the defined area). The fence at Québec City 2001 FTAA was 2.5 kilometers long, while the fence at Heiligendamm 2007 G8 stretched 12.5 kilometers. Also, the construction of the fence has been steadily improved and is standardized according to the security handbooks of transnational police agencies. Fences are higher and more massive, with cement foundations, and are often equipped with movement detectors and surveillance cameras. These no-go areas prevent dissenters from actually articulating their protest at the place where global governance decisions are made. In urban areas, walls composed of shipping containers are assembled during the days preceding the summit meetings in order to protect certain objects, to enforce the no-go areas, or to channel protest marches.

Preparatory spatial arrangements do not stop here, however. Already at Genoa 2001 G8, the red zone was surrounded by a yellow zone. For Québec City 2001 FTAA, protest groups even negotiated with police to establish several green zones, where protesters could gather—impotently far from the red zone and purportedly safe from police action. These zones were ultimately breached not only by tear gas floating in from the saturated yellow zones but also by police combat teams. At Heiligendamm 2007 G8, the red zone was inside the fence, and a three-kilometer-wide concentric zone surrounded it. In this zone, protest and assemblies were banned by a "general directive" issued a few weeks before the summit. Dissenters who entered this yellow zone, despite not having trespassed a fence and although they were still quite far from the meeting itself, could be prosecuted for committing a criminal act. The sea and air space were subdivided into high- and low-security zones, as well.

At Strasbourg 2009 NATO, the three cities involved in the summit—Strasbourg, Kehl, and Baden-Baden—were organized into leveled security zones. The cities of Strasbourg, Kehl, and Baden-Baden, which hosted the NATO summit, were subdivided according to a three-level security-zone concept, in which the borders of the "flexible security zones" could be adapted to meet emerging police requirements. The highest security zone could be accessed only by local inhabitants; the next zone could be accessed but was a no-protest zone. In the third zone, registered protests were permitted, but there were constant identity controls. In addition, the German police manipulated the protest preparations spatially by not allowing for any protest camp on the German side. Protesters coming for several days thus had to get to the protest camp on the French side, with no chance to participate in the protest events on the German side because of the intensifying border controls. The border crossing was further complicated by the temporary reintroduction of border controls between EU member states, a suspension of the Schengen agreement. This suspension has become a habitual practice since Genoa 2001 G8.

While the spatial divisions for controlling space discussed so far are all of a preemptive type, other tools are employed *during* protests in order to maintain spatial control. These tools vary with national or local police culture and include: police strategy, mobile blockades, and the reduction of anonymous and safe space.

Police strategy. For Heiligendamm 2007 G8, the federal criminal investigation police were responsible for securing the space within the fence, while the national police forces were responsible for the no-protest zone outside the fence. The region around the no-protest zone was subdivided into areas secured by designated police units from various states. The major highways leading to the biggest city nearby, as well as big train stations and airports, were secured by the federal police and the army. In preparation for Miami 2003 FTAA, law enforcement divided downtown Miami into relatively small surveillance grids to monitor marches and protesters. Each grid contained undercover officers who reported to the Operations Center via radio. With their information, law enforcement was able to track the movement of "spontaneous direct actions."[17] In addition, the U.S. Federal Bureau of Investigation provided a live video feed to the Operations Center to further monitor protesters.

Mobile blockades. In addition to using semipermanent blockades made of fences and containers, police mobilize flexible barricades composed of rows of police vehicles (e.g., cars, motorcycles). These are used to define, seal, and change routes of marches and protests; prevent moving groups from meeting one another (or from arriving at the designated starting point); blocking, delaying, and directing dispersal; and protecting vulnerable access points unprotected by other means. While police vehicles are used in all countries, Genoa 2001 G8 is one of the best examples of this tactic. The militarized police forces called *carabinieri* used their cars not only to block roads and to encircle demonstrators but also to disperse them with a tactic called "carousel," whereby a police vehicle drives fast in a circle in an area occupied by protesters.

Another tool available to authorities is the bodies of police officers. Police use their bodies to separate and divide space so that protesters remain isolated either from other protesters or from the public. This is accomplished in several ways. For example, police isolate and separate snake marches. This style of march, avoiding predetermined marching routes, "snakes" around in and out of streets spontaneously, a tactical maneuver that make traditional policing more difficult and the disruption of traffic more likely. In response, police sometimes use large numbers of officers to surround the entire march, thus defining two territories that can be reshaped on the move: inside the protest space and outside. The inside space contains protesters, who are now isolated within this space. The space outside remains relatively undisturbed, but the public remains separated from protesters. In effect, this division of space prevents protesters from mingling with the public and prevents individuals in the public spontaneously joining in the march. It also prevents protesters from departing the protest to stop for food or to go to the bathroom.

In Germany and the United Kingdom, this tactic is called "Kessel" (kettle). Several lines of police officers corral dissenters or an entire demonstration. While for demonstrations this normally means that the march is accompanied by lines of police, with smaller groups it normally means that the march is stopped for several hours until everyone is identified, checked, or even arrested. When police used this tactic during a big demonstration in Hamburg just a few days before Heiligendamm 2007 G8, the organizers of the demonstration aborted the march. Totally enclosed by several lines of police for hours, the demonstration was both invisible (because of its immobility) and very unattractive (because of its appearance of criminality). After the demonstration was aborted, several hours of confrontations between dispersed dissenters and police forces ensued. In another form of separation, police prevent two marches from joining up. At Miami 2003 FTAA, small "feeder marches" were prevented from joining the main march.

Police use similar tactics to ensure their control of permitted marches. At New York City 2002 WEF (World Economic Forum), police surrounded and isolated a large protest. Facing an estimated ten thousand marchers, the police had used the permit process to establish a route for the protesters. Knowing the protesters' route, the police used barricades, officers, bikes, and motorcycles to confine the march to a predetermined path. At one point, we observed what appeared to be the entire march contained between motorcycled officers on one side and a three-foot barricade stretching for many blocks on the other side. The police ensured that marchers remained on the established route. Ultimately, all ten thousand marchers were largely isolated from the public, again reproducing an inside and outside protest space.

At Gleneagles 2005 G8 British police units focused on containing protest events during the summit by strategically hindering the entrance to certain spaces and objects of protest by installing long lines of heavily equipped riot police. Dissenters who still insisted on making their way to the enclosed space were forced to find ways to break or circumvent the police lines, which rarely happened. At the opening demonstration of Gleneagles 2005 G8, hundreds of thousands of protesters in Edinburgh were channeled through the inner city, their mobility restricted for most of the route by metal fence constructions. Once started, there was simply no way to go other than following the flow of the masses in one direction. There were few opportunities to get out of the demonstration during the entire march. One protester commented that day that he "felt like a sheep being directed to the fields."

Knowing the endpoint of a permitted march, U.S. law enforcement often use a series of pens at the end of the march that can hold thousands of people. This method is most common in New York City, where police officers use metal barricades to mold the space. In some instances, police build several corrals, allowing only a specific number of individuals into each space. This allows them to break down a march of twenty thousand people (or more) into segments of two thousand or fewer. The Washington, D.C., police used the same tactic during 2002 IMF/WB (International Monetary Fund and World Bank). A fortified and barricaded space with hundreds of officers dressed in riot gear awaited the marchers at the final destination point. Once the march arrived at its end point, the timed permit for the route ended, and those outside the pen were urged to disperse. The pen then remained the only "protest space."

Reduction of anonymous and safe space. Both constant police observation and the use of cameras contribute to this strategy, which clearly reduces the feeling of activists that they can move freely and therefore lowers the probability of disruptive actions. Police habitually surveil spaces crucial for the infrastructure of dissenters, such as camps, Convergence Centers, and independent media centers. In addition, during marches themselves, dissenters are subjected to constant photo and video surveillance. Besides reducing the space where dissenters can move and assemble anonymously, this is also a tool for gathering evidence for possible legal prosecution after the summit. Anonymous space is reduced further by constant identity checks, which begin on the routes toward points of assembly. Police often control the assembly areas, allowing people to enter only if they show their identity cards. Entering into protest space, then, implies leaving behind privacy, anonymity, and security.

Another tactic for reducing anonymous and safe space is the sabotage of crucial activist infrastructure. Alterglobalization movements rely on a lean but sophisticated infrastructure of Convergence Centers, often operating a week or more before the protests start. This infrastructure includes independent media centers, legal support offices, camps, food kitchens, training centers, art workshops, and information points. It provides a context for flexible coordination of various political actions, a safe space for retreat and recovery, and opportunities for different modes of political participation. Authorities have acknowledged the strategic capacity of these infrastructural projects and often frustrate the creation of such places in advance by not cooperating in allowing legal ways to establish them. In one example, the German police forced individual property holders to contact the police before they could provide land to the camps Heiligendamm 2007 G8. During the protests, infrastructure is often raided or destroyed by the police. This happened at the Convergence Center at Prague 2000 IMF/WB, at the Hvitfeldtska School at Göteborg 2001 EU, and at the Independent Media Center in the Diaz School during Genoa 2001 G8. It occurred also at the Évian 2003 G8 Independent Media Center in a squat in Geneva. Targeting the working and sleeping places of dissenters, authorities can disrupt activists' preparation for action and restrict their capacity for (unexpected) movement. When their camp was surrounded during the night and a whole day at the Gleneagles 2005 G8, dissenters had to find a way to get out of the camp and approach the G8 meeting without being snatched by the police. Similarly, police forces surrounded camps of Heiligendamm 2007 G8 dissenters during the night.

Sabotaging protesters' safe spaces is complemented by counterposing sanctioned spaces to activist infrastructures. While protest camps, independent media centers, and Convergence Centers are frequently monitored and raided by police, the authorities happily facilitate the organization of countersummits consisting of discussions in large buildings, often far away from the summit site. This way, dissenters are channeled into the more easily manageable spaces of a countersummit rather than gathering at the spaces where disruptive actions are prepared. This clearly demonstrates that the tactical division of space aims not at avoiding protest but at channeling it into certain spaces that are easy to control. Global dissent is reterritorialized into striated and anticipated spaces.

Controlling Individuals' Movement

Zones, barricades, and encirclements, whether used preemptively or during a protest, are control mechanisms aimed at direct physical control of groups. Another approach to reterritorialization mobilizes policies and legal barriers to impede individuals' movements to express their dissent. A whole series of regulatory tools preempts the movements of the activist network: ban orders, travel bans for foreign activists, daily obligatory registration, preventive (mass) detention, imposed spatial restrictions for demonstrations and assemblies, and (the reintroduction of) border controls.

Ban orders are a legal instrument to restrict movement and to extend the spatial regime of no-go and no-protest zones. This instrument was widely employed at Gleneagles 2005 G8 and Heiligendamm 2007 G8. In Scotland, an extraordinary legal paragraph, Section 60 of the Criminal Justice and Public Order Act, originally intended to prevent minor football disturbances, was mobilized in order to enforce ban orders. It resulted in dissenters receiving ban orders during the protests in the days before the opening of the G8 meetings; the orders covered the entire region surrounding the summit's venue. Dissenters whom the police identified as being in this region after being "banned" were subject to being charged with criminal activity. Ban orders normally last until the day after the summit. German police banned certain activists who participated in actions in the region of the summit's venue, sometimes even months in advance. This way, the participation of targeted dissenters was incapacitated even before the actual summit protests started.

In order to frustrate the movement of foreign dissenters, authorities coordinate internationally to impose travel bans on activists who allegedly pose a risk. As early as Prague 2000 IMF/WB, a trainload of Italian activists was held at the border of the Czech Republic because authorities claimed to have identified among them persons who had participated in an international preparatory meeting some months before. For this reason, officials did not let the train enter the country. Before Genoa 2001 G8, Berlin's senator for internal affairs imposed a travel ban on at least sixteen activists because they posed a potential risk. This assessment was based on their legal records; one of the persons, for example, had been fined for graffiti painting. These dissenters had to register in person every day for a week at their local police department. During the week of protest in conjunction with Heiligendamm 2007 G8, 556 people were turned away at the German border. In some cases, the decision was based on additional information requested from authorities in the dissenter's country of origin; in other cases, simply carrying a black hoodie in one's luggage was deemed sufficient grounds for police to deny entry to Germany.

This points to another tool being reemployed by authorities: massive border controls. Internal border controls have been abolished by the Schengen agreement, implemented in 1995, but this agreement is temporarily suspended for summits in Europe. The Schengen agreement was suspended for Genoa 2001 G8 and Heiligendamm 2007 G8. (For Gleneagles 2005 G8, this step was not necessary since the United Kingdom is not part of the Schengen agreement.) The border controls during Genoa 2001 G8 and Heiligendamm 2007 G8 were massive. At the border to Italy, cars on the highways were supposed to line up in a special queue for foreigners heading toward Genoa. At the same time, the airport and two train stations in Genoa were shut down in order to restrict and contain the dissenters coming by train. In both cases, nearby ports were also heavily controlled. The Italian authorities turned away a ferry with 135 Greek dissenters at the port of Ancona.

Another measure for controlling people's movement is the imposition of conditions for demonstrations and assemblies. While Donatella della Porta and Herbert Reiter[18] stress the advantages of this aspect of a negotiated management approach of policing protest, they do not analyze the wider implications for the social control of dissent. In Germany, it is now common for authorities to determine in advance not only which route a demonstration is allowed to take but also where it will start and where it will end, how long and how high the banners may be, when the demonstration may start, and, sometimes, even how many people may participate. If demonstrators disagree with these imposed conditions, they may either perform an illegal action, go to court to assert their right to protest (which can take several months), or not do an action at all. The police, meanwhile, define the criteria that determine whether a demonstration or assembly is behaving "well" or "badly." If people are deviating from the preestablished route, or carrying excessively large banners, or jumping, or disguising their faces, the police now have a reason to intervene or even to dissolve the assembly. Assemblies that are "negotiated" and that stick to the imposed conditions are defined as "good," while assemblies that are spontaneous or that do not adhere to the "negotiated" rules are defined as "bad" or even "violent" and so criminalized. Criminalizing a demonstration allows police to invoke regulatory measures to outlaw, disperse, and assault dissenters.

A final preemptive tool available to authorities is detention. During Göteborg 2001 EU, the police surrounded the Hvitfeldtska School, a space that was legally granted to protesters for sleeping and coordinating activities, and arrested about four hundred people before the protests were to start. Mass arrest can also be used to incapacitate groups of dissenters during protests. Six hundred detentions or arrests were made at Seattle 1999 WTO; 859 at Prague 2000 IMF/WB; 1,115 at Göteborg 2001 EU; 310 at Genoa 2001 G8; 600 at Washington, D.C., 2002 IMF/WB; 700 at Gleneagles 2005 G8; 1,140 at Heiligendamm 2007 G8; nearly 2,000 at Copenhagen 2009 UN Climate Conference;[19] and 1,000 at Toronto 2010 G20 (the largest mass arrest in the history of Canada).[20]

Distinct from mass arrest, snatch squads may intervene at any moment to grab an individual, often with force. Sometimes these are individuals who have been surveilled and selected in advance, and other times they are chosen spontaneously.

Authorities use preemptive exclusion of foreign and veteran activists to reduce the likelihood of creative, uncontrolled activist reterritorialization (disruption) of the summit. On a symbolic level, it also deprives local activists of the encouraging experience of international solidarity.

Militarization

One of the most immediately striking visions of summit meetings is the militarization of the space surrounding the event. It is not hyperbole to say that the space becomes a war zone, with officers dressed in sophisticated military gear and accompanied by armored vehicles. The closer to the actual meeting location, the more militarized the space becomes.

Over the past couple of decades, the policing of protest has witnessed an increase in the use of both military tactics and military equipment. The growth and normalization of police paramilitarism is well documented in the criminology literature.[21] Peter Kraska and other scholars have clearly demonstrated that the line between police and military institutions is becoming less distinct.[22] As a result, it is now increasingly difficult to distinguish between war and law enforcement. For evidence on the militarization and militarism present in U.S. policing, Kraska points to the spread of SWAT teams trained in military tactics and armed with assault rifles and armored vehicles. Originally designed for hostage rescue or for engaging heavily armed criminals, SWAT teams are now used in less dangerous situations, such as raids on houses of accused drug dealers.

The militarization of policing that began in the 1970s continues to impact the policing of protest today, sometimes with devastating consequences. The "less-than-lethal weapons" used in policing protest (such as bean bags, pepper bullets, and acoustic weapons) were used first by militaries for "peacekeeping" purposes and then diffused into police departments. An example of the flow of technology from the military to the police is the recent use of sound cannons. Sound cannons (technically called Long-Range Acoustic Devices, or LRADs) are weapons that emit high-frequency sounds intended to stun and paralyze humans. They were first developed by the U.S. Navy to prevent ships from getting too close to each other. This technology crossed the military/police boundary in the United States for the first time during Pittsburgh 2009 G20. Subsequently, Canada threatened to use it during Toronto 2010 G20. In addition to alterglobalization protests, police also threatened to use the technology in Oakland, California, after a contentious trial involving the police murder of a young man in the local train system. All this supports Kraska's claim about the blurring of police and military.[23]

Mainstream journalists use the phrase "war zone" to describe the militarization they witness in the days before the start of an event, often noting that the setting does not look like a space for a peaceful global gathering but rather like a city preparing for civil war. Each such observation threatens the legitimacy of global governance. Rural areas provide the option of avoiding these images, because the military reorganization of space, while present, is less dense, striking, and photogenic. The erection of the fence around Heiligendamm 2007 G8 revealed its dramatic intrusion in a rural and forest context, but few journalists took photos. Moreover, militarization of a seemingly generic rural area shocks fewer residents and does not have the same charge as the disruption of a familiar urban (often touristic) site used regularly by millions of citizens.

Summit security zones are depopulated of their usual users (businesses and organizations are often required to close) and repopulated by an overwhelming number of police and military officers in combat gear:

5,000 at New York City 2002 WEF; 5,000 at Kananaskis 2003 G8; more than 3,000 at Miami 2003 FTAA; and more than 20,000 at Heiligendamm 2007 G8 (18,000 police officers and 2,500 army soldiers).

The use of actual military units further blurs the line between law enforcement and the military. Several thousand soldiers of the Swiss army were employed for Évian 2003 G8 (Évian is in France but is close to Switzerland). Heiligendamm 2007 G8 involved the largest military operation at a summit in Europe, triggering a public debate in Germany. Officially, the involvement of the army in internal security operations is constitutionally prohibited. However, the German authorities framed these operations as legally permitted "administrative assistance" in case of an emergency situation. During security preparations the German army was involved in the construction of an emergency road and several observation flights with Tornado airplanes. The highway from the airport to the summit venue was overseen by observation tanks of the army, a Tornado overflew a protest camp at a height of only eighty meters, and military personnel were posted at a civil hospital in Bad Doberan. Canadian Forces fighter jets also patrolled a no-fly zone over the Kananaskis 2002 G8 security zone.

While the preparation of a militarized war zone for a summit often takes several weeks, if not months, the reconversion into a "normal" state of affairs goes much quicker. Often, a few hours after the official summit ends and the delegates leave town, police and military have also left the city. Fences and barriers are removed, graffiti are cleaned, protest posters are removed, and broken windows are repaired. Global governance meetings impose a geography, changing the city, and then leave. For those who participated in protest marches a few days before, it looks as if the protests had never taken place, as if nothing had happened. Activists who walk through those streets can still see the action as if superimposed on a landscape surreal in its demilitarized quiet. It suddenly is possible for anyone again to walk freely through the streets without being observed, checked, or arbitrarily arrested. In some ways, the protest has been erased, made meaningless. In another way, the city is forever changed, because the image and the possibility of its militarization are burned into the minds of every witness. Even years after a protest, it can be surprising to find access points open and unguarded. This is the "ghostly remainder"[24]—or reminder—of global governance.

Yet, this demilitarization is only partial. The reality for the local population is that the space is forever altered, because some of the security apparatus is left in place. While the most obvious fences do come down, what remains behind are the security cameras, the equipment that police purchased, and the police mentality resulting from the hours that officers spent training to control crowds. While the local population may not know it, this same apparatus will likely be turned against them if they mobilize for better wages or cleaner air or to protest police brutality.

> *In Cancún, only one day later, we found ourselves walking "freely" but in disbelief over the bridge at km 0 where we were held, rudely, nine kilometers away from the opportunity to express our dissent to the Ministerial itself. Not only was the militarization gone; also gone was the huge shrine to the farmer Lee Kyung, who had died in the protest. It had seemed permanent when we gathered there last night. These disappearances themselves felt violent and dishonest. We felt deceived to be allowed to travel across that bridge, because such freedom denied the ghosts of the fence and the soldiers, the decision to revoke our freedom and to silence our dissenting presence. The bridge was no longer just a bridge. The bridge reeked of the possibility of restriction. That space now contained a series of questions: "is it open now?," "Will it be open later?," "Is there another way to get there, or not?," "Will they let us pass?"*

After a summit, the location is no longer a space for questioning global governance. How precious, although also terrifying, that time seems, when the shadow that is economic globalization affixes itself to a building and can be pointed to and screamed at. A few men meet in a room surrounded by armies, brutally uninterested in the voices outside, revealed for what they are. But as their summit recedes from physical space, it becomes ethereal, and its haunted witnesses speak of an otherworldly military visitation, unbelievable in their "free" city. The summit leaves scars on the psyches of the witnesses, but we cannot point to it any more. The time of protest/war is erased from the spatial memory and does not even survive as historical episode. The only time protesters were able to reclaim a summit place as a contested site of global governance came in November 2007, when severe sentences were announced against activists resulting from the protests at Genoa 2001 G8. About sixty thousand people rallied there, with the slogan "We are history."

Channeling Dissent

The networked and decentralized character of alterglobalization movements contributes to a deterritorialization of global governance. Summit protests open a space for global conflict by making it difficult for existing political institutions to govern. Spatial tactics of protesters exemplify the process of deterritorialization. Direct actions during summit protests rely on a decentralized model, giving various groups a chance to apply their favored tactics in a certain place, while at the same time profiting from the cumulative effects through the temporal simultaneity (and distribution) of these decentralized actions. Such a mode of resistance coincides with what Deleuze and Guattari have called deterritorialization. Summit authorities work to reterritorialize social conflicts in order to make dissent manageable. They attempt to regain control over space through location decisions, division of the space, regulatory controls imposed on individuals, and militarization.

As we have demonstrated in this chapter, global governance is bound to its manifestation in space. Dissenters from all over the world gather at IMF, WTO, and G8 meetings to express their concern about corporate globalization, while simultaneously attempting to undermine the legitimacy of global governance by blockading and disrupting the flows of summit meetings. To regain and maintain control, police have developed a set of spatial strategies, choosing geographically defensible and socially isolated locations, dividing space, controlling individuals movements, and, militarizing the space. All of these actions affect the legitimacy of global governance, so that its spatial practice make it both visible and vulnerable.

Examining these mechanisms together, we see that the spatial control of globalized dissent is increasingly organized in a preemptive way. The social control mechanisms do not aim so much at only protest avoidance; they seek to channel protest into preestablished spaces and predictable flows in order to foreclose the potential for disruption of the summit space. Whereas the disruptive capacity of movements is incapacitated preemptively by eliminating anonymous space for unpredictable actions, entire cities or rural regions are manipulated spatially in order to guarantee a smooth functioning of the flows (of people and material) involved in a summit meeting, while holding protesters at a distance.

Foucault describes such mechanisms of spatial division as a form of social control. He shows how "modern" institutions such as jails, schools, and hospitals rely on a similar refinement of the techniques of enclosure, segmentation, subdivision of function-related units, and ranking. Control over activities is gained through the techniques of a daily schedule, the temporal construction of actions, the coordination between body and action, and the instrumental codification of the body, which ultimately leads to the maximum possible exploitation of the body. These mechanisms, according to Foucault, organize complex spaces that not only fix movement but also allow for circulation.[25] That is, power organizes the flow and circulation of bodies and products. Control, then, is not only about restriction but, importantly, about channeling flows in more convenient directions. Effective protest engages public discourse by directing itself to authorities and fellow citizens. It is most effective when it disrupts official flows. It requires mobility, movement, and flow in order to achieve these tasks. Spatial controls transform protest flows into ordered, contained, restricted channels more convenient and less disruptive to the summits.

The spatial control of dissent focuses on the avoidance of what Foucault has called "an undesired event."[26] By precluding the possibility of disruption, authorities ensure the flows involved in a summit meeting. Foucault points out how the avoidance of an "undesired event" hinges on making the flows of goods and people predictable. Gilham and Noakes argue that police strategically incapacitate the movement of some protesters, while allowing others to move freely. This "strategic incapacitation" is generally aimed at those protesters whom law enforcement deems dangerous or views as potential problems; their movement is then temporally incapacitated.[27] Our study, however, demonstrates that the incapacitation of movements" in order to avoid undesired and unpredicted events, does not happen—or does not happen primarily—*during* protests. Police and authorities have developed an entire arsenal of techniques to organize the contested spaces for the manifestation of global governance and to incapacitate spaces of resistance preemptively. Dissent is spatially relocated and preempted long before people gather in the streets.

However, let us not forget that the spatial dimension of control remains inextricably linked to the symbolic dimension of governance, and therefore to its contested struggle for hegemony. The farmers of Heiligendamm may have been right-wing, but when their fences were mistaken for the summit's, they did not blame the activists. Spatial controls particularly perturb residents who are divided from their accustomed flows and occupied by their own militaries.

3

Toward a Political Economy of the Social Control of Dissent

In the light of the remarks of the French President, can the Minister reassure the House that good Scottish food will be served at the Gleneagles Summit?
—British Lord Wallace of Saltaire[1]

Over the past thirty years, an industry has developed around securing global ministerial and summit meetings, such as the G8, G20, World Trade Organization (WTO), International Monetary Fund (IMF), and World Economic Forum (WEF) sessions. As the meetings became increasingly contentious through the 1980s and 1990s, the responsibility for "securing" the summits became more important for the states to hosting the gatherings. As a result, greater funding was allocated for security, leading to a large infusion of monies to local law enforcement agencies. Some of this money is spent on overtime salaries, extra personnel (including private police),[2] city services such as transportation and waste management, and federal services, such as special deployments of military and border agencies.[3] Some of the money is invested in new technologies, which are left behind with local police agencies long after the event. This arsenal of new technologies and weapons includes new surveillance technologies (such as aerial surveillance and fixed street cameras),[4] "less-than-lethal" weapons" (such as beanbag shotguns and acoustic weapons),[5] and the latest riot gear.

This chapter examines the political economy of the social control of dissent. By political economy we mean the politics of mobilizing and using resources. To that end, this chapter provides a preliminary analysis of security costs of summits. Such analysis can aid in revealing the power dynamics of the social control of dissent.

This is a preliminary analysis for several reasons. First, there is almost no previous scholarship examining these expenditures.[6] While some attempts have been made to examine G8 and G20 costs by a research group at the University of Toronto,[7] no similar attempts exist regarding other organizations, such as the WTO, the IMF, and the WEF. Second, host governments rarely disclose detailed information on expenditures. In those cases where budgetary data are provided, they are given in the aggregate and without much detail. When we have interviewed law enforcement officials about funding, they either are not forthcoming or do not have access to the information. When details are given, they are not comparable across summits. We have in one case the cost in police overtime hours and in another the costs of renting the venue, inclusive of catering. Thus, the work here is a first step, enticing but frustratingly incomplete. Enters a new analytic approach, we hope that other scholars will help us uncover further information.

In the first section of this chapter, we assemble the available data on expenditures. Next we explore the most visible manifestation of power relations—tensions about who pays. Finally, we offer some conclusions about what these expenditures mean for the social control of dissent.

What Does It Cost?

Despite the limited information available to us, it is staggeringly clear that security budgets for international summits are extravagant. New York City 2002 WEF spent approximately $11 million for police overtime alone. Expenditures for Washington, D.C., 2003 IMF/World Bank were $14 million; for Miami 2003 FTAA, they were approximately $23.9 million; for London 2009 G20, $30 million.[8] Approximately $1 billion was spent on Toronto 2010 G8/G20,[9] making it the most expensive event to date. After Toronto, a debate unfolded in the media regarding the high cost of security. This could open up some much-needed discussion on the budgets for these meetings. However, as of now, it does not appear that the costs will decrease.

John Kirton and colleagues have documented the increasing costs of G8 and G20 summits from 2001 to 2010, as summarized in Tables 1 and 2.[10]

TABLE 1.

Cost of "Securing" the G8

Year	Location	Cost
2001	Genoa, Italy	$40 million
2002	Kananaskis, Canada	$93 million
2003	Évian, France	No data available
2004	Sea Island, Georgia, United States	$40 million
2005	Gleneagles, Scotland United Kingdom	$140 million
2006	St. Petersburg, Russia	No data available
2007	Heilgendamm, Germany	$124 million
2008	Toyako, Hokkaido, Japan	$280 million
2009	L'Aquila, Abruzzo, Italy	$124 million
2010	Toronto, Canada	$309 million

TABLE 2.

Cost of "Securing" the G20

Year	Country	Cost
2008	Washington DC, United States	No data available
2009	London, United Kingdom	$28.6 million
2009	Pittsburgh, United States	$98.7 million
2010	Toronto, Canada	$574.6 million

To date, the Canadian government has been the most forthcoming with information about security spending. Table 3 shows the total cost of security expenditures per department and agency for Toronto 2010 G8/G20. Although the government did not release detailed information about how the money was spent, the data do show the diversity of law enforcement agencies involved in security operations, including both police and military agencies, as well as a number of nonlaw enforcement organizations and even private institutions (noted in the table as "Industry," without further specification).

There are three types of expenditures: those for security itself, operational costs of a secure summit, and collateral costs to the locality.

TABLE 3.

Costs for securing the 2010 G8 & G20 Summits in Toronto[11]

Department/Agency	Spending (in Canadian dollars)
Royal Canadian Military Police	$507,459,400
Public Safety and Emergency Preparedness	$278,310228
National Defense	$77,570,00
Canadian Security Intelligence Service	$3,137,483
Health	$2,266,619
Canada Border Services Agency	$1,180,070
Transport	$1,240,581
Canadian Air Transport Security Authority	$399,399
Public Health Agency of Canada	$583,330
Industry	$2,829,000
Contingency Reserve (Fiscal framework)	$55,000,000
Total	$929,986,110

Security

Examining the overall budget of summit meetings, one observes a significant rise in costs after Seattle 1999 WTO, perhaps because law enforcement in Seattle was criticized for not having spent enough time and money to study the tactics of the alterglobalization movement.[11] In the protest following the conflict in Seattle, law enforcement agencies responsible for policing summits took their work more seriously.

As noted earlier, a portion of the security-related part of the budget goes to payment for police officers hired to supplement the local staff. A report to the Canadian Parliament after Toronto 2010 G8/G20 states that one of the drivers increasing G8 security costs is the relative numbers of law enforcement agents in regular employment near the venue. If the number is low, perhaps because of the rural nature of the location, then the costs are higher because it is necessary to import officers, soldiers, and military equipment. G8 summits deploy approximately twenty thousand security personnel.[12]

Another aspect of the costs directly involved in security concerns equipment, including the increasingly longer and more robust fences being constructed. For Heiligendamm 2007 G8, the costs for the twelve-kilometer-long perimeter fence came to €12.5 million. Police and material equipment are coordinated at the national, provincial, and local levels. In the case of Évian 2003 G8, for example, one hundred warplanes were mobilized to surveil the summit area. Use of military equipment is very expensive; a one-hour flight of a German army Tornado, such as those used at Heiligendamm 2007 G8, costs €41,804, plus the costs of the pilot and other personnel.[13]

In addition, new equipment, such as new police cars, helicopters, boats, night-vision sights, protective clothes, and communication technology, is needed for police operations. The cost to the federal government of renting a digital police radio network in Heiligendamm was €3.6 million.[14] Summit meetings are a welcome occasion to improve the equipment of local police forces.

Other material preparations are related to the provision of accommodation and catering for the police forces. In the case of Heiligendamm 2007 G8, the costs for catering were €630,100. The money spent on renting buildings for the police operations amounted to €1,074,600.

Operations of a Secure Summit

Smooth transport of summit participants has become a costly and complicated operation. To avoid mixing delegates with dissenters, helicopters and boats have become common vehicles for daily transport of delegates during summit protests. The transport costs for Gleneagles 2005 G8 amounted to £1.5 million, including buses, luggage trucks, cars, and helicopters for approximately 4,400 delegates and media persons. Moreover, the airport of Prestwick had to be upgraded to security standards; £35,000 was required for the team planning these adaptations. A temporary structure cost £197,000, and £635,000 was spent upgrading areas of the apron tarmac; such investments are not required for normal airport operations.

The costs for official summit delegations' accommodation, catering, and entertainment are diverse. At Prague 2000 IMF/World Bank, approximately $67 million was spent converting the "Palace of Culture" into a conference facility. For Genoa 2001 G8, $2.89 million was spent on a luxury cruise liner that served as accommodation for the political leaders. These costs are normally paid by the national governments, since they are the official hosts of such meetings.

The most complete budgetary information in this regard is available for Gleneagles 2005 G8. Although 2,375 delegates were accredited to the summit, only 475 had access to the hotel in Gleneagles, and only half of these stayed at the hotel. Rent for the Gleneagles hotel (including catering for the guests) for seven days cost £1,085,000. The cost of setting up the conference facilities (meeting rooms and offices), through the company Jack Morton Worldwide, was £2.2 million. In addition, there were costs for interpreters (£145,000), printing of conference handbooks (£31,000), installation of a secure IT network at the summit site (estimated £66,000), transport and catering for inspection visits (£6,000), installation of backup generators (£26,000), and compensation paid to the facility owner to make up for the unavailability of the other rental properties during the period of the summit (£63,000). Preparation and breakdown rental time cost £104,000. Additional catering, together with a twenty-four-hour snack bar, cost £39,000. Meals for the prime ministers themselves (two working lunches and two dinners) were covered by the government hospitality budget and cost £10,000, including wine and flowers. The parallel program for the spouses of the G8 leaders amounted to £22.000.

As we discuss further in later chapters, media strategies are an increasingly important dimension of the social control of dissent. For Kananaskis 2003 G8, the Royal Canadian Mounted Police hired a public relations firm, GPC International, a partner company of Fleishman Hillad and a major global player in the world of information consulting, to design an information campaign. The expenditure for this service is classified as national security secret, but a contractor working with the company told us that it was substantial.[15] GPC International was involved in the planning of the event from the onset, developing a multilevel communications operation that targeted different types of "stakeholders," such as the global media, local residents, and national protesters. GPC International was involved in the planning process months before the protest. Its task was to add a communications layer to the overall policing strategy.

In their effort to control the message coming out of these summits and the protests against them, summits have an interest in keeping journalists inside, covering the news of the summit itself, rather than outside, covering dissent. At Gleneagles 2005 G8, more than 3,000 journalists were accredited (about 2,100 of them actually collected their security badges). Inside the summit security zone, media centers provide workspaces with internet connections, edit suites, radio booths, and space for press conferences given by authorities and summit officials. Including catering provided for journalists, the British government spent £3,852,000 on media facilities and £1,454,000 on transportation for journalists. For Heiligendamm 2007 G8, the German federal government spent €15 million for the press center,[16] which was constructed for the summit. The press and information office of the federal government obtained an increase in its annual budget for cover the cost of executing the G8-related press tasks, including €81,000 for police public relations work.[17]

Collateral Costs to the Locality

The political economy of summit meetings also places demands on local resources. The German administrative district of Bad Doberan spent approximately €600,000 for Heiligendamm 2007 G8. The federal government refused to take over these costs, which resulted largely from the construction of two ambulant treatment centers and cost of labor. Fire brigades from Rostock and Bad Doberan put in a total of 14,053 hours on the G8 summit, and an unknown number of hours was put in by the brigade of Bad Güstrow. The volunteer and employed rescue services worked a total of 63,243 hours.[18] In addition, officers from emergency units from other German provinces, the "Technisches Hilfswerk" (Technical Relief Organization), and the German Army contributed to the emergency response operation during the G8 summit. The provincial government paid for these extra working hours, although the responsibility for emergency response was with the city of Rostock and the surrounding administrative counties. In total, the money spent for the emergency response services added up to €3,786,200.[19]

Another negative effect of summit meetings for local resources comes from preventive closure of businesses, sometimes explicitly recommended by authorities, often necessitated by road closures or fences which restrict access, and always implicitly stimulated by the scare tactics in the media. It was difficult to purchase food near the Carlini stadium, where many of the protesters found accommodation at Genoa 2001 G8, because most local stores were closed and even barricaded. Similar scenes accompany summit protests elsewhere. Yet, for small-scale enterprises, one or more days of closure can be significant. For these reasons, the German authorities encouraged shop owners in the city center of Rostock to keep their shops open during the days of Heiligendamm 2007 G8. Nevertheless, the president of the Northeast German Retail Association, Heinz

Kopp, confirmed that many retailers saw their profits reduced by as much as 80 percent during the week of the summit.[20]

Yet another loss of profit for local business can emerge from property damage. Shops (and especially their windows) can be the victim of confrontations between police and protesters. At Québec City 2001 FTAA, many shops cannily boarded up their windows while remaining open to do business with and provide services to dissenters. At Heiligendamm 2007 G8, it was the local farmers who lost profit. According to the provincial minister of agriculture, eight farms were directly affected by the police-protester interaction in the fields surrounding Heiligendamm, resulting in an estimated damage of €32,000. Other damages to local business and public infrastructure were assessed at €100,000.[21] Costs from property damage are often not covered by the federal government.

Évian 2003 G8 exemplified the complexities and delicacy of international "cooperation" around summit security. In some cases, it is less costly not to police or enforce the law. For instance, during a planning meeting, Micheline Spoerri, head of the police in Geneva, admitted that local law enforcement had received orders not to intervene to prevent possible property damage in the city of Geneva (which expected protests during the summit). The order was based on a cost-benefit analysis. The municipal government in Geneva reasoned that to prepare for a large protest, it would have to pay foreign police from other cities for their services. This would be true regardless of whether or not any property damage resulted from protest activity. In other words, having foreign police officers in Geneva ready to confront protesters would be expensive, in fact too expensive for the local municipality to cover. Tolerating widespread property damage was the cheaper option, since this potential damage would likely represent a smaller loss to the city than the substantial bills the city would have to pay for French and German officers.[22]

Officials often justify various summit expenditures by citing an anticipated increase in tourism arising from the worldwide attention a region receives during such summits. The possibility of attracting future investment is a recurring theme that circulates before summit meetings. A study by Deloitte and Touche before Prague 2000 WB/IMF predicted a summit-related profit to the city of $26 to $79 million, with another $188 to $413 million coming through extra investment in the following five years.[23] In a debate in the British parliament, the Baroness Royall of Blaisdon pointed out that the first minister expected the benefits to Scotland to be around £500 million, ten times the costs of security.[24] To convince cities that these benefits were realistic, expenditures for Toronto 2010 G8/G20 included $2 million for a fake lake designed to promote tourism in the area.[25] The Italian government produced approximately $100 million to "spruce up" the city before the delegates arrived in town for Genoa 2001 G8.[26]

However, these increases in tourism may never materialize. As a local tourist agency from the region of Gleneagles 2005 G8 confirmed, the expected increase in tourism failed to appear. Despite glossy magazines in the English language about the prospects of the region and a regional collaboration in the special "information office for economy for the G8 summit," the tourist sector of Heiligendamm could also not attest to a significant increase in the two years after the 2007 G8. Similarly, the Gleneagles Hotel, which hosted the 2005 G8, could not report a rising profit rate after the summit. Potential rural venues that host global summit meetings may suffer the same fate as urban venues: they may realize that instead of being seen as the charming center of the world, they can easily be made to appear as a heavily fortified war zone. Laura Tartarini, a lawyer from Genoa, pointed out that there was no increase in tourism in Genoa after the 2001 G8 and added that the city is famous now for the police murder of Carlo Giuliani, an alterglobalization activist, and the police violence that took place during the summit, rather than for its tourist attractions. Although the federal Italian government compensated the city for its financial losses resulting from the summit, the inhabitants of Genoa felt as if the soul of their city were being raped for a summit that had nothing to do with their city.[27]

This lesson is not lost on other cities. After Genoa 2001 G8, fewer cities queued up to host the next meeting of the global elite.

Tensions

As often happens with projects that require large pools of money, the complexity of spending the funds increases the chances of conflict between local agencies participating in the event; conflicts may arise between police departments or between police departments and city government. An instance of such conflict occurred during the planning for Washington D.C. 2003 IMF/WB. Expecting fifty thousand protesters, law enforcement agencies were asked to develop a policing strategy to control large groups to ensure that the disruptions that occurred at Seattle 1999 WTO and Washington D.C. 2000 IMF/WB would not reoccur in

D.C. To make this possible, the agency hired thousands of police officers from nearby cities, scrambling to find the funding to pay overtime. Two months prior to the protest, the D.C. police chief, Charles H. Ramsey, expressed concerns about the impact on the department's annual budget. He warned that, without federal assistance, police "might be forced to patrol a smaller area, restrict delegates' movement or seek more help from federal law enforcement agencies or the National Guard."[28] The *Washington Post* reported that police jurisdictions approached by the D.C. Police Department were "reluctant to send officers to Washington because . . . the District might not be reimbursed for the cost of the extra police protection—and thus might not be able to pay officers from other departments."[29] This funding problem was resolved by creative financing; the Clinton administration proposed that the federal government earmark $15 million from the national budget to cover IMF security costs.

While the example of Washington, D.C., 2003 IMF /WB revealed intercity conflicts, these conflicts can also be international. Évian 2003 G8 offers an odd case of international tensions over who would pay for security. At the official level, France organized, planned, and coordinated the summit meeting. The biggest part of the French budget for the summit went to building a heliport for those leaders who were flying directly to Évian over Lake Leman (£225,000). However, because the summit site was close to France's border with Switzerland, Swiss and German police were involved in the security operations. Switzerland provided ten thousand extra police and soldiers, spending an estimated €16 million. The costs for the deployment of the Swiss army already added up to €4.3 million. Germany supported the operations with 1,015 police.[30] Switzerland was also confronted with the costs of damages that resulted from clashes in the nearby cities of Geneva and Lausanne, which amounted to several hundred thousand euros.

A dispute developed after the summit regarding political responsibility for the costs and lasted for several years.[31] Debates over budgets are common during the planning phases for summit security, and the disputes sometimes even make the national newspapers. When observers ask who is going to pay for security, local, regional, and national governments point to one another. The exorbitant cost of securing Évian triggered a public debate about the appropriateness of G8 summits in general.

Évian 2003 G8 was not the only occasion that led to conflicts about who would pay for extra police support. For Gleneagles 2005 G8, even before the summit meeting there were significant disputes involving the

Scottish Tayside police, the Scottish government, and the central British government in London. The skirmish involved payments for the extra police officers and the material support requested from the London Metropolitan police and the British army. The dispute was not settled in advance, since the entire cost of the G8-related security operation had not been made clear yet. After the summit meeting, however, the British Ministry of Defense demanded compensation from Tayside for an unpaid bill of nearly £400,000[32] for equipment provided for the policing of two international summits in Scotland (there was also a British-Irish summit).[33] Tayside police passed the responsibility to the Scottish authorities, who responded that the British government was responsible for costs related to the G8 summit.

The British government had made its position on supporting local policing costs for major events clear in advance, stating, "There are normal arrangements which apply to the costs of security wherever it is. The costs are dealt with in the normal way. If every time there was an international summit or a major event the security costs were all paid by Whitehall, we'd end up forking out an awful lot of money."[34] Moreover, the spokesperson for the Ministry of Defense stressed that what was happening was not a political conflict between the central government in London and the Scottish government but a normal bureaucratic procedure based on an agreement between the British army and the Scottish police under the framework of "military aid to civil authorities."[35]

At Heiligendamm 2007 G8, a conflict ensued between the provincial government of Mecklenburg-Western Pomerania and the federal government, which had initially promised to contribute €22.5 million for the summit, as well as some of the necessary security operations. It soon turned out, however, that the costs would vastly exceed this contribution. The construction of the huge perimeter fence had already cost €12.5 million. In December 2006, the estimated security cost for the summit—€92 million—was made public.[36] The provincial government had to adjust its annual budget for 2006 for about €126 million, €69.5 of which was reserved for the G8 summit. Approximately €10 million in G8-related security operations by federal police for border control and the army was covered by the federal government, which, however, refused to cover the costs for police forces, arguing that police responsibilities are the provinces' responsibility.[37] This left Mecklenburg-Western Pomerania facing the costs for supplemental police officers from other provinces.

Because funding for summit security comes out of national and local revenues already strained by other economic needs, the tensions between increasing summit costs and responsibility for the bills will likely become more acute. These tensions will, we hope, provoke intragovernmental and public debate about the budgets necessary for securing the agendas of global elites and for criminalizing dissent.

Political Economy of Social Control

Summit social control operations are expensive because of their multidimensionality. They cover not only crowd control but extensive coordinated and international surveillance operations, extending to border control. They include not only policing but also ensuring a high level of security for every aspect of the summit. They include not only security but also public relations and the costs of consultants to develop communication strategies and a luxurious physical containment of the media.

When we examine its political economy, we discover the institutional makeup and character of the social control of global dissent and find that it looks less like protest policing and more like a new version of Low-Intensity Operations (LIO, also called Low-Intensity Warfare). Generally, police actions are internal to the nation-state and are focused on order maintenance regarding domestic issues. In contrast, military actions are generally external to the nation-state and aim to eliminate and destroy the enemy. LIO refers to international military deployments without a declaration of war and also covers domestic military deployments.[38] LIO fall short of full-scale warfare, mainly to avoid the appearance of repression. As such, they often involve the use of less-than-lethal weapons, public relations campaigns, and the extensive gathering of intelligence. Moreover, they seek to intimidate sympathetic observers, persuading them not to join the targeted social movement.

Lest observers believe that the military involvement is limited to loans of some intimidating equipment and a few advisers, we would point out that the security budgets demonstrate that militaries are fully involved in these operations, which are directed at controlling domestic dissent. A member of the military planning team for Kananaskis 2003 G8 described the "security methodology" as "pretty aggressive stuff. We [the Canadian security forces] were flying fighter planes en masse. If anybody got anywhere near the meeting, they would have been shot down; same thing with anybody that tried to infiltrate the areas where the leaders were gathering. We made it very clear to everyone that we had soldiers with live weapons."[39] LIO stretches beyond the use of police and military resources to involve an assortment of government agencies that contribute other low-intensity work to the operations.

Summits are microcosms of global governance. Operational and security budgets climbing toward a billion dollars reveal to us the value of the legitimacy of the neoliberal project to promoters of global governance. Localities, regions, and even member nations to invest with increasing reluctance. The struggles over who is ultimately responsible for paying for the security of global events suggest the internal contradictions of the neoliberal economic model whose touted benefits are increasingly dubious. They also reveal the much-debated uncertainty around the role of the nation-state in the context of globalization. Most nation-states still maintain a domestic monopoly of force, and this is why they are useful partners in mounting summit meetings. Yet, nation-states also face the costs of economic globalization; these costs are crystallized in summit security, whose striking budgets contrast rudely with related contractions in the maintenance of employment and social services. Interestingly, some of the same parties that disrespect dissenters may also denounce summits.

4

Policing
Alterglobalization Dissent

*By all reports, it's a day to wear diapers. We don't. 3 a.m.
Washington, D.C. April 2001. Spring joint meeting of the
IMF and World Bank. It's very complicated loading the
vans. Our unarrestable jail support team are the only ones
carrying their driver's licenses, so they have to drive. But
one is a very nervous driver. And the energy in the van on
the way to our dawn position after an all-night meeting, no
coffee, and two hours of sleep is haphazard and frantic. B
and I have the map and we're in the lead van, but squeezed
in the rearmost seat, which, with the nervous noise, is actually out of the driver's earshot.*

*This is the first action after Seattle. We know it will
be different. Word on the street yesterday was that they're
going to arrest everyone in sight. No point carrying signs
and banners, water, cameras, or backpacks. We'll lose
everything, so just go with necessities in your pockets. I'm
relieved that since we're not anticipating tear gas, I don't
have a stinky vinegar-soaked kerchief draining out of a
ziplock into my jeans. Our legal support is well prepared.
We're ready. But tension is high in the vans because everyone is worried that we won't get our moment in the street
before getting scooped. We drove two thousand miles to
be here. We want to be present, to manifest our rage and
dreams by standing in the street for at least a few minutes
before the police ritual enfolds all the meaning.*

*As we drive through the deserted streets, excessively
alert people shriek at every shadow. Phantasmatic police
come at us at every intersection. B and I are trying to navi-
gate from the floor of the van, where the flashlight won't be*

seen from outside. Periodically, someone yells "duck", bod-
ies crash down on us, and flashlight and map are disori-
ented. We have to start over figuring out where we are on
the map. Finally, we breathe relief. We're on a wide road
with a straight shot at our destination.

Someone shrieks. "Cop car! Turn right." Our driver
responds meekly, "But it's a bridge." "Doesn't matter. Get us
out of here!" We peek out the window, then get back down
to the map. Shit, now we're in Maryland. We have to turn
around and go back. Our driver nears collapse. Everyone is
shouting at her. "Don't make any illegal turns!" She finally
maneuvers us through a Marriott Hotel valet zone and
back across the bridge. Now we're within about a mile, on
another straightaway. "Stop screaming at the driver!" The
energy calms. She can do it. It's just a little further. Then,
ahead of us, two cruisers, parked on opposite sides of the
wide boulevard. Doom. We're so near the zone now, 24 kids
in two vans. They'll snatch us for sure and we go straight to
jail. "Turn!"

"Pull in here!" "Everybody out!" "Behind the dump-
ster!" Suddenly the two ex-marines in our group have
taken command. "Get the vans out of here." "Go! Go!"
They send the drivers away. Great, now we're behind a
dumpster in an alley a mile from the location where
people are waiting for us, the vans are gone, AND we'll
have to cross the street with the cruisers to get there.
The marines organize us two by two and release us at
one-hundred-foot intervals. They take the front. S and
I take the rear. We have the group's one cell phone, so
we can report arrests to legal. We watch the pair in
front of us make it across the boulevard and into the
darkness on the other side. Our turn. We're so obvious.
I'm shaking hard as we cross that street. We make it
to the other side, and I look back at the cruisers just
as a cop comes out of a store, moving gingerly toward
his car carrying a six-pack of coffees and a big box of
donuts.

In this chapter and the next, we work to expand the conceptualization of protest policing. We begin with a brief review of the literature. In the remainder of this chapter, we present a thorough inventory of policing, including and beyond the streetscape. In the following chapter, we move to an empirically grounded analysis of the effects of these police tactics, presenting a series of theoretical interventions that grasp the significance of police actions with regard to social movements.

As Jennifer Earl points out, studies of protest policing alternately try to explain repression (treating it as the dependent variable) or try to explain movement resiliency (using repression as an independent variable).[1] Earl herself prefers to examine the dynamics of repression: the institutional positions of repressive agent (private or state agents, categorized according to tightness of linkage with and control by national political elites); the character of repressive action (coercion or channeling); observable or unobserved police action (not synonymous with "covert" and "overt").[2] Similarly, Wilson focuses on the dynamics of criminalization of dissent: completeness, severity, and extensiveness.[3]

Some scholars focus on what we think of as the "supply-side" dynamics of repression (how repression produces itself). In this vein, della Porta and Reiter identify police strategies: coercion (violent? preemptive?); persuasion/negotiation; cooperation/collaboration; information gathering and use as weapon; selectivity (different policing for different groups, from soft/tolerant to aggressive); political opportunity structures (political, institutional, and cultural); police knowledge/images/perception of protest issue and protesters (e.g., good/bad); police officers' view of their own role in society; and external forces (civil rights and law-and-order coalitions).[4] P. A. J. Waddington focuses on the troubles of repression for the police themselves: "on-the-job trouble" (risky or dangerous operations); "in-the-job trouble" in which the reputation of the police is at risk due to bad press or investigations (this explains police officials' motivations for negotiation); and "die-in-a-ditch" situations in which the police will risk both kinds of trouble.[5]

Other scholars focus on what we think of as "demand-side" dynamics, seeking the explanation for repression in the actions of protesters. Earl summarizes the variables used in these studies: the degree to which the movement threatens political elites; movement weakness; media coverage that protects the movement; the political opportunity cycle; and the volatility or stability of the political opportunity structure.[6] Wilson also identifies variables than can be used to study how movements' own character influences repression: attitudes, mobilization, goals, and organizations.[7]

The diverse approaches of these studies are further complicated by the complexity of each variable. Even the seemingly straightforward variables used by scholars may be more intangible than they appear. How should the severity of various police actions be measured? Earl has pointed out that the impact of arrests may have been underestimated as being less severe than the impact of police violence,[8] and Gary Marx's extensive work on surveillance has shown it to be as incapacitating as any other form of repression, despite a lack of force or even direct interaction.[9]

A common recognition of the literature is that *sometimes* repression has a "backlash" effect, spurring increased mobilization.[10] This is often the case in response to police violence; however, the effect is hard to track. Earl's study shows that the effect of repression depends on its timing and the phase of a social mobilization. Karl Opp and Wolfgang Roehl observe a "micromobilization" response to repression and find some movement-side variables associated with increased likelihood of such backlash mobilizations.[11] But the literature on surveillance, which owes much to the prolific Marx, shows consistently isolating and divisive impacts.

Della Porta has gathered scholars for two important edited volumes on policing of protest, the first of which appeared in 1998, just prior to the emergence of the alterglobalization movement (although after the emergence of direct-action confrontations by Autonomen in Europe) and the second of which was published in 2006, well after the emergence of alterglobalization. The earlier volume happily determines that negotiation had for the most part replaced escalated force in Western Europe and the United States. This shift was accomplished by the increasing use of three tactics: "underenforcement of the law, the search to negotiate, and large-scale collection of information." The variables identified to explain protest policing were political opportunities (police institutions, state political context, and political culture), civil rights or law-and-order coalitions, and police knowledge (ideas and images about protesters). In summarizing the findings, della Porta, Peterson, and Reiter conclude:

> The dominant protest policing style in Europe is selective, that is, different police styles are used for different actors. In this way, "brutal" and repressive styles have survived. These styles are connected with the same kind of stereotypes about professional disturbers of the peace, conspirators, and so on, as before. The difference today is that these stereotypes and protest policing styles are now applied only to a small minority among the protesters, whereas historically they

were used against large sections of the population, such as the members and associations of the working-class movement. It is this kind of continuity in the role of the police, in the range of options theoretically open to them, and in the mechanisms with which they individuate and label "dangerous" enemies that makes arrest or reversal of the trend toward "softer" and more tolerant protest policing styles a possibility.[12]

Eight years later, della Porta, Peterson, and Reiter assert that policing of the alterglobalization movement involves "new strategies [that] challenge social scientists' approaches to protest policing."[13] The later volume addresses two questions. The first asks whether the escalated force model has been reimplemented or whether "a new repressive protest policing style" has been developed; the second asks whether the negotiated model was ever really in ascendance or whether its use was always selective.[14] On these questions, there is far less agreement among contributors to the book than in the first volume, with some authors arguing for novel policing strategy and others maintaining that alterglobalization policing used existing elements of "emergency" policing,[15] as well as negotiation, its oddities connected to variables of police knowledge and disorganization within police institutions. The 2006 study reconfirms the 1998 findings that "the massive use of intelligence" is "legitimized as an alternative to brutal intervention on the street."[16]

Most striking to us in the later volume is Abby Peterson's description of Copenhagen police chief Kai Vittrup's strategy, which involves an offensive paramilitary plan designed to "maintain the initiative during the summit, determining the time and place for the anticipated events and controlling their development" through a combination of the "tactic of exhaustion" and negotiation under contrived and theatrical conditions. Peterson notes that in both Denmark and Sweden,[17] police sought to "undermine . . . nonviolent civil disobedience actions."[18] We are convinced by this chapter's answer to the volume's question about the prevailing model for policing protest: there has been a shift to preemptive policing, selective to be sure but not reserved for violent or extremist activists. We note that the shocking "Miami Model"[19] is, in fact, the Vittrup model.

The 2006 della Porta et al. volume identifies additional important findings with regard to policing alterglobalization. First, the transnational nature of the protests has led to momentary reversals of global integration, such as the closure of borders, which violates the EU Schengen agreement to abandon internal border controls.[20] Second, the multilayered police agencies, including multiple local agencies (mobilized to increase the size of the force but not always willing to act under joint command), as well as various national and even foreign agencies, have difficulty agreeing upon strategy and also coordinating or even operating together in a hierarchical command structure. At Seattle 1999 WTO; Göteborg 2001 EU; Genoa 2001 G8; and Miami 2003 FTAA, this caused severe disorder among the various police units.[21] Third, the direct-action communities are not recognized by police as a "political subject" (instead, they are persistently treated as a "public-order problem"), and police may therefore refuse to collaborate with the negotiated model of policing.[22] The refusal by the police (and the state) to recognize certain protesters as "political" affects relations with the moderate and cooperative sectors of the alterglobalization movement, as well. (Another possible interpretation is that alterglobalization is rejected as a political subject *ideologically*, and its tactics are used as an excuse to delegitimize it.) As Peterson points out, for the Danish and Swedish police, nonviolent direct action itself was a source of significant concern, and they sought to preempt its occurrence through raids and Vittrup's "tactic of exhaustion."

Della Porta et al. imply that alterglobalization protest *needs* more specialized policing. They argue that the models used by the police at Genoa 2001 G8 (based on tactics used to handle other "emergencies," like football riots, activities organized by the Mafia or by other organized-crime groups, and terrorism) were inappropriate.[23] In her chapter, Peterson examines inappropriate policing, particularly officers' unfamiliarity with chain-of-command operations, since most of them have been trained to work alone or in small teams. Noakes and Gillham determine that neither "escalated force" nor "negotiation" fully captures what is going on. Instead, "rearrangement," detention, and disruption are used to accomplish "strategic incapacitation," particularly of protesters who are "transgressive" (that is, who refuse negotiation and predictable forms of protest).[24]

These scholars agree that police riots occur as a result of several factors: police unpreparedness and disorganization; demonization of "bad protesters"; and aspects of police culture and psychology (fear and/ or the rush of physical conflict), which whip them into unplanned and undirected violence.[25] We must wonder, however, just how unplanned or unintentional such violence can be when police are armed with paramilitary gear and deployed in military formations. Della Porta and Reiter's volume relies on a presumption we view as doubtful—that riots are unde-sirable for both sides.

Alongside della Porta and Reiter's efforts, a great deal of the research conducted to date about social control of the alterglobalization move-ment has been done by legal collectives, activists, and sympathetic non-academic observers.[26] The U.S. National Lawyers Guild compiled a multi-event analysis and concluded that the negotiated model has shifted to a preemptive model focused on blocking access, intimidating activists, conducting broad-scale [illegal] searches, raids, and mass arrests, and confiscating or incapacitating protest resources.[27]

We organize our inventory of police tactics into five arenas: regulatory and legislative dimensions of policing, intelligence, event policing, crimi-nal prosecution, and transnationalization. Tactics implemented in these areas may overlap.

Regulatory and Legislative Dimensions of Policing

The very meaning and significance of "negotiation" have changed as cit-ies have developed regulatory mechanisms to preemptively control pro-test. In advance of protests, city governments have used legislative and bureaucratic mechanisms to reduce or restrict constitutionally protected political activity and speech. As activists prepare for a protest, they receive word that wooden sticks and bike locks have been defined as "ille-gal" during the protest period. They will not be able to get within a given distance of the meeting site. The city has assembled and budgeted for tens of thousands of police and is prepared to arrest and detain thousands of demonstrators. The city proclaims a regulatory environment that is not only aggressive but volatile. If we imagine the law as the ground beneath the feet of a democratic society, the behavior of cities in advance of a pro-test is a legislative period of earthquakes, inducing anxiety and uncer-tainty. Anything can happen.

As discussed in chapter 2, city governments work with global gover-nance agencies and with the police to define and build "security perim-eters." Massive metal walls distort the geography of the city, sometimes dissecting neighborhoods, even though the erection of barricades and checkpoints is a profound and questionable act of governance. Residents are required to carry pass cards. Parts of the city become off limits to all but "official." credentialed participants in summits. Hotels and businesses are forced to close, and tourists' access and movements are limited.

Another regulatory tactic is the passage of city ordinances directed at a specific protest. In advance of Miami 2003 FTAA, the Miami City Council defined two or more persons moving down the street as a "parade" and eight or more gathered outside a structure for more than thirty minutes as an "illegal assembly." For Heiligendamm 2007 G8, a "General Directive" banned protest in the zone immediately outside the security fence. Ordinances also restrict protest materials and defensive equipment, such as gas masks. By limiting the diameter and materials allowed for sign support sticks, ordinances render illegal lockdown equipment used for human-powered barricades and most puppets, which require strong supports. At Heiligendamm 2007 G8, even the maximum length of front banners (carried perpendicular to the direction of the march) was restricted, and side banners (carried along the edges of the march parallel to its direction) were entirely forbidden. During a related demonstration in Hamburg, the police conditions for permitting a big demonstration of several thousand people even included a prohibition against jumping up and down.

Miami removed the special "parade" ordinance (section 54-6.1) from the law immediately after the event (indeed, the ordinance itself included a sunset date, November 27, six days after the 2003 FTAA meetings ended), but some restrictive ordinances have no expiration and can result in new limitations on local protest activity long after the protest is over. Moreover, the experiences of summit protests may lead to new ordinances, such as occurred after Göteborg 2001 EU, when Swedish authorities quickly introduced a ban on the wearing of masks during political assemblies. After Heiligendamm 2007 G8, German authorities tried to include face makeup as used by the Clandestine Insurgent Rebel Clown Army in the list of prohibited forms of masking during demonstrations.

Old laws may be resurrected. At New York City 2002 WEF, the city threatened to charge masked protesters under an 1845 law "originally adopted to thwart armed insurrections by Hudson Valley tenant farmers who dressed and painted themselves as Native Americans to attack law enforcement officers over rent issues."[28] The law has been intermittently resurrected to criminalize queers (1965), the Ku Klux Klan (2001), and alterglobalization protesters (2002).

More recently, the city of Toronto resurrected and used the Public Works Protection Act to expand police power during the 2010 G20 protest. The legislation was first enacted in Ontario, Canada, during World War II, in 1939. The act defined a "public work" as any railway, canal, highway, bridge, or other public resource that is either owned or operated by the government of Ontario, including any public work constructed by any board or commission, municipal corporation, or private enterprise. The act also includes any public building or place designed as a "public work" site by the lieutenant governor in council. In sum, the definition of "public work" is sweeping and nimble, easily applied to a variety of locations. Perhaps for this reason, the government of Ontario used the Public Works Protection Act to temporarily give police extended power; it accomplished this by designating the area around the G20 meetings a "public work" space. This reapplication of the law not only extended police powers but also transformed the type of activity that occurred prior to and during the protest. The exact nature of what powers were given to the police was never clear. Prior to the event, local media reported that police could require identification and question and detain anyone within six feet of the security fence. Civil liberties organizations proclaimed this unconstitutional. Regardless of the legality of the extended power, protesters on the ground felt the effects, since the media reports made it unclear what was and was not a legal act during a march.

Requiring permits is another way to legally constrict dissent. Through the permitting process, police collaborate with the city government bureaucracy in systematically restraining lawful protest by restricting use of public space for rallies and marches. Preparing for New York City 2004 RNC (Republican National Convention), United for Peace and Justice (UFPJ) requested a permit to use the Great Lawn of Central Park, a traditional place for large political gatherings. The city denied the permit and tried to locate UFPJ's rally on a distant highway, instead. Sometimes the normal role of the local government is superseded entirely. The special police departments created in Germany for Heiligendamm 2007 G8 and Strasbourg 2009 NATO were given temporary authority over legal issues related to political assemblies. These special agencies assume the authority to allow and forbid demonstrations, a responsibility normally carried out by the *versammlunsbehoerde* (the "assembly office" of the city or region). This development shows not only the manipulation of law to control protest but also the suspension of civil authority in favor of police authority.

Permitting may also require social movement organizations to pay for insurance, portable toilets, and garbage cans and to take responsibility for the behavior of people who join the protest. Protest organizers may have to provide their own police (called "marshals" in the United States), who patrol the edge of the march route and confront straying participants. (For example, if the march has a permit to close only one lane of traffic, the marshals, rather than local police, may be responsible for keeping marchers confined to that space.) Often permits define "protest areas" or "pits" (discussed in chapter 2). Since the permit covers only these areas, stragglers or those reluctant to enter the caged zone are not protected by the terms of the negotiated agreement covering the protest or rally. Consistent with the agreement, those outside will be hassled, dispersed, or herded into the protest pits.

Such state "structuring of protest"[29] forces activists to choose between impotent permitted activities and more transgressive ones. Permit holders that have entered into a contract with the state sometimes try to control other protesting groups, which creates tensions in the alliance between them. Several times, this has resulted in major friction and mutual accusations among groups of protesters. At the opening demonstration of L'Aquila 2009 G8, we observed demonstration organizers physically attacking a group of black-clad protesters who insisted on continuing the demonstration after the police had blocked the march. Such incidents influence possibilities for future cooperation between groups.

Another civic action is the preparation of detention facilities. At Philadelphia 2000 RNC, a derelict jail was "reopened" to house protesters. At Genoa 2001 G8, the Bolzaneto military barrack was used as detention facility, and at Heiligendamm 2007 G8, various state buildings, including youth prisons, were emptied to create places to hold arrested summit protesters. Other cities construct holding facilities or arrange for the use of stadiums. In press releases before the demonstrations begin, cities announce their capacity and their willingness to engage in mass incarceration of protesters.

Intelligence

One of the most significant scholarly studies on surveillance is David Cunningham's analysis of memos from the U.S. Federal Bureau of Investigation (FBI) Counter Intelligence Program (COINTELPRO). From 1956 through 1971, counterintelligence missions designed to "expose, disrupt, misdirect, discredit, or otherwise neutralize"[30] various political organizations were official FBI policy. However, the "normal" intelligence activities of the agency before, during, and after the official program included much of the same activity, with very similar effects on targets.[31] Histories of surveillance, police action, and incarceration of political prisoners clearly reveal the violence of the state against political activists. But COINTELPRO was explicitly organized to disrupt political organizations associated with several *social movements*. The FBI's unit of analysis was the movement. And it used a range of tactics calculated to have psychological and social effects to meet its goals of "neutralizing" targeted movements.

State surveillance inhabits a shadowy realm of public affairs, often secret and barely legal. Cunningham explains that intelligence operations can serve two goals, investigation of federal crimes and (more controversial) precautionary monitoring through information gathering about organizations. Counterintelligence operations may have a preventative goal, to "actively restrict a target's ability to carry out planned actions," or they may take the form of provocation for the purpose of entrapment—catching targets engaged in criminal acts.[32] Some of the "normal intelligence" activities routinely undertaken by the FBI outside official COINTELPRO that nevertheless had a preventative counterinsurgent function were harassment by surveillance and/or purportedly criminal investigations, pressured recruitment of informants, infiltration, break-ins, and labeling or databasing, which harmed groups' reputations and impacted their abilities to communicate with the media, draw new members, and raise funds, "exacerbat[ing] a climate in which seemingly all mainstream institutions opposed the New Left in some way." Using infiltrators who act as agents provocateurs is, according to Cunningham, part of normal intelligence operations.[33]

Surveillance—certainly in the case of social movements protesting corporate globalization—can also be organized by nonstate actors, in this case multinational corporations. John Stauber and Sheldon Rampton document a number of cases of corporate infiltration of social movement groups.[34] However, corporate social control is even more difficult to investigate than state involvement because corporations are not legally accountable to citizens. A case that did not become public until a few years afterward was the corporate infiltration of local ATTAC groups and of an antirepression group in Lausanne, both in the context of Évian 2003 G8.[35] ATTAC (an organization that aims to raise awareness and to educate the public by using nonviolent methods for often symbolic street interventions), along with many other groups, was campaigning against Nestlé because of its involvement with biotechnology.

Since associations and social movements endure for decades, they have interests separate from those of their participants. The literature shows that knowledge (or fear) of surveillance and infiltration forces organizations to direct their energies toward defensive maintenance and away from the pursuit of their broader goals.[36] In addition, activists may respond by turning from overt collective forms of dissent and engage in more covert, individualistic forms of dissent[37] or forge more militant, even violent, factions.[38] Organizations' funding and their relationships with other organizations, the press, and the public may be affected, as well.

Researching the surveillance of alterglobalization and antiwar groups in the United States in 2006, we were surprised to find that it included nonviolent targets at a level comparable to that which occurred in previous eras.[39] However, as Cunningham has documented, the lack of a criminal standard or test as a basis for surveillance is nothing new. And Frank Donner traces the recent history of "terrorist" accusations against pacifist organizations to the targeting in the early 1980s of antinuclear, anti-death-penalty, and Latin American solidarity organizations.[40] This targeting was performed by both local police and federal agencies. Disruptive, counterinsurgent activity against organizations that have not met a criminal standard was officially forsworn with the closure of COINTELPRO. Yet, we documented that the same activity is still underway, now by a network of law enforcement organizations.

So surveillance is more than "police knowledge";[41] it is a policing tactic which aims to quell or weaken political activity. Technologies of surveillance include direct surveillance, such as observation and visits by officers, recording of automobile plate numbers, raids, questioning, and burglary; electronic surveillance, such as phone taps, audio eavesdropping, tracking of e-mail, and monitoring of Internet and other computer activity; use of video, photo, and car-tracking devices; undercover surveillance, including by police in disguise, and the use of informants, infiltrators, and agents provocateurs; and databasing and the sharing of databased information.

It is inaccurate to categorize direct and indirect technologies solely as overt or covert methods of observation, as most of these technologies can be employed either way as part of a counterinsurgency strategy. The exceptions are raids, which cannot be done covertly, and the use of long-term infiltrators and agents provocateurs, who must remain covert so as not to be expelled. But most of the other technologies can be used either way. For example, telephone surveillance can be conducted seamlessly, without alerting the surveilled person, or it can be conducted obviously, in order to signal the surveilled person that he is under surveillance (e.g., sounds on the line, disruption of service, purportedly inadvertent play-back of tapes on the line). "Clumsy" operations suggest to activists that law enforcement officers intend for them to be aware that they are under surveillance. This dimension is part of the counterinsurgent function of surveillance. Even an overt revelation of long-term infiltrators can be a useful counterinsurgency technique, as it disrupts trusted relationships and decreases communication in networks.

Overt direct surveillance is a threat similar to the brandishing of weapons and functions as an immediate discouragement to protesters. People arriving at a meeting may be surprised and alarmed to find a watchful police presence outside. This watchfulness may take the form of an around-the-clock guard or frequent, visible drive-bys. People arriving at a protest may be unsettled to find police videotaping demonstrators. People playing roles of increased responsibility in the protest, such as speakers at rallies or those who work as marshals or medics, may find themselves the subject of close-up surveillance photography or video.

The threat has different significance for various people. People planning to engage in gray-area activity may be discouraged from doing so, knowing they can be identified on videotape, or may be forced to protect themselves better. First-time protesters may be concerned that their employers or others will find out about their political activities. People attending meetings may doubt the reputation of the group in whose meeting they are participating because surveillance suggests the group is illicit. People may feel uneasy about taking a visible role in organizing.

During major protests, overt and constant surveillance is common near activist spaces, such as sleeping and eating spaces, medical centers, educational events, art workshops, and meeting and organizing spaces. (Activists often organize a central meeting space, where decision-making "spokescouncils" are held; these places are often called "Convergence".) At Sacramento 2003 Biotech, outside a spokescouncil meeting, several officers stood on the sidewalk near the door so that activists had to carefully move around them to enter the meeting. (Circumnavigating officers on a sidewalk is not a trivial matter, as activists have been charged with felony assault on an officer for inadvertent physical contact such as jostling or brushing against police personnel.) Meanwhile, several police vehicles were stationed directly across the street. Once the meeting started, the police trained a vehicle-mounted searchlight on the building. At such short range, this powerful light was a striking intrusion into the space.

Persons approaching the door to enter the meeting found themselves spotlighted. The light also shone through the windows, eerily illuminating the meeting space. There was also a helicopter hovering over the building, and patrol cars circled, their sirens screaming, inducing in meeting participants anticipation of impending assault on the building. Waves of rumors were circulated and quelled, but the three hundred activists in the room became jumpy and had difficulty concentrating. Many left. There was no raid, but the meeting was made ineffectual. Meanwhile, a few blocks away, at the "Welcome Center" (a small warehouse with a media center and an information table), volunteers continued to compile a list of all the different kinds of vehicles doing drive-bys at their facility. Helicopters circled overhead, while cars, motorcycles, and vans passed slowly at all hours.

At Heiligendamm 2007 G8, police mobilized a new form of militarized surveillance. Tornado planes from the German army (allegedly without bombing equipment) flew patrol flights above the action camp in Reddelich and the region around the fence in order to take pictures. Although the first flights preceding the protests went unnoticed, the flight on the day before the blockades shocked the entire movement. One of us, along with an elderly activist, was giving an interview about the historical development of action repertoires of social movements in Germany and their use of violence and comparing that history with the violence of the state. The elderly activist had just pointed out how the state was establishing a threatening state of emergency in order to criminalize dissent when the Tornado passed above our heads, making an incredible noise (apparently the plane was flying below the legally required minimum height of 150 meters). Interrupting the interview, the camera immediately swung up to catch the Tornado. After it had passed, the activist smiled and said: "You see, this is what I am talking about." According to the authorities, the pictures taken were intended to detect transformations of the ground and potential depots of explosives. However, pictures taken by the plane and released to the public after the protests seemed focused on persons and vehicles in the camp.

Electronic surveillance is very easy for law enforcement authorities to implement. They can join listserves and view websites to gather information on events, meetings, and plans. They can automatically trawl the Internet and intercept satellite-based communications (ECHELON). They can access remotely the personal computers of targets. Not much is known about exactly how governments are using these technologies and how often they secure warrants for use. In Europe, the extent to which electronic surveillance is used became apparent only after a study of the dossiers of the criminal investigation police in the case of the "Militante Gruppe" (militant group). Lawyers had requested access to the dossiers of a number of persons facing trial under the antiterrorist legislation Article 129a. By tapping the e-mail communication of only a few persons, intelligence agents and the criminal investigation police actually collected the e-mails of several hundred activists (those who communicated with the tapped persons either personally or through mailing lists). Such operations can also take either an invisible or a clumsy posture. Interviewees reported to us that, in meetings with local police, departments agents have announced "we read your e-mail." Another clumsy form of computer monitoring with counterinsurgent impacts is theft of activists' laptops.

The partner of Andrej Holm told an insightful anecdote during the 2007 Chaos Computer Club Conference about the period after the arrest of her partner on charges of terrorism. In the weeks after Andrej's arrest, she did not dare to switch her cell phone off because this could have been interpreted as suspicious behavior aimed at avoiding surveillance. However, the electronic surveillance of her cell phone interfered with her television reception, making it practically impossible for her to watch television anymore. One evening, when she felt like watching one of her favorite television series, she phoned her mother to make clear to the intelligence services that were tapping her conversations that she was going to switch her cell phone off in order to be able to watch the show. The unexpected outcome of this phone call was that the interference between phone and television stopped for a few hours without her having to switch off the cell phone.[42]

In the United States, the alterglobalization movement has experienced extensive undercover surveillance. Some believe that aspects of movement culture, such as the emphasis on anonymity and the use of pseudonyms, facilitate undercover operations. However, movements with different cultures, such as the Black Panther movement, suffered the same kinds of infiltration. A number of long-term infiltrators have been identified, some through their roles as prosecution witnesses in the 2006 Green Scare (a series of investigations and prosecutions aimed at environmental activists in the United States). Some have lived in "activist houses," compiling data and at times attempting to provoke militant actions. One affinity group at the Philadelphia 2000 RNC learned that their van driver was an infiltrator when he drove them into a police blockade, where all on board were arrested.[43] In Europe, long-term infiltration seems to be more difficult or is simply harder to discover. What is well known, however, is that intelligence services try to recruit informants. These attempts become known only when activists refuse to cooperate and make public the invitation they received. Prior to Heiligendamm 2007 G8 and Strasbourg 2009 NATO, several such attempts became public, and activists discovered one case of successful recruitment.

Undercovers also join short-term actions, such as nonviolent civil disobedience actions. Meetings and rallies are rife with poorly disguised police officers. Infiltration has become so pervasive that activists now assume that most meetings are infiltrated. Given the other kinds of surveillance easily available to police, activists wonder why they engage in elaborate (but still clumsy) personal surveillance of nonviolent events. Police even infiltrate groups and actions regarding which—if the police actually have any prior intelligence on the action planning—there is no basis for suspecting violence or property crime. Activists, sure that no information-gathering purpose is being served, conclude that the infiltration serves the specific counterinsurgent purpose of disrupting the bonds of trust among groups. But some activists suggest that the participation of undercover agents enhances the moral authority of the movement, since police, having observed the planning sessions, know well that the actions are designed to be entirely pacific.

In early 2006, the U.S. federal government began a series of indictments and investigations of environmental activism. The resulting prosecutions, dubbed "the Green Scare," were based on electronic surveillance and information from long-term infiltrators. They also utilized another surveillance technology, grand juries, which gather information secretly and under duress from entire communities. Communities know who has testified, but they do not know what has been said, because grand juries are not open court proceedings. They also know that testimony is exacted under threat of jail time and that witnesses do not have recourse to the Fifth Amendment protection that allows them to remain silent under questioning. (If witnesses refuse to testify, they can be imprisoned.) Grand juries are a form of community surveillance that has the counterinsurgent impact of disrupting networks of trust and solidarity. By isolating and threatening individuals, grand juries pit them against their communities. Anticipating but never knowing about the next group of witnesses to be called, communities preemptively freeze information and action.

Another form of surveillance is raids or house visits. Purportedly with the intention of acquiring information, a police team will visit a home or office. They may or may not have a search warrant. They may be heavily armed. They attempt to search the premises and question those present, using threats and bribery to gain cooperation when acting without a warrant. A couple of months prior to New York City 2004 RNC, multiagency forces visited several activist houses in the U.S. Midwest in riot gear but without warrants and accused residents of planning acts of violence at the convention. News of the visits spread quickly through activist circles. These raids were a first strike against RNC protesters, before much planning had even taken place. They sent the message that protest would not be tolerated. Raids and eight arrests took place in advance of Minneapolis 2008 RNC; activists were charged with "conspiracy to riot in furtherance of terrorism."[44] In advance of Heiligendamm 2007 G8, federal police searched forty houses, social centers, and activist projects in several German cities. Computers, address books, and genetic materials were confiscated. The victims were accused of "formation of a terrorist organization" under Article 129a of the German Criminal Code.

But counterinsurgent surveillance is more than intelligence gathering. Information is also organized and stored. Surveillance databases have expanded qualitatively with the digitization of information and increased interagency collaboration. Law Enforcement Intelligence Units (LEIU) facilitate direct and international (among the United States, Canada, Australia, and South Africa) interagency collaboration and database sharing.[45] In the EU, there are increasing attempts to establish a fully unified and shared database of "political troublemakers" (although the commission working on this has not so far agreed on a definition of the category). Moreover, the automatic exchange of collected data (such as flight details) between the United States and the EU has been implemented in the context of antiterrorist legislation. In conjunction with the qualitative expansion of databasing, categories are being created that collapse politics, crime, and violence. These include categories such as "domestic terrrorism," "criminal extremism," and "eco-terrorism," which are applied to political organizations and their members, including pacifist organizations such as the Quaker American Friends Service Committee. A 2003 conference of the LEIU in Seattle attracted protesters seeking to expose its private (but federally funded) "network" nature, its collection of data on noncriminal activities (such as protests), and its low evidentiary standards.[46]

Video and photo surveillance is omnipresent at rallies and public events. Some of this visual material is used in court cases when activists are prosecuted. Some goes into databases. The collection of this material is alarming because it creates a law enforcement/criminal record based on the act of dissenting. It is of notable concern to youth, immigrants, and others who may be concerned about their criminal records and decreases their comfort expressing dissent.

Event Policing

While traditional approaches to protest policing focus on the battle in the streets, today's strategies include legislation and public relations. Police promote these activities as part of a "model" of protest policing inseparable from what happens—and doesn't happen—in the streets. Nevertheless in this section we will focus on actions in the streets, where an array of policing tactics are used in seemingly erratic combinations.

According to the Vittrup strategy of "exhaustion," in the days and hours immediately prior to the protest, individual activists and small groups are stopped, questioned, detained, and searched without probable cause. This policing communicates to dissenting groups the pervasive, saturated nature of policing. Activist spaces receive inordinately punctilious fire inspections. On various pretexts (including building code violations discovered without the aid of the relevant regulatory agencies), police surround organizing spaces, cut off entry and egress, arrest those inside, and confiscate art and educational materials.

At Genoa 2001 G8, masked police raided a media center and a sleeping place, beating the activists they found there. More than sixty people, three of whom were in comas, were hospitalized. Activists fear raids because they feel vulnerable to the risk of being trapped inside a building by the police, with no hope of media witnesses, and also because they don't want to miss the political events they are preparing for. The threat of raids builds tension and a sense of constraint before the protest has begun. Activists get the sense that moving around or even having a meeting is going to be difficult. But face-to-face meetings are essential for multiple reasons: to evade electronic surveillance, to verify and authenticate information and plans, and to allow people who may be working together for the first time to build relationships quickly.

Only part of protest policing involves physical control. The police spend a great deal of effort on performative activities designed to intimidate dissenters and to distract or divert mobilized groups from completing their plans. Groups of police in extreme militarized costume and posture "patrol" the neighborhoods in which activists are meeting and organizing. At Sacramento 2003 Biotech, large SUVs were mounted with runners, on which between three and eight riot-gear-clad cops would ride, combat-ready, as the vehicles slowly circled the residential neighborhood where activists were organizing. Police often choose the moment of a large meeting at Convergence to mass a large force nearby. Activist watchers observe this massing, and, as the information is passed on, rumors of an impending raid disrupt and redirect activists' energy. (Entry, exit, and business at Convergence are regularly disrupted by the building's own security team vigilantly "locking down" the building in anticipation of police visits.) Even when there is no action going on (but often when a meeting is under way), police assemble a collection of vehicles and rush around the area with all sirens blaring, implying imminent action ("siren parades").

At Los Angeles 2000 DNC (Democratic National Convention), the activist legal team won a rare injunction against raids on the Convergence Center. But, given the instability of the legal landscape regarding protests, activists had little confidence that this injunction would hold, so the space was still vulnerable to siren parades, massing reports, and rumors, leading to waves of fear and security lockdowns every few hours.

Once people have assembled in the streets, police use several strategies to disrupt activity. They declare assemblies illegal, even in locations and at times that have been prenegotiated and that are permitted. Protesters are often perplexed by the lack of any immediate pretext for voiding negotiated agreements. Having declared an assembly illegal, police then threaten or engage in mass arrest or violence. At a demonstration of ten thousand people during Heiligendamm 2007 G8, protesters were prevented from participating in the permitted march before they even left the gathering place. Police provided illogical reasons; they claimed that the number of people would exceed the number mentioned in the permit and that protesters were masked (which was disproved by video recordings and observers). The march started only after several hours of waiting and was not allowed to follow the initially agreed-upon route.

Police are supposed to issue an audible "dispersal order" and give time for people to disperse before taking action against an assembly. However, it is common for the order not to be given or to be given inaudibly or, even if it is both given and audible, for inadequate time to be given for dispersal. A striking example of this occurred when the police abruptly curtailed a rally in the protest pen at Los Angeles 2000 DNC. They issued a dispersal order, but the pen's one exit was laced with concrete traffic blocks. Rally attendees were shot in the back with rubber bullets while attempting to disperse around the blocks. Likewise, at Miami 2003 FTAA, a rally at the courthouse was issued an inadequate three-minute dispersal order and then immediately surrounded and subjected to mass arrest. At New York City 2004 RNC, police used nets to capture hundreds of people, who were subsequently arrested.[47] Police use their bodies, standing shoulder to shoulder, clad in riot gear and using supersized nightsticks or bicycles, as dual-purpose moveable fence and battering instruments.

The mass surround-and-arrest tactic often results in the arrest of passersby, people coming out of work onto the sidewalk, journalists, and delivery workers. Mass arrests are often disorganized, infuriating observers and protesters trying to disperse. Moreover, they often do not produce convictable charges and therefore serve primarily to detain activists so that they cannot engage in protest for some hours or days and, secondarily, to endanger them gratuitously in an effort to discourage them from future dissenting activity.

Political arrestees—the vast majority of whom are arrested for crimes that would not ordinarily be arrest-worthy, such as jaywalking—are often held in unusual and illegal conditions. Protesters are deprived of their legal rights to counsel, same-sex searches, phone calls, access to bathrooms, blankets, heat, beds, timely arraignment and release, and standard bonds. They are also subject to cruel and unusual punishment while in custody, such as denial of medical care, excessively tight handcuffs, beatings, sexual abuse, death threats, and being held at gunpoint (particularly unwarranted for U.S. protesters, who are never charged with violent crimes). At Miami 2003 FTAA, a large number of arrestees were pepper sprayed at close range, then arrested and detained in confined spaces, without any chance for recovering and cleaning their eyes and faces. Political arrestees are also often held in unusual facilities that are unsafe, exposed, condemned, or otherwise inappropriate. Arrestees at New York City 2004 RNC were held in a set of cages erected in a building with extensive toxic residue.[48] At Heiligendamm 2007 G8, hundreds of protesters were kept for hours, sometimes days, twenty to a cage, in a provisional detention facility. They were under constant camera surveillance, subjected to 24-hour light, allowed no contact with lawyers, and given only a thin mat and blanket as they slept on the floor.

The day prior to the courthouse mass arrest at Miami 2003 FTAA, although no "terrorist" appeared, there were the fence was not breached, no roadways were blocked that were not preemptively closed by police, and no windows were broken or other property crime committed, at 3:53 p.m., activists remaining in the streets after the end of a union-sponsored march were told by a police representative with a bullhorn that the demonstration could continue "until there is violence." Just under seven uneventful minutes later, a wall of police moved on the protest, firing rubber bullets and tear gas and hunting protesters indiscriminately and violently for hours, moving thirty blocks on a path well away from the summit site. They systematically drove protesters into the Overtown neighborhood, where residents told activists that they had been encouraged by police to rob protesters with impunity.

Permitted and pacifist demos are regularly attacked. This was particularly noticeable at Genoa 2001 G8:

> Saturday. An enormous peaceful march of 150,000 people. . . . For around ten minutes the police, seemingly without any aim or reason, fired canister after canister into the crowd. A crowd that was not even heading towards them. Until then . . . people were raising their hands in the air. . . . Soon protesters were throwing the tear gas back at the police. . . . Those most angry with the gassing moved to the front and began to fight back.[49]
>
> This clearly shows the falsity of the idea that militant sections of the crowd "provoke" the violence of the police and that if only we were all pacifists then the police would leave us alone. It is a ridiculous presumption in a way to believe that we can 'decide' how the police will react to us. We had ensured we were going to get a violent response by gathering in the streets in such large numbers and announcing our intention to get inside the Red Zone. This is a provocative and confrontational stance to take, whether or not you are throwing molotov cocktails. Then the black block[50] get all the blame for the violence on account of being the only people actually prepared for the violence that the entire demonstration has inevitably provoked. . . . The police respond to the level of violence you threaten and to your effectiveness. If you are ineffective but violent, you will probably get a response from the police, if you are ineffective and non-violent then you will probably not get much response from the police, but if you begin to be effective, whether you are using violence or not, then you will be met with a violent response.[51]

Police action is often indiscriminate, but sometimes it is targeted. Targeted groups are followed by helicopter wherever they go and are frequently surrounded, questioned, harassed, and arrested. The police also attack preemptively groups from which they expect confrontation in order to control the time and place of the conflict. An observer of Genoa 2001 G8 notes that "The attack was clearly pre-planned and designed to make things kick off well away from the Red Zone."[52]

In addition, police target well-known organizers and people with easily identified infrastructure functions (people doing communications, providing medical care, supplying music or water, using bullhorns to provide information or keep spirits up). These people are more likely to be picked off for arrest or shot at. "Snatch" arrests (in which a tight phalanx will rush a crowd and extract one undistinguished person) may also be arbitrary. At Philadelphia 2000 RNC, the housing activist Camilo Viveiros was subject to an extraordinary assault by Chief of Police Timoney, who then charged Camilo with assault and other crimes carrying a total of a thirty-year prison term. Despite the fact that Timoney couldn't tell a consistent story in court, the framing and fabrication of evidence against Camilo was not resolved until 2004. Such arbitrary targeting instills terror. (Of course, such tactics also enrage and politicize both activists and observers.)

There is some evidence in the United States that police may also introduce the possibility of violence indirectly, by encouraging opposing groups to attend protests. A number of groups we interviewed described the appearance of counterprotesters or opponents at events that had not been announced to the public. This method is reminiscent of third-world governments' use of paramilitaries or the private armies of the local elites to suppress rival political groups. (When two opposing political groups are present, it is always interesting to note to which group the police trustingly turn their backs.) Even if these confrontations do not result in violence, they may incite arguments, which, although they tend to be small-scale, become central to media coverage, creating an impression of strife, even if the dispute is quite marginal to the event itself—and, moreover, may have been created by the police. This artificial introduction of conflict changes the social context for assemblies and steals the strategic action frame from protesters.

Weapons used by police at protests include striking weapons, chemical weapons, electric weapons, projectiles (plastic, rubber, and wooden bullets), water cannons (sometimes with pepper spray in the water, which has a high rate of dispersal and which, unlike tear gas, is invisible), and concussion and shock grenades (the former meant to make a scary explosive sound, the latter used to simultaneously create a disturbing flash of light; both have been linked to severe injuries when they land on or close to people). Sonic weapons were used for the first time in the United States at Pittsburgh 2009 G20.[53] The U.S. National Institute of Justice is planning to implement the use of microwave weapons developed by the U.S. military for crowd control.[54]

In contrast, there has not been a single case of weapons preparation or use by alterglobalization protesters in the United States, and only a few Molotov cocktails have been used in Canada. On the few occasions when police have seized what they claimed was a weapon, they have had to withdraw the charges. U.S. and Canadian protesters do return tear gas canisters. (One justification for this is that the exploding canisters are less of a public hazard behind police lines, since the police have gas masks, unlike the general population.) European activists do use Molotov cocktails and similar weapons that can be used to start fires behind police lines. Europeans also throw cobblestones and other materials at police. This is a regular dimension of European labor and other protest, not unique to the alterglobalization movement. However, neither North American nor European protesters carry any firearms, knives, or other personal weapons. A European protester writes:

> I see our weapons as almost being tokenistic, symbolic—it illustrates the depth of our discontent. . . . But come on—a stone against a helicopter, a stick against an armoured car—and they call us violent? To be honest there is no comparison—they are the real butchers, they are the ones whose hands are covered in blood.[55]

Purportedly "less lethal" police weapons are often used counter to instructions. A number of protest participants and observers have suffered severe head injuries from projectile weapons whose "less lethal" status stipulates that they be aimed below the waist or at the ground. Gases are often misused in enclosed spaces with inadequate exits. Moreover, tear gas is not to be used as a projectile weapon. In a similar way, water cannons are a means for dispersion and may not be used to target individual protesters. This rule, along with the requirement that police aim at the legs of protesters and not above, was violated by police dissolving a blockade at one of the entry gates to the red zone at Heiligendamm 2007 G8. A protester, injured by a strong water jet, was blinded in one eye. At

Genoa 2001 G8, police used large amounts of CN gas, a form of tear gas prohibited by the Geneva Convention on War but not forbidden for public order policing. While still not allowed in most EU countries, rubber, plastic, and other alternative material bullets are regularly used in the United States.

As use of these weapons increases, their lethality is becoming more apparent. A total of 334 people died after having been attacked with a taser in the United States or Canada between 2001 and 2008.[56] There have also been more than one hundred deaths in custody associated with pepper spray, although the U.S. Department of Justice accepts as an extenuation that some of the victims were asthmatics or had previously been subjected to choke holds, so therefore their deaths were not due to pepper spray itself.[57] Protesters who have been shot with tear gas canisters at close range have suffered permanent, debilitating injury, and a woman leaving a baseball game in Boston was killed by impact of a pepper-spray projectile. Police departments, community coalitions, and government officials are investigating these weapons.[58] Meanwhile, other "less lethal" weapons are developed by the military and then quickly passed on to police.[59] A Police Chiefs' Association project encourages the adoption of these weapons.[60] Weapons proliferation is much more rapid in the United States than elsewhere in the world. Weapons deployment is also more chaotic in the United States than in Europe, and European police tend not have such a wide array on hand at a given protest.

European police have, however, used live ammunition at protests. At Genoa 2001 G8, Carlo Giuliani was shot at close range and killed. Activists described this event as an assassination, but the 2009 judgment of the European Court of Human Rights—while criticizing the Italian authorities for their handling of the subsequent investigations—held that the police officer had acted in self-defense. An attempt by activists to reconstruct the event using the video and photo material that became available through the trials, however, convincingly makes the point that the police officer aimed first at a fellow protester who was not threatening him directly and that Carlo, probably trying to do something to prevent his mate from being shot, grabbed a fire extinguisher lying on the ground, and ended up being shot himself. Just a month earlier, protesters had been shot at Göteborg 2001 EU; one almost died. At the same event, Swedish police, armed with semiautomatic rifles with laser sights, forced several hundred unarmed people, including a breastfeeding mother, to lay down outside the Schillerska School (the Convergence) for nearly an hour.[61] The reason provided for this operation was that an armed German terrorist was supposedly inside the school. However, neither the terrorist nor weapons were found during this intensive operation.

Prosecution

Very few activists charged at summit mobilizations in the post-Seattle era have been convicted. The majority of arrestees have had their cases dropped, not prosecuted, or have been offered incidental charges involving fines, such as a traffic citation. Among those prosecuted, most are not convicted. Unchanged since Isaac Balbus's 1973 study is the police privilege of using mass arrest as a method of control without being held accountable by the courts for providing reasonable charges and evidence.[62] Serious prosecution of activists arrested at summit mobilizations focuses on a handful of cases. These are of two types. Some involve high-profile activists whose conviction would simultaneously rid the state of a skillful opponent and discourage others from taking his place out of concern for the increased penalties for effective political action. Other cases involve ordinary protest participants. For both types, prosecutions tend to rely on inflated charges and chaotic evidence. The incredible budget, multiagency security apparatus, police violence, and mass arrests at Miami 2003 FTAA did not result in a single conviction of an activist.

In late 2007, in contrast, twenty-five activists from Genoa 2001 G8 were sentenced to a total of 110 years of jail time (the state asked for 225 years). According to Media G8way Gipfelsoli Infogroup "There have never been such high sentence demands for street clashes."[63] On November 17 of that year, about sixty thousand people marched in Genoa to protest the trials of the activists and to seek prosecution of the police for the violent raids and the detentions of activists at the summit. A statement from supportolegale points out that "25 people can't shield an inconvenient historical passage that questioned so strongly our lifestyle and society."[64] Prosecutions related to Göteborg 2001 EU resulted in an unusually high rate of convictions, usually on the charge of "breach of the peace" or "violent revolt" (*valdsamt upplopp* in Swedish). By 2003, sixty persons had been convicted and sentenced to a total of forty-five years in prison, and Eric Wijk claims that the total amount of years people served was 50 years.[65]

Activists are also sometimes arrested and charged preemptively. Eight activists planning to participate in Minneapolis 2008 RNC were preemptively arrested and charged with conspiracy to riot in the second degree and conspiracy to damage property, with terrorism enhancement. If convicted, they faced sentences of 12 years.[66] Under community pressure, the terrorism enhancement was dropped. Charges were dropped against three of the accused. Five accepted plea agreements for gross misdemeanor convictions. Four served no jail time.

Prosecutions of U.S. activists charged for opposing national or international events take place in the local courts, relying on evidence supplied by inexperienced local police working in an unfamiliar situation, fraught with interagency power struggles and hierarchical relations with other agencies. European prosecutions work with an integrated architecture of national riot police, who can more easily be prepared or unified around strategic cases.

Social justice activists are also experiencing increased prosecution for protests that do not involve summits. In 2001, routine prosecutions of protesters for repeated acts of civil disobedience (demonstrating too close to the U.S. School of the Americas) resulted in sentences of six months in prison—shocking outcomes for symbolic, negotiated, pacific trespassing. Three elderly Dominican nuns received sentences ranging from thirty to forty-one months for the "symbolic disarmament" (involving their own blood and a household hammer) of a Minuteman missile in Colorado in 2002.[67] Charges are also increasing against persons involved in effective, high-profile direct action, such as banner hangs, despite the peaceful and safe nature of this activity. Trespassing and property damage, traditional gray areas of civil disobedience, are being recast as severe and violent crimes or even terrorism. A good example is the so-called Tarnaq case of November 2008. Nine persons were arrested in the French town of Tarnaq as part of antiterrorist investigations because they allegedly had sabotaged train tracks in the context of the annual protests against the nuclear waste transports from France to Germany. One of the arrestees was held in custody for six months without initiation of a trial.

Most striking is the FBI's Operation Backfire, a major federal prosecution project that indicted fifteen people for various environmental property crimes, such as freeing animals from fur farms, damaging biotechnology field trial crops, and burning SUVs at automobile dealerships. Activists call this wave of indictments and related investigations "the Green Scare." In none of these cases was there risk to human life; yet, this type of activism was categorized as "eco-terrorism" and "domestic terrorism." In early 2006, as mentioned earlier, the FBI began indicting people for a series of such actions. Indictees were offered plea bargains in exchange for providing the names of other participants, and many cooperated in order to reduce the huge sentences with which they were threatened. They knew that these threats were serious because Jeff "Free" Luers had been sentenced to twenty-two years and eight months for the burning of three SUVs.[68] (The fact that Luers's sentence was longer than Oregon's sentence for rape insulted the feminist community, which joined in the campaign to free him.) Although the median sentence for arson in the United States is five years, many of the Operation Backfire sentences are much longer, because of "terrorism enhancement."

Another part of the Green Scare was the case against the SHAC 7, a group of activists who worked with an organization called Stop Huntingdon Animal Cruelty and organized against a company called Huntingdon Life Sciences. Charged not with any criminal activity but with conspiracy to encourage others to engage in activities such as protesting at company owners' homes, they were sentenced under the Federal Animal Enterprise Protection Act (formerly the Animal Enterprise Terrorism Act) and the electronic civil disobedience (for activities such as sending black faxes that use up the time and ink of the receiving machine). The SHAC 7 were sentenced to one to six years in prison, with all but one of the defendants receiving three or more years.[69] Sherman Austin served a year in federal prison (and was threatened with a great deal more) because of the links he posted on his website.[70]

During the Green Scare, grand juries were running in many U.S. communities, hearing evidence from extensive electronic surveillance and cooperative indictees. Much of the Left disassociated itself from the accused movements and did not stand by the arrestees or oppose the grand juries. The isolation and uncertainty of this time, along with the sudden and severe criminalization of former gray-area activity, caused activists to feel unsafe in every space and relationship.

Similarly, Germany's Article 129a antiterrorist legislation has been used against activists accused of property crime. Seven people, including three journalists, were detained in October 2007 and their friendship networks interrogated.[71] After the arrestees were held in isolation for three weeks, the federal court rejected the warrant for the sociologist Andrej Holm, who was being investigated because of similarities between his writings on gentrification and anti-imperialism and the manifestos of an antimilitarist group that had taken credit for burning some military vehicles. Other arrestees included his coeditors of a book on Venezuela.

The criminalization of nonviolent activity is shaking activists deeply. Our interviewees stated, "When people are being thrown in jail for twenty-five years for destroying vehicles, it means that we are just supposed to follow orders." The U.S. reclassification of military recruiters as federal officers makes interfering with them in any way a felony (thereby criminalizing pacifist actions at military recruitment centers). Activists suspect that creeping criminalization is happening in part because current social movements refuse to be violent; to justify the arrests and other interference, either the violence has to be invented or nonviolence has to be reclassified. Another interviewee proposed that "People aren't committing the crimes that they want them to commit. They can't throw them away, lock them up, so they will invent . . . charges."

One other category of prosecution aimed at dissenters is criminal suits brought against organizations in an effort to prevent them from participating in various protest activities. The U.S. government, for example, sued Greenpeace USA, holding the organization responsible for the civil disobedience of members who had already been tried and sentenced as individuals. Greenpeace was acquitted in 2004, as the prosecution failed to prove any violation of the obsolete 1872 "sailor-mongering" law in question, but questions regarding the First Amendment and selective prosecution issues were not addressed.[72]

Transnationalization of Protest Policing

Steadily, protest policing is taking on a character specifically directed at alterglobalization. Personnel and agencies are increasingly federalized and specialized and their strategies for managing activist citizens transnationalized. The Italian *carabinieri* assigned to control protest are military police. The French and Canadian riot police are federal police. The German Kavala that policed Heiligendamm 2007 G8 was an agency invented for that purpose. Although the U.S. military is constitutionally forbidden from taking domestic action and protests are generally policed by the local police, the National Guard was mobilized to handle the "emergency" of Seattle 1999 WTO. Even before the advent of the "war on terrorism," the U.S. Army's "antiterrorist" Delta Force was attending alterglobalization events; it was present in Seattle before the arrival of the National Guard.[73] Policing of Miami 2003 FTAA was a multiagency effort involving forty law enforcement agencies, seven of which were federal, in what was infamously described by Miami mayor Manuel Diaz as "the model for homeland security":

the largest mobilisation of German police (17,000) since the end of the Second World War made the headlines . . . deployment of the army and air force against demonstrators . . . a gigantic rehearsal for a civil war, an operation that was systematically prepared for over a year and a half, and whose methods and measures either tested or fully overstepped legal boundaries . . . 1,100 army soldiers deployed were also used against demonstrators.[74]

In Europe, international coordination of policing is under development by various transnational agencies. Three important ones are the research program Coordinating National Research Programs on Security during Major Events (EU-SEC), the United Nations Interregional Crime and Justice Research Institute (UNICRI), and the International Permanent Observatory on Security during Major Events (IPO). EU-SEC was initiated in 2004 as a response to Göteborg 2001 EU and Genoa 2001 G8. The main object of this research program is to coordinate police operations within the EU member states and with Europol. As part of this effort, EU-SEC publishes a handbook for security at summit protests, which is an attempt to set and disseminate standard security procedures to be followed at summit gatherings and to provide standard criteria and methods for risk analysis. EU-SEC itself is coordinated by UNICRI, a United Nations institute consisting of several working groups concerned with security. UNICRI publishes the "Counter-Terrorism Online Handbook." IPO is part of UNICRI and advises governments as they make security preparations for major events. The services of IPO are free to national governments. Founded in 2006, IPO was been involved in the preparations for St. Petersburg 2006 G8, Heiligendamm 2007 G8, Singapore 2006 IMF/WB, and Hanoi 2006 APEC (Asia Pacific Economic Coordination, another Free Trade Agreement). IPO is planning to publish a handbook for G8 member states.

Beside directly assisting and advising the respective governments on how best to coordinate security at summit, these agencies aim to standardize the criteria for security operations. The two handbooks that have been published include criteria for selecting summit locations. These official agencies are supported by the increased cooperation between the police forces and the secret services of various countries. The U.S. intelligence services, for example, now participate in evaluations of potential summit location from an early stage.

5

A Taxonomy of
Political Violence

How is it possible to assess the relative impact on dissent of the bodies stopped by water cannons in proximity to the fence and those stopped in their own kitchens by publicity about the funding and building and guarding of the fence? In this chapter, we present an analysis refined through ten years of direct experience, observation, theorization, and praxis undertaken alone, with fellow activists, and together as a research team. After refining many iterations of our analytic framework, we distilled a series of concepts that capture the dynamic effects of social control on dissent. We believe that scholars and litigators should focus on these concepts.

The multifunctional operations of the fence and its infrastructure require consideration of the connections between physical constraints and psychic perceptions, between individual reactions and social networks. Even the most tangible forms of social control, fences and force, also function indirectly as psychological operations, Foucault's "biopower." Meanwhile, some of the least forceful forms have the most direct and immediate effects: "I'm not going to the protest because I don't want to be on videotape."

These complex and subtle interconnections are articulated well by Alberto Melucci. He challenges the common instrumentalist conception of social movements that focuses on how formal organizations mobilize resources to take advantage of political opportunities by mounting strategic campaigns and staging disruptive protests. Instead, he focuses on the "submerged networks" in which "new ideas" are nurtured through decades of development and experimentation, eventually leading to social change:

> networks composed of a multiplicity of groups that are dispersed, fragmented and submerged in everyday life, and which act as cul-

tural laboratories. They require individual investments in the experimentation and practice of new cultural models, forms of relationships and alternative perceptions and meanings of the world. The various groups comprising these networks mobilize only periodically in response to specific issues. The submerged networks function as a system of exchanges, in which individuals and information circulate. Memberships are multiple and involvement is limited and temporary;[1] personal involvement is a condition for participation. The latent movement areas create new cultural codes and enable individuals to put them into practice.[2]

In this passage, Melucci summarizes several important concepts. First, he theorizes connections between the individual and the social and how each contributes specific work to movement development. The social creates a suggestive laboratory, which individuals experience through shifts in perception and meaning. Second, he emphasizes the role of discursive space through which information and ideas circulate. Third, he highlights the physicality of activity, experiments, and practice and their need for space. The body is crucial, but it is only one site of action. The mind, communication, and complex physical and nonphysical social spaces are equally important. And, clearly, the action is not all at protests, although these dimensions of social movements are expressed there.

In articulating a new analytic framework for understanding the social control of dissent, we draw on Melucci's analysis to consider violence not only against bodies but also against minds and social space. Traditional notions of political violence have focused on the body. Space is, of course, geographic: assemblies require public territories, and groups require rooms to meet, construct art, provide services, and so on. But Melucci's analysis of social movements also defines space as having particular institutional qualities that nurture social movements, such as privacy, independence, and undirectedness (so as to be open for experiment). And there is a third meaning to space, which is yet more subtle. It is the possibility of finding networks through which to ask questions and to propose, define, practice, and develop identities, cosmologies, cultures, and codes. How do we understand the kind of space that trust needs? What would constitute violence against the space for "alternative perceptions and meanings"?

Social spaces . . . independent of the institutions of government, the party system and state structures. . . . In them the signifying practices developed in everyday life can be expressed and heard independently from formal political institutions . . . individual and collective identities are able to exist; 'soft' institutionalized systems favoring the appropriation of knowledge and the production of symbolic resources; and open systems in which information can be circulated and controlled.[3]

Melucci also argues that the political action takes place in "everyday life." Does this mean that protest space is not particularly important? On the contrary, it means taht the psychological and social dimensions of politics are critical and vulnerable points. If the heart of social movements is the shifting, informal social networks through which people "ask questions about meaning," slowly articulate "conflicts" with social orders, and create new "knowledge" that ultimately changes society, then we need to be deeply concerned about the health of marginal, informal, prearticulate politics, not just formal, public, committed ones. We need to be concerned with forms of social control that limit, discourage, or redirect—whether they manifest at marches or in the newspapers.

In our work on the effects of various forms of policing, we have found it nearly impossible to distinguish between the effects of various police tactics and to track separately those effects on individuals, organizations, and communities. Assorted tactics used by the police arrive in the political consciousness of individuals and groups in one lump. Generally, interviewees' discussions of experiences of police violence seamlessly integrate urban security architectures and media campaigns with street-level policing. The analysis in this chapter explores the effects of policing tactics on social space, including discourse, and on the social and individual psyche of activists and the wider group of dissenters. We consider the marginalizing and preemptive effects of police action, the accumulative effects of police tactics, the disastrous effects of fear on political consciousness, the vulnerability of collectivity itself to police tactics, and the evisceration of discourse, culture, and history. We conclude the chapter with a strong proposal regarding the meaning of political violence. Please recall that, as in the rest of the book, all uncited quotations are from our own primary research.

Marginalization

A powerful indirect effect of protest policing is the marginalization of political activists. Each policing tactic reviewed in chapter 4 has a public relations function. Police tactics function to identify protests as criminal and, therefore, as illegitimate. This portrayal collapses the purported interests of elites and nonelites while trivializing and dismissing protesters' politics. It also communicates to protesters and would-be protesters that what they are doing is not—as they may have believed upon setting out—crucial to their society's well-being but is instead incomprehensible, bizarre, and unsafe. Activists cannot help internalizing these messages. They may respond by trying to make their protests sane, relevant, cheerful, and popular. They may respond by embracing a subcultural identity that scorns mainstream perspectives. They may do neither but subtly accept the idea that their views are not a valuable part of public life and their politics are an annoyance and inconvenience to fellow citizens.

Activists we interviewed described their experiences of marginalization, or what Foucault would call "technologies of the self." They explained, "Even the word 'activist' is stigmatized. People have disgust for what you do. You're not a committed, responsible citizen." Activists recognize how their skills are delimited. They cannot function normally. "When you're socially isolated, it's hard to be an organizer. If you're in that kind of fear level it attacks . . . your ability to relate to people." They even see themselves as toxic to other activists: "I must look suspicious. I was vague about myself. I [imagine] myself as an infiltrator."

Policing tactics communicate several key concepts. The first is that public dissent is, as argued by critical criminologists, criminal behavior. The use of surveillance cameras, intensive police presence, special armored vehicles, advance planning, and excessive budgets present as fact that the planned protests are a criminal matter requiring the advance preparation of security arrangements to protect the general population (since that is what the police are supposedly for). Second, the protests are not just a criminal matter requiring the attention of the authorities (like, for example, counterfeiting or double parking), but a matter of violence, aggression, and imminent general danger. The whole population of the city must prepare for large-scale violence, from which the good citizens are to be protected by security checkpoints, fences, militarized police, and patrols. Dissenters reconceive themselves not as political participants but as targets of a crackdown operation. They camouflage themselves, protect sympathizers from reprisal, and reduce communicative action so as not to draw police attention.

> *Traveling to Québec City for the FTAA protests in 2001, we took every precaution. We had prepared too much to let them turn us back. We knew about the fence. We knew about the border controls. We disguised ourselves in two SUVs traveling separately, in which we drank Pepsi and read People magazine. Every item in the car had been vetted. No political t-shirts, only Gap and Banana Republic. Not too much black. Not a single item of FTAA or globalization literature. All of our training material disposed of at a rest stop more than a hundred miles from the border. No crucial maps of the city where we'd be protesting. Only trail maps of our purported camping destination. At a diner, we had emptied our wallets, looking for political and social references. We had reprogrammed our cell phones, disguising all relevant information and political contacts. The guys tucked long hair into baseball caps and sat in the back seat for good measure. We did all of this with punctilious gusto, knowing we'd only have one chance to get across the border. We made it. We were clean. Clean, that is, of our reason for being there. We failed to anticipate what it would be like to prepare to protest without the accoutrements of political culture, and we had made no preparations for rebuilding it.*

Policing of protest also creates a division and a false dichotomy between "good" and "bad" protesters. The state constantly asserts its respect for the rights of "peaceful," "law-abiding" political expression. Those who refuse to follow the rules of protest permits, routes, and styles do not deserve the state's respect. Thus, by definition, all those who disturb in the slightest the channel provided by police are threats, are violent, unpredictable, preternaturally out of control, beyond the bounds of social mores. Political policing cleverly merges social decorum with the architecture of state control. Without public consideration of the amount of space and inconvenience to be granted to dissent, the state draws an arbitrary line. Those who transgress it are faulted with an assault against society itself. They are "anarchists," those who defy what the state says—whatever that may be today, no matter how absurd it is. The popular/hysterical use of the word "anarchy" captures the merge: Action transgressing the state's dictums, no matter how benign or trivial the transgression (such as feeding people in the park), is promptly portrayed as an explosive, corrosive virus. Anarchy will invade your house and will turn you into an anarchist; neighbors will be at each other's throats in a moment.

Marginalization and criminalization isolate those who are active. An interviewee explains how "five people's homes being raided leads to intimidation of millions of people. It needs to be clear that a goal of such activity is to isolate the movements that are being repressed, using the fear of millions of people to create that political isolation." This isolation changes everything about political action. "People are staying home to avoid being on a list, so then it feels like nobody cares." When police drive by groups' meetings regularly or engage in other tactics such as writing down license plate numbers, "This intimidates people from coming to our meetings." Not only does it reduce participation and preempt solidarity relations between organizations and movements; it also demoralizes activists who renarrativize their politics as marginal.

Meanwhile, the focus of protest policing on the immanent violence of protesters provides another kind of marginalization. The political target disappears from view. Global governance, already unaccountable, hides under a fake bush. The paraphernalia of militarization takes center stage and is rationalized. The established violence of debt holders, multinational corporations, and their chartering governments is not up for discussion, only the purported violence of some youths presumed to be on a train somewhere, headed this way.

Preemption

It is always "difficult," in the words of one of our interviewees, to "assess what doesn't happen." The absence of an occurrence is multiply determined—and activists are the first to admit this. But the preemptive effects of police violence are not difficult to find. Activists who have experienced militarized protest or citizens who have been subjected to advertisements of impending militarization see public streets and plazas as spaces of immanent violence too—but by the police. Public space, supposedly free for assembly and expression, is reshaped by police preparations into a dangerous zone. This restricts and reduces the fundamental political opportunity of public assembly as a social movement strategy. Even experienced activists become discouraged to organize and participate in demonstrations. Interviewees explain, "It gets tiring when you are shadowed by forty cops ready to beat your ass down when there are no illegal actions planned. It's just a protest." Another explained, "We barely did anything and got fucked with by the cops. . . . It affects people's motivation. They become apathetic, depressed, alcoholics. Depression and alcoholism are on the up and up. Political activism is on the down and down."

Inexperienced activists, on the other hand, are easily put off by a single show of force. In Colorado, just as the movement against the war in Iraq was becoming strong and diverse, a dispersing rally in Colorado Springs was inexplicably teargassed by police. This was one of very few acts of violence to occur during a global day of protest, February 15, 2003, which was dubbed "The World Says No to War." The violence put a little march in Colorado on the international newswire (of the eight hundred cities with marches, fewer than five experienced police violence that day). But many Colorado activists, who had been emboldened by the war and by new organizing, were thereafter terrified to attend another rally. They had brought their children. They were packing strollers and kids back into their cars when it happened. "I can think of three or four individuals who have gone to more spiritual activities, like meditations, prayers, and conversations and will not participate in public rallies." We heard this story over and over again from Colorado organizers who immediately saw a massive decline in turnout at events.

Vittrup's strategy aims to control the emergence and unfolding of a protest by blocking and redirecting assemblies. Counterinsurgent surveillance also aims to prevent political activities. However, many police strategies have indirect preemptive effects. The simplest measure of this is activists' frequent use of the term "intimidation," a description of police action that indicates an essence both preemptive and effective. When activists adjust their plans on the basis of their perceptions or expectations of the police or prosecutorial response they are likely to evoke, they are enacting "anticipatory conformity." They have already assaulted, contained, charged, or convicted their own hypothetical actions. Anticipating police repression at Heiligendamm 2007 G8, ATTAC tried to convince the Block G8 alliance to abandon its blockading concept in favor of a symbolic march toward the fence.

Another preemptive control tactic is creeping criminalization. As activists learn that formerly legal activities are being prosecuted, they don't know what will be defined as illegal next. The line of legality becomes phantasmic, varying according to activists' perceptions of state intolerance. If property crime is violence, then surely formerly gray-area activities, such as civil disobedience, will be excessively prosecuted, as well. And this phantasm is real. Creeping criminalization, in conjunction with conspiracy charges, chills discourse about currently legal activities that may not be legal next week.

Security perimeters, permitting, and protest pits make planned protest seem meaningless by restraining it to areas far away from its target. Permitting requirements preemptively discourage protest by magnifying the expense and difficulty of organizing. Protest-related legislation discourages protest by creating and advertising pretexts for police criminalization of lawful speech activity. Discouragement is a form of preemptive social control.

Publicity of large-scale surveillance databases, along with codes and tags such as "criminal extremist" and "domestic terrorist," have caused many dissenters to fear participating in even completely legal political events. Interviewees explain that "People who might be sympathetic are now either just completely neutral or don't want to know." Their reluctance to participate impacts donations to organizations, the number of participants at events, readiness to sign petitions and public statements, volunteerism, and willingness to receive educational newsletters and announcements.

Activists are punctilious in acknowledging that quantitative shifts in membership and level of activity are multicausal. Many said, "Well, you can never really know" why someone doesn't participate anymore or why fewer new people have joined this year. Despite this cautiousness, nearly everyone we interviewed in 2006 in the United States was able to think of people they know personally who had explicitly stated that they were ceasing political activity because of their fears of surveillance. Several interviewees stated that they personally knew twenty to thirty people for whom that was the case. When asked to count specific people they knew well who used to be active and whom they knew or suspected had curtailed their activism because of their fear of surveillance, every interview participant counted at least two people; many counted five to ten.[4] One insisted that s/he could list three hundred people. Another interviewee explained, "I would not want to give you a small number because it is my conviction that almost everyone that I know in [this city] doesn't want to come out." We observed a similar effect in the context of L'Aquila 2009 G8. Many activists did not even consider traveling to Italy because they were still in shock from Genoa 2001 G8. As one activist remarked during an interview, "It's sad, but the strategy of Genoa worked. I definitely don't want to be confronted with a *carabinieri* [Italian military police] anymore."

A number of our interviewees stated their suspicions that "leaks" of database information to the media, as well as Freedom of Information Action (FOIA) releases (files acquired under the U.S. Freedom of Information Act), are not what they appear to be. They believe this "information" is strategic law enforcement activity designed to cause potential participants to think twice about political action. Activists who have reviewed a lot of released files observed that "the redaction was deliberately inept," which they interpreted as a counterinsurgent act. Enhanced law enforcement databasing increases information collection with no opportunity for subjects to purge or correct errors or to challenge interpretations. Rapid information sharing among jurisdictions (including internationally) exponentially increases the impact of criminal and terrorist tags. The implications of databasing raise serious dilemmas for established organizations. Knowing well that mailing-list members and donors may be spooked and withdraw their support from the organization, interviewees wonder if they have an obligation to inform members and donors about the possibility of surveillance. This may explain why organizations sometimes pretend not to know or don't want to find out whether they are being watched.

Permeation and Accumulation

Social control tactics cannot be analyzed discretely because they are rarely employed separately. The tear gassing during the 2003 antiwar demonstration in Colorado Springs is an exception. Many of those affected had not experienced other police tactics and were thus able to describe the specific effects of that one police tactic. Typically, dissenters participating in a single summit mobilization experience ten or more tactics, from the constraining effects of the permitting process to menacing militarization, accompanied by several types of surveillance; they also witness unnecessary arrests and distorted descriptions of events in police statements to the media.

Moreover, social control actions interpenetrate. Frightening confrontations and selective prosecutions are often evidence of surveillance. Police arrange an array of tactics with suprarational relations. If it weren't truly frightening, their array of weapons and surfeit of cameras might be humorously absurd. Overkill ensures there's something for everyone.

As activists and groups become more experienced, they are exposed to more tactics. New activists may not immediately be aware of police tactics. As the tactics come into focus, however, their effect is cumulative. Vittrup's strategy of "exhaustion" describes the accumulation of experiences over time and space. Often activists prize their experiences of evident surveillance, police violence, and unpredictable prosecution as a badge of seriousness and commitment. But the accumulated effect of police tactics takes its toll in brittleness and a peculiar vulnerability. The impacts are not proportionate or predictable. Some activists ended their political work after experiencing police violence. For some, it was prosecution. For yet others, it was infiltration, for still others an affected friend. For one protester, the experience of hearing cops read her diary during a house search was the last affront.

This accumulative effect does not require sophisticated, multiagency coordination. This is not to say that social control is unstrategic or untargeted. In 2000, a diverse coalition of global justice activists was converging in the Denver/Boulder region of Colorado. Including long-time civil disobedients and younger direct activists, the coalition was working effectively to attract activists from the peace and justice, international solidarity, and student movements that were part of the emerging U.S. alterglobalization movement. The coalition was quickly destroyed when participating nongovernmental organizations (NGOs) were investigated in connection with an act of political vandalism that some believe was masterminded by an agent provocateur. Whether or not the act was contrived, the investigation was conducted as an act of collective punishment of the coalition, and it had lasting divisive effects. The coalition did not survive, and longstanding organizations have still not fully recovered. Activists' willingness to collaborate across tactical differences was destroyed.

Dispersed implementation of social control tactics has another impact, which is to convey a sense of permeation even when the tactics are not, in fact, pervasive. The indirect effects of police action gain their power through the phantasm of total presence—a reality imparted not only through history but also through seemingly haphazard particularity and the omniscience it implies.

> *The June night of the 2004 RNC raids, I arrived home, which at that time was an activist house. My roommate greeted me, ashen, and whispered, "They just raided two houses in Denver." We knew that if a house was to be visited in our city, it would be our house. We convened the residents in the backyard, where we made a list of every possible thing in the house that could be intentionally misconstrued as weapons related. This was Colorado, so we were looking for things like camping fuel and hunting knives. One of the nonactivist housemates was frustrated and didn't believe that he had to dispose of his hunting crossbow. We made a rapid, shaky, and silent cleanup of the house, moving offsite all activist paperwork and meeting notes and our computers (which we couldn't afford to replace if they were taken). We threw out literature from groups we didn't want to be associated with. And then we locked the door and sat waiting. The next day, sure enough, a member of our group was visited at his place of employment. Our house was not visited, but it might as well have been. Believing we lived in a rationalized technocracy, we anticipated that raids were approaching all houses comparable to the ones raided, which meant houses where activists involved in nonviolent direct action lived. We readied ourselves for the costs of that visit. We had enough time to impose the terror, inconvenience, and restraint upon ourselves.*
>
> *We lived suspended, jumping at the unfamiliar and terrifying sound of knocking on the usually unlocked door, unable without our computers to do any work. Clearly, they didn't need to raid us. The desired effect was already produced. We were much too tense to organize for the RNC. Although only five activist houses were raided that week, the message was sent loud and clear that the federal government was already accusing us of terrorism, knowing full well that we were not armed or violent organizations, simply because we were planning to participate in protest against the RNC.*

Political Consciousness and Terror

Political consciousness is the outcome of political dialogue. In Flacks's words, it is personal narrative and logic that lead people to decide to "make history," taking the risks and inconveniences that entails.[5] These decisions are sustained by immediate and extended communities that share analysis, hope, vision, and strategy.

Parallel to the development of political consciousness and political experience is the deepening of the experience of social control, which moves from discouragement and a sense of being misunderstood, to acceptance of marginalization and distortion, to a sense of danger and risk. Although trajectories are diverse, we can conceptualize layers of recognition of marginality and insecurity:

- My dissent is not valued by my purportedly democratic society and government. I am marginalized, trivialized, treated as an inconvenience.
- As a dissenter I am an enemy. My dissent impedes the "rights" of drivers.
- As public space is subject to violence, I feel that to express myself is a risk.
- As pacific actions are forbidden or assaulted, I feel that there is no space, no tolerance for dissent.
- As social control touches my everyday life, I feel an ongoing, personal sense of violence. The state is at war with me/us.
- I experience trauma at what I have witnessed/experienced.
- I face the ultimate, existential political choice. I cannot have a life because of state repression. I must choose between politics and my health or the safety of my family.

Simultaneously with the personal effects, social spaces and flows of communication are affected promptly by the fear and uncertainty induced by social control. These effects are well documented in Jeffrey Juris's book *Networking Futures*, in which he describes the transformation of Genoa 2001 G8 from a protest site to a space of terror.

It is not an uncommon view among activists that one of the most important aspects of mass demos is that participants are exposed to arbitrary police violence. It is often argued that this is one of the more reliably radicalizing experiences. In addition, it is often argued that this experience crystallizes issues of power, order, and discipline in society and forces people to address with clarity how their society functions: "We left our copy of the European Convention on Human Rights behind agreeing that a lemon would be more useful."[6] However, this knowledge brings with it a dark reversal of prior beliefs, that is, the understanding that social control is the defining feature of the interaction, not the political conversation of perspectives, values, ideas, and vision.

Many interviewees told us that social control has caused them to see the government as lawless. Criminalization of dissenters is an unstable fault line threatening to swallow them. An interviewee explained, "Rendition without charges . . . I think that enters into people's subconscious, like every moment of their day." Another said, "Like stepping off the sidewalk, those are only civil infractions and only circumstantially illegal . . . it's so often arbitrary. Sometimes you can march in the streets. Sometimes you can't. That's the area most affected for people. Their political imagination gets curtailed by repression." A young activist said, "It is scary that maybe one day the police will just walk in my door and take me or I'll have a bunch of charges that I don't know are accumulating, legitimate or illegitimate. The way the government is operating now it doesn't seem to really matter the accuracy of the data."

As the ground of criminality shifts, activists can protect themselves only by avoiding vaguely defined risk—places, organizations, topics, and people. What is striking, again, is that the activities avoided are not illegal. "I have really shifted the things that I'm willing to work on from anything that was progressive and radical to things that are more peace and justice," one person told us. Another interviewee explained, "I'm cautious about people I meet. I met someone from Pakistan and I have his card. But now I am choosing to get rid of materials associated with him because he's in the Middle East." An interviewee described how seeing one's every action as surveilled and subject to criminalization discourages any and all political activity: "It'll be easier for me to hang out and drink beers instead of being passionate and political. . . . At this point I assume the FBI will know whatever I do: [so I always think] Is this worth it being on my FBI file?" Through on our 2006 research, we learned that many U.S. activists had been largely pacified.[7] "There was a time in my life when I felt like I was going to do something powerful. *We* were going to do something powerful. And it was all taken away. And now it feels like I'm just going through the motions. I'm just verbalizing it, I'm not living it."

Even more difficult to handle than one's own risk is the recognition that one's activism puts others at risk, as well. This experience reframes activism as selfish and individualistic, counterposed with the well-being of family, friends, and communities—those for whom one is fighting in the first place. Activists come to see themselves as a toxin. After the house searches undertaken in connection with Heiligendamm 2007 G8, two activists explained how guilty they felt about not having encrypted their computer hard drives, which had been confiscated. They were afraid that all their contacts might be targeted, as well.

The collective dimension of political consciousness is the production of formal and informal discourse that supports analysis and ideology. But we find that, with increased awareness of social control, groups are censoring in advance their expressions. They are redesigning their communications for the police, not for fellow dissenters. "The assumption that everything is being read puts pressure to word things carefully to make sure it's clean. . . . We spend a lot of time reworking and rewording simple statements." What do they mean by "clean"? It's not about violence or illegality; they are "concerned about seeming inflammatory [or] confrontational. . . . We now have a department devoted to that." Everyone in the group interview laughed at this statement. But the joviality evaporated, and they became grave, describing the significance of this vigilance as "an accepted dimension in how we operate." Another organization even reconceptualized its assemblies: "We don't hold 'protests' or 'demonstrations'; we hold 'public awareness rallies.' Our language has changed. We have to be more precise. You can't talk like a regular person . . . if you're chatting away you might say the wrong things." Groups are also discouraged from associating themselves with others' ideas: "I don't like even talking about politics . . . because I don't want to get either of us confused in each other's business. If someone is being watched for something I'm not being watched for, I don't want to talk about politics with them."

In the United States, a major event that discouraged political association and solidarity was the mediated prosecution of Professor Ward Churchill. After an assault by conservative talk show hosts who sensationalized a small, nonacademic essay he wrote in response to the events of 9/11, Churchill's university investigated him with the intent to revoke his tenure. Radical allies scattered to the winds. One of our interviewees summarized the mood. "Anyone associated with Ward Churchill is contaminated. If you honestly come out and say, 'I think that Ward was right,' you're a pariah." The state's overt lesson was that even tenure could not protect leftists. But the covert lesson was equally chilling. The left was too scared to enact its own sacred watchword—solidarity. And leftists were perfectly willing to blame the victim to bulwark the fantasy that careful wording (counterposed to Churchill's purportedly rash prose) could protect them from a similar fate.

But many activists are well aware that watching your words is a feeble defense. Groups don't need to generate evidence of criminality in order to be assaulted. State counterinsurgency projects will invent the evidence, or simply demonize and criminalize words and acts formerly considered legitimate. And it takes only one episode of police action to scatter would-be participants and supporters, severing lines of communication and political development. Police tactics benefit from the irrational power of fear, which dramatically amplifies those tactics' effects.

When organizations are marginalized and isolated from one another through fear of contamination, they also lose the cross-fertilization of multi-issue analysis and organizing. (In Europe, this strong cross-fertilization developed directly from the movements of the 1960s. In the United States, movements first took a detour through single-issue politics and only later forged a new multi-issue "politics of difference.") Social movement groups continue to be challenged by one another to address "multiple oppressions" and seek amelioration not only of working conditions but also of "everyday life" itself.[8] In order to develop continuous analysis of new issues (e.g., biotech, water privatization, immigration), social movement groups need to trust one another enough and to interact with one another enough to learn from one another—capacities endangered by the intense fear induced by police tactics.

Collectivity

Sociology asserts that human collectivity is unassimilable into biological, economic, or philosophical theories. Social movements scholarship is built on the recognition that collective popular responses to social problems differ fundamentally from individual responses. Social movements literature wrestles with the perversely unpredictable phenomenon of the peculiar collectivity that is the formation, diffusion, and dissipation of a social movement.

By asking the question of how individuals and groups make sense of their action and how we may understand this process, we are obliged to shift from a monolithic and metaphysical idea of collective actors towards the processes through which a collective becomes a collec-

tive . . . (i) Collective identity as a process involves cognitive definitions concerning the ends, means, and the field of action . . . (ii) . . .
to a network of active relationships between actors who interact,
communicate, influence each other, negotiate, and make decisions.
forms of organization and models of leadership, communicative
channels and technologies of communication . . . (iii) . . . a certain
degree of emotional investment is required. . . . Collective identity
is never entirely negotiable because participation in collective action
is endowed with meaning which cannot be reduced to cost-benefit
calculation . . . passions and feelings, love and hate, faith and fear . . .
particularly in those areas of social life that are less institutionalized,
such as the social movements. To understand this part of collective
action as "irrational," as opposed to the parts that are "rational" (a
euphemism for "good"), is simply nonsensical. There is no cognition
without feeling and no meaning without emotion.[9]

As described so far in this chapter, social control affects individuals
in complex ways. It also affects collectivities. Of course, here, again, we
cannot draw a clear boundary. What happens to collectivities also affects
individuals who are connected (or who could be connected) to them. And
an event that affects one individual can ricochet through a collectivity, as
well, frightening others almost as if it had happened to them, while taking
on collective dynamics as group history, a shared story, and a crisis point.

A special category of collectivity is the social movement organization
(SMO). These include formal organizations, such as churches and nonprofit organizations, but much social movement work happens outside
formal organization, in various informal groupings that are also SMOs.
Temporary groups organize around events (affinity groups and event
conveners). Other informal groups are long-term friendship-based associations better described as communities.

Social control sullies the reputation of organizations—that is the
public relations function of criminalization. Without any prosecution
having occurred, simply through overt police attention, potential participants, donors, and supporters are led to perceive an organization
as criminal. Social justice groups that are part of religious congre-
gations find that their implied criminalization distorts their relation
with their communities. An interviewee explained, "If we were being
watched and beat up, then there must be something not right about
what we're doing. . . . As if we're not really [religious people]. . . . Our

reputation was tainted. If the police don't trust you, something must be wrong with you."

As recognized by scholars, organizations under surveillance tend to shift their agenda from projects to self-defense.[10] Interviewees described this repeatedly as "a distraction." An interviewee stated, "What I want to be doing is on the street holding a sign and doing my protesting. But we got pulled off into being concerned with countersurveillance." An interviewee observed that the new leadership of his group "avoids anti-war and antimilitary and protest. But we've always been about war and peace and nonviolence!" Members of other organizations described their struggles against the criminalization or restriction of demonstrations. The most striking example of this shifting agenda came from a church member whom we interviewed. The church's governing board, he said, was so spooked by surveillance that it curtailed charitable donations made from its endowment. Fellow interviewees from his group expressed their shock that the church refused even to give money for aid after Hurricane Katrina.

Once the immediate self-defensive activity is over, the agenda of the organization may be permanently shifted. A long-time board member of a twenty-seven-year-old peace and justice organization reflected on the aftereffects of overt surveillance six years after it happened (the interview took place in 2006): "It scared us from sponsoring events," he said. "My sense is we would have been much more active against the [2003 Iraq] war. As an organization we've avoided initiatives. . . . We've participated in other groups' events, [holding] banners. . . . I think we've stayed away from contentious issues. We haven't said anything about immigration or about the war."

We found that police tactics had a widespread chilling effect on internal communication in organizations. Regardless of the legal status of the activities they participate in, members of nearly all of the groups we interviewed have reduced their use of e-mail and the telephone, instituted "complicated" communications systems, and try to have their meetings in person. Typically, a pacifist group explained, "We did not use e-mail at all, for anything. We set our meetings at rotating locations, and everybody knew where the meeting was going to be. We wouldn't communicate by phone." An interviewee joked self-deprecatingly, "It totally changes the character of any conversation. 'Do you remember that meeting we talked about last week? Well, it's happening tonight. What's it about? I'll tell you later.'" Interviewees were quick to point out how much this "slows us down." Because of the difficulty in communicating, "things that take a lot of planning don't ever happen."

Strategic campaigns require extensive logistics, interdependencies, coordination, and timing. Surveillance disrupts the elements of relationships and communication that make strategic planning possible. Scared to be creative, wary of trusting anyone, aware that no conversations are private, organizations have great difficulty generating strategic plans. An interviewee explains the "paralysis" that results when efforts to be strategic and creative to plan effective actions are affected by "worry about the heat you're going to get for even trying—for even talking about it . . . if we do *anything*, we are going to be watched, hammered down." An intervewee from another organization says, "We couldn't think creatively."

A German activist relayed to us a telling anecdote about Berlin 1988 IMF/WB. Although many groups had been preparing action for several months, during one of the last general meetings preceding the protests, no group wanted to reveal its plans. The fear of infiltration and of the resulting criminalization was overwhelming. The meeting became known in activist circles as the "hush meeting." A participant at St. Petersburg 2006 G8 explained how planners had to organize meetings in the middle of the night at cemeteries because they lacked other available spaces that were free of surveillance. That this is not only a problem for activists in postcommunist countries became evident during Heiligendamm 2007 G8. The last few action planning meetings were organized outside the camps; participants moved to several different places during each meeting in order to avoid infiltration and surveillance. Besides inducing a constant feeling of insecurity, this also turned out into a time-consuming and exhausting maneuver.

Events and campaigns depend on organic leadership development and on volunteerism. Several interviewees had observed police targeting of people who are stepping up and taking responsibility for logistics, outreach, or safety roles (e.g., marshals and medics). Police surveillance puts a criminal taint (by implying accusations of agitation or conspiracy) on logistics roles and on volunteerism in general. Moreover, long-term relationships with organizations seem risky, so affiliations become more temporary and less committed, with the result that "I've noticed a big shift from long-term strategizing and community building."

Conservative decisions on the part of organizations are understandable in light of the costs of surveillance to organizational resources. Governments provide little to no administrative mechanisms of accountability for false accusations, improper or unwarranted investigations, or erroneous surveillance. One organization that was illegally searched spent more than 1,500 hours of volunteer time dealing with the fallout for its membership and its relations with other organizations. Of the seventy-one surveilled organizations in our U.S. study, only two had managed to take legal action related to surveillance.

Organizations rely on networks of supporters for material resources as well as for analytic development, as discussed in the section on political consciousness. A U.S. pacifist group in our study had been meeting in a church hall. After the media revealed that the group was under surveillance, it was no longer welcome to use the church, and its relations with that congregation have been strained because it was viewed as having put the church at risk. Groups that rely on their solidarity with other groups may even become wary of social associations: "As soon as your organization's name is linked with another organization, . . . then there's this sense of we're going to trigger the alarm bells . . . just because we had a picnic with these folks." Regional networks can be disrupted by social control in one area of that region. "People say, 'I don't want to go [to do political action] in [city]. It's scary, it's dangerous there.' When you hear that, you realize that the surveillance on [city's] activists has worked. . . . You shouldn't have to stay home to be safe. You should feel safe wherever you go to express yourself."

In the United States, 9/11 and the Green Scare broke ties of generosity and solidarity among organizations. With federal accusations of violence and terrorism attached to a wide range of organizations, formal and informal groups became islands reluctant to associate with or to issue statements in support of others. These associations might sully their reputation, frighten their donors, or endanger their ongoing (although much reduced) campaigns and membership. And many of these groups' political work was primarily education and communication—sharing their information, analysis, and vision with the larger society. After listing the paralyzing effects of social control, an activist concluded pithily, "And you're trying to communicate with millions of people!"

Meanwhile, social movement organizations have persisted in rationalizing surveillance and repression. Rather than opposing government repression, many organizations have worked to articulate a hard line between legal and illegal political activities (a distinction also claimed by the organizations that refused to be interviewed by us on these grounds), expending extensive resources in "careful wording," which they believe will keep them safe.

In Europe, many direct-action groups of the early wave of summit protests have meanwhile become NGO-like organizations focused on information gathering and awareness raising. Pretending to support critical civil society, European governments effectively pacify dissent by making it dependent on state money. Instead of fearing surveillance, former activists worry now that their organization's funding will be cut and they therefore refrain from organizing disruptive or transgressive activities.

Groups concerned about the creeping criminalization of gray and formerly legal activity take extreme precautions, forgoing inclusivity and destroying written records of their work. Groups also reported not taking notes at meetings: "We're afraid to have a piece of paper with anything written on it at the end of any meeting," said one activist. Further, many interviewees, having internalized the general concern about undercovers, said that they don't want to be seen writing anything down, because it would make them look as if they were surveilling the meeting. In addition, concerned about future investigations, they do not keep diaries. This lack of archiving is the destruction in advance of the history of the movement, and it has implications for social movements' capacity for active reflexivity.

Space and Discourse

We use the concept of "space" to combine several other concepts. "Political opportunity" is a concept that has been used to describe the confluences of constraint and creativity that structure (and exclude) possibilities that social movements might use strategically. Movement space shelters the communion that recognizes these opportunities, as well as communication and connection between people. A third kind of space is the "laboratory" (formerly conceptualized as a "resource") in which social movement activity is prepared, prototyped, and practiced. This may be a physical space, but may take other forms as well. Meeting rooms, though mundane, are crucial, other kinds of physical space equally so. These three kinds of space are interdependent and inseparable.

Today's system of social control has communicated to dissenters that their societies are not open to dialogue, no matter how peaceful. Reflecting on police seizure of art materials, an interviewee explained: "There's a strong statement: 'Our threshhold for your dissent is so low, it's way down here. We're not going to tolerate perfectly legal building of perfectly legal things."'

Activists also perceive a foreclosure of political space formerly available for civil disobedience. Civil disobedience includes negotiated symbolic actions such as crossing through a fence onto a military base (ready for a prompt and docile prearranged arrest). Civil disobedience also includes activities such as the creation of street art, mass bike rides,[11] and squatting; these are legal "gray-area" activities that have been subject to escalated police action and criminal charges. Members of several pacifist groups we interviewed said that the groups had been infiltrated during civil disobedience actions. (This was surprising, because civil disobedience is not covert, indeed often prenegotiated with police, so there is no need for infiltration.) Interviewees reported that going through the intense experience of preparing for arrest and then finding out that one of their fellow arrestees was an agent had shaken them deeply. After that, "you don't want to get your friends and nuns and old people involved." Civil disobedience relies on the judicial system, which has in part closed off opportunities for protest by imposing increasingly harsh sentences and by refusing to allow the political motivations for acts of civil disobedience to be considered in court proceedings (eviscerating the political content of trials and forcing the defense to rely on apolitical technicalities).

Social space for discourse and connection has also been reduced. "We're scared to openly and honestly talk about issues in our community. The state is using that information to crush legitimate movements." A middle-aged person in a peace group told us, "My mom is scared to talk to me on the phone. . . . She's not sure what she is allowed to say and not anymore." A member of a peace group reported on the changes its members had made since experiencing social control: "We used to be a lot closer. Now we sometimes talk in code, we're more cryptic, share less information. We're all a bit more reserved in terms of our speech." Another activist says, "People are scared of the implications of just being radical. There's almost no space that we consider safe. . . . People just stopped expressing those views entirely."

On one hand, the spatial control of dissent works like Foucault's disciplinary gaze. This powerful gaze places the burden of discipline on the observed, thus interiorizing the power of observation to the point where activists become their own observer, each person regulating his or her own behavior. This strategy seeks to reduce feelings of anonymity, producing more pacified forms of dissent. The reduction of anonymity for the purpose of policing is not new. According to Foucault, the thrust of modern power lies behind the seemingly simple idea of surveillance and internalization that now permeates modern society. This impulse away from anonymity is ever-present in contemporary society, from community policing tactics[12] to national security investigations. Of significance here is that reducing anonymity in specific spaces can directly impact how people act in those locations. In the end, these techniques of power produce (obedient) individuals and subjects, rather than people who must be "repressed."[13]

The consequences became painfully apparent at L'Aquila 2009 G8, where the lack of safe spaces caused people to stop expressing their views. In the weeks preceding the summit, activists in several cities suffered several waves of house searches; social centers were also targeted. At nearly all the social centers, activists hastily announced that they had nothing to do with G8-related activities and that their social center was not available for protest coordination or as a meeting place for international protesters.

Feeling Culture

"The cultural turn" in sociology, alongside the emergence of "new" social movements, has emphasized the significance of culture in shaping social problems and providing the material for (and constraints on) mobilization for social change. "The culture of protest" recognizes that social movements contain and nurture their own cultures, including particular styles of interaction and expression. Ron Eyerman and Andrew Jamison argue that cultural change is always the ultimate goal of social movements and thus the medium in which they work. Melucci considers everyday life as a site of political development; needs are first felt, articulated, and shared at the level of the mundane. They are then collectivized and elaborated as cultural movements in the process of politicization.

Social control at times takes the form of fearsome spectacle, with epic stage sets, elaborate costumes, loud explosions, and intense drama. But social control, too, has an "everyday life." Endless judicial proceedings drain the energy of participants and erode the place of politics in the courtroom. Surveillance induces a jittery unreality that, when internalized, trails targets far beyond their agents' assignments.

Among our methodologies is the use of our own bodies as observational devices for studying the social control of dissent.

> *Normally and decisively resistant to what we view as self-aggrandizing paranoia, Luis and I [Amory] fell victim to it while conducting our 2006 study of surveillance in the United States. Seeking to be "responsible," we designed detailed precautionary practices to protect our interviewees' identities, to avoid data loss, and to prevent project delay. We kept our appointment calendars only in our minds, backed up data in three places every night, never left our laptops in cars, and didn't discuss the data on the phone. The one night I left my laptop in the hotel room and went out dancing, I carried a copy of the day's data taped to my body.*
>
> *Exhausted from travel and intense interviews, I found myself looping in my security logic, unable to clearly distinguish what needed to be protected or even what could be. I wasn't able to get a reality check and support from Luis because we weren't going to discuss or revise security procedures over the phone. When I stumbled across my organization's name while reading an interviewee's FBI file, I had no way to seek any support. Back home after the research trips, I fought the urge to feel safe in my own home and maintained security procedures for nearly a year until we had submitted our first article. Several times during the year, I spent hours looking for things I had successfully hidden even from my own memory.*

When people believe they may be under surveillance, ordinary life takes on a funhouse quality, full of gross distortions, absurd oversights, and looming combustion. This can make you crazy, fast. It can also make you inefficient and temperamental.

> *I'm dragging my laptop through the grocery store. I have CD data in the small of my back. Every time I leave my home, I'm aware of its vulnerability. An activist with a project, running a hallucinatory (but not unrealistic) obstacle course of social control, I was determined to make it through, to deliver the goods. My daily life has been transformed, infused with fear*

and caution, evacuated of open celebration of struggle, ready
for assault, and neutralized by the ambition to "run clean" so
as to survive it.

This is not a culture of dissent. This is a culture of fear.[14] Activists call
it "security culture." In an interview, an activist explained to us that security "was the first thing we talked about, even before our name or what
we're going to do." The fundamentals of organizing culture are inclusivity
and solidarity.[15] The focus on security has, in some instances, had devastating impacts on inclusivity, solidarity, and the production of friendship
bonds necessary to build a healthy activist community. Many of our inter-
views suggest that security culture has in fact replaced organizing culture,
mainly because of the effects of state surveillance. An activist explained,
"When I see people I don't know, I get excited. When I first saw the undercovers, I was amazed that we had attracted folks that don't fit in, and I
was sad when I found out they were undercovers." Another interviewee
described how people who fit in too well with the group, as well as people who don't fit in, arouse suspicions. The hallmarks of security culture
are exclusion, wariness, the withholding of information, and avoidance of
diversity. An activist described his group as showing "paranoia, freakiness,
and unwelcomingness that results from the fear." Another activist jokingly
described security culture as the "icemaker," which has replaced the community building "icebreaker." The person went on to explain: "Like handing
out a signup sheet . . . people are not only afraid to sign up, but afraid of
asking for it." A new activist described the experience this way: "What's the
opposite of unites? When I'm suspicious or they are, it creates a tension,
conscious or not, about who people are and what their intentions are."

Another interviewee described the issue this way: "Secretive planning
is a disaster in community building." The person added, "New people can't
get involved. It's hard to build a movement on community when secrecy
is an important thing." Another interviewee pointed out that security culture has become so common that people are using it for actions that don't
need to be protected: "There's confusion over what actions need to be
clandestine and what doesn't."

Again, we draw on the lived experience in our own bodies and con-
sciousnesses. And knowing the ravages of security culture doesn't make
us immune to it. Even at nonactivist gatherings, we instinctively bristle
when we see a "sign-up list" at the entrance of an event, we give a fake
e-mail address, we feel uncomfortable when people ask for more than a

first name in a meeting and when even a friend asks for too much detail about a project over the phone. When the friend is an activist, the person hears the reluctance to be specific and understands. And we both see how damaged we are.

In addition to the displacement of organizing culture by security culture, we found other distinct dimensions of cultural change in protest movements. Cultures of protest rely on trust, bonds of friendship, and community. After an infiltration was revealed, "people were tense, held back, uncommunicative, not feeling good about themselves and other people. . . . [There's] something insidious about destroying the trust." An activist described how the intimacy and urgency of political community was disrupted by infiltration: "We're lonely in our churches and organizations where we work. So there's an incredible sense of community when we meet [other peace activists]. We're hugging and learning to protect each other." An interviewee who learned that a long-term and close friend was an FBI informant described the effect of the experience: "If this friend of mine could be an informant, then anybody could . . . anything could be true. My entire reality was disrupted . . . all my friendships and alliances thrown into question." The result?: "I'm not really doing much anymore."

Social movement communities learn through "cross-pollination." Experienced activists pass on what they have learned, and people travel to share strategies and tactics. But if people are afraid to be associated with each other or can't trust each other, these networks of information-sharing stop cold. "It was nice to be able to tell stories of like I worked with this organization and can I help you build. . . . Here's what we did that you all might be able to do. . . . Now . . . you can't help them out, you can't tell them stories of things you've done before. Because if they were a snitch you'd be in a really bad situation."

Another cultural shift is the avoidance of historical reflection, including debriefing, which would necessarily indict individuals for their roles in events that might be criminalized sometime in the future. Reflection is intentionally reduced as a protective measure: "Here, we can only talk about what's going on here. Next week we can't talk about this anymore. And we can't talk about something else until it's sure who's going to be part of it." If actions cannot be discussed later, the strategy of the movement no longer advances. There are too many witnesses; better destroy the history and the possibility of memory. Something might have happened, but no one will know exactly what it was, or who did it, or how it was done. There will be no expertise to draw on for the next time. Social control effectively provokes an erasure of collective memory: minutes of gatherings are often not kept anymore, websites are dissolved immediately after a mobilization. This way, activists effectively administer their own marginalization. They have turned into "people without history."

Many social movements aim to create what scholars call a "prefigurative" cultural practice (which enacts the liberation they strive to achieve) as a dimension of their work on campaigns and projects.[16] These very prefigurative practices, such as openness and equity, make them easy to infiltrate (although some believe that these practices function like jujitsu to redirect agents who must participate in progressive practices to maintain their cover). But the agenda-reorienting, fear-cultivating pressures of social control may well elicit a reduction of prefigurative practices, particularly when those practices are used as hallmarks to target participants and movements.

Cultural communities may slowly become social movements through the process of developing meaningful practice to continually embody their values. But, as this practice verges on the political and is targeted as part of social control, its use may be reduced. We interviewed a church group whose members described how the pressures of social control caused the congregation to question (and ultimately to largely abandon) its formerly growing belief in a "Christian obligation" to social justice.

One of the most popular forms of prefiguration is participatory democracy. Under the pressures of social control, movements committed to participatory democracy and transparency resort to secretive planning (which they describe as elitist). Group members we interviewed were communicating much less and across fewer media: "There isn't that constant discussion, which can be really beneficial. Then you get everybody's opinion if you can talk to everyone." Many groups reported that they were no longer maintaining their former level of inclusivity in decision making: "Sometimes a handful makes decisions, and it never used to be that way." The loss of transparency also means that members cannot hold leaders and groups accountable. In addition, people don't have the information they need to make informed decisions. Not only are the decisions made by fewer people, but they are made by a group whose diversity is constrained by suspicion: "There's not as many people involved, there's not as many voices in the decision making, there's not as many people from different walks of life." Participatory democracy links accountability with transparency. Activists are well aware that secrecy can be toxic to their values; in seeing secrecy as unavoidable, they know they have surrendered much of what they stand for. The cultural loss of the living values of transparency and inclusivity is personally and socially devastating.

Political Violence

If social control disrupts the health and activity of social movement groups, we might understand it to have "maimed" the social movement. As we summarized in chapter 1, dissenters require a sense of entitlement, efficacy, organizational networks, trust in government, a sense of hopefulness, and space. We have shown how social control affects individuals' comfort and sense of efficacy in expressing their dissent, the development of political consciousness, fundraising, networks, the redirection and usurpation of agendas and plans, the displacement of strategic framing, the foreclosure of space and dialogue, and the disruption of culture.

In addition to these more or less linear effects, we have also identified irrational ones, those that result from fear. Like solitary confinement, social control threatens the sanity of people and organizations. Fear coursing through them, individuals become paranoid, and groups undermine their own values and abandon their projects. And they avoid one another, justifying this abandonment as essential for survival. Later, wasted by adrenalin and redirection, they default to actions and methods that represent mere dispirited shadows of their former ambitions. They rationalize it all. They will be safe if they just don't inflame the authorities. Since they usually didn't do anything wrong in the first place, this belief verges on irrationality. Can we use the phrase "organizational insanity" to describe an organization that has lost its ability to pursue its own objectives—or, indeed, to recall them faithfully?

Rather than finding the customary dualism in which hardcore activists become more militant while other activists become more moderate,[17] today we find signs of pervasive pacification in the United States and Europe. In lieu of going "underground" to continue their actions,[18] many social movement groups are abandoning gray-area civil disobedience activities and moving toward exclusively educational and permitted activities. Yet, knowing that even educational events are under surveillance, groups do not feel safe undertaking even this most pacific type of action. We heard from all types of groups that strategic and ideological dialogue have been both reduced and self-censored. L'Aquila 2009 G8 demonstrated the dramatic decline in popular willingness to participate in protest. In contrast to Genoa 2001 G8, where a hundred thousand people took to the streets, the major demonstrations in 2009 brought out just several thousand protesters. This is not an unambiguous tendency, and there are some signs also of increasing militance. Strasbourg 2009 NATO was dominated by property destruction and confrontations with the police.

Regardless of the apparent response of activists (which are determined by many factors, including the increasing number of events to be protested), our focus is the political reality of social control. Even when participating in state-sanctioned actions, organizations are weakened. Confronted with a "protest pit," would-be dissenters are discouraged to the point of feeling they are wasting their time. Social control works psychologically, and this includes menacing police costumes and formations, surveillance months before the event, and Kai Vittrup's negotiations in the streets. Psychological methods are by far the easiest and least controversial way to police a protest. People just stay home.

Can we propose that social control can be fatal when it does not kill a *person*? We are alarmed to find security culture displacing organizing culture in most groups, including peace groups, pacifist groups, and other groups that undertake only legal activities. We are also concerned by the reduction of free communication and the loss of both living history and written archives. Communication and archiving are essential functions of organizations, without which they become something less than an organization, incoherent and episodic. Organizations that cannot organize, communicate internally, establish relationships, or maintain archives are in critical condition.

Melucci emphasizes "collective action as a social production, as a purposive, meaningful and relational orientation."[19] Associational life depends on membership, donations, and access to space in which people feel comfortable engaging political ideas. Assaults on organizations that deprive them of resources and democratic space and that burden potential participants with excessive risk amount to what is conceptualized on an individual level as an assault or an excessive use of force. If we can show that social control debilitates, disables, and destroys not only activists but political organizations, does it make sense any longer to describe social control with a term other than "violence"? If political violence includes a range of activities directed against political organizations and if we can observe these activities regularly in Western Europe and in the

United States, can we continue to make sense of an analytic tendency that reserves the analysis of state political violence for "dictatorships"?

Purportedly democratic modern states are engaged in a good deal of violence, not only in their external relations with other states but also in the way they manage their own populations. This includes what is seen as the legitimate, spontaneous use of force in apprehending suspected criminals (sometimes executing them in the process). Violence is routine in the administrative management of detainees, prisoners, and migrants. Militarized police operations against organized groups, such as squatters and separatists, are supposed to be taken under judicial directive. Violence is also used to secure the "public order" against large, disorganized, and anonymous crowds, such as sports fans or paraders. States engaged in civil war mobilize violence through the police, prisons, military, and vigilante organizations.

Violence against political dissenters in situations that do not involve civil war is sometimes conceptualized as a "public order" conflict. It sometimes takes the form of criminalization and judiciary-directed military action. When dissenters are categorized (usually by political, rather than judicial, means) as "threats to security" or "domestic terrorism," state violence may involve federal agencies and military resources.

"Political violence" is a concept that has been used to study social movement tactics[20] and totalitarian societies.[21] There is a fair amount of political territory between these concepts. Research on state political violence against social movements in democracies has not gone much beyond forceful protest policing.[22]

Citizens and residents of modern democratic states can enact violence against the state, including individual acts of rage, seemingly spontaneous insurrections, strategic sabotage, guerrilla attacks, or military action. All of this action is political; it is dissent by other means. The most outstanding recent examples of violent confrontations with the state were the riots in several poor suburbs of Paris in 2005 and the upheavals in Greece in 2008 after the police murdered a fifteen-year-old boy, Alexandros Grigoropoulos. In both cases, the violence consisted widely of mass confrontations between the police and citizens, who threw stones, rockets, and Molotov cocktails; burned cars and used rubbish bins to erect barricades; trashed shop windows; and looted. The concept of violence can produce heated debates among activists and scholars alike, each using different definitions and coming from diverse ideological perspectives. In particular, Black Bloc tactics[23] produce strong reactions. Appendix B in this book contains an e-mail dialogue between two scholars, John Holloway and Vittorio Sergi, that focuses on these tactics and their relations to violence. The dialogue is included because it clearly shows the complexity of the issue and will likely prove useful for the reader.

Our research shows that overt, bodily violence against protesters is part of a dense continuum of state activity. The density is important because bodily violence is neither distinctly the worst thing that can happen to an activist nor yet entirely separable from other forms of repression, over which it looms as an explicit or implicit threat. Repression is a multimedia assault that arrives in the psyche all at once. By referencing each other, both bodily violence and other forms of repression have a cumulative force and impact, as documented in studies of state terror. While we do not intend to diffuse the meaning of "violence" or to enter into debate about its proper understanding, it is apparent that less overt forms of state repression wreak comparable damage.

We are cautious about undermining the usefulness of the concept of violence by expanding it. Nevertheless, when considering state violence against dissenters, we feel the need to ask about the meaning of political violence. Is political violence the subset of overt bodily violence that has a political source, or does political violence refer to damage to political rights?

- If a dissenting group is restricted by legislation, permitting conditions, or metal barricades from access to public space to such an extent that its ability to create a meaningful challenge is eliminated or curtailed—although no bodies are injured—is this political violence?
- If a dissenting group whose members, although marginalized, have expressed enthusiasm for political expression now finds that the environment of protest has changed such that these same members are now frightened or newly impotent to express their planned dissenting view—although no bodies are injured—is this political violence?
- If a dissenting group whose members have embarked upon a manifestation the planning of which has been surveilled such that the police know there are no plans for any violent actions, is pestered by searches or finds its access to the start point restricted or rerouted, is terrorized at gunpoint, or has its members arrested—although no bodies are injured—is this political violence?

✦ If a dissenting group finds that it receives extensive media coverage it has not initiated that associates it with property crime or violence and that seeks to convince the public (including persons concerned about the substantive issues the group works on who may have considered attending events organized by this group as an opportunity to learn more or express their views) to view the group as criminal and to avoid contact with its ideas and members—although no bodies are injured—is this political violence?

✦ If a dissenting group finds that it has been labeled a "domestic terrorist" group in government databases such that donations and receipt of literature from it will attach a similar label also to members, recipients, and donors and if this labeling has a sharp detrimental effect on budget, audience, and operations of the organization—although no bodies are injured—is this political violence?

What kind of subjects can experience political violence? Organizations? Communities? Social movements? If some of these subjects do not have "bodies" or legal "standing," how must we conceptualize violence? This is a question of unit of analysis. Civil rights protections embrace not only individual speech, which may be made impossible or discouraged, but also rights of political association and assembly. Bodily violence is not the only (and not necessarily the most powerful) method of disturbing the exercise of these rights.

This recognition identifies a need for a legal concept that can establish standing for informal political organizations and social movements. If corporate political donations are protected as a form of "free speech," then surely such assaults on membership-based organizations must be understood as a form of political violence. If private enterprise is protected by tort law from libel, denial of service, and interference with customer access to premises (tortious interference), then nonprofit organizations and civil society groups should also be protected from interference with advantageous relationships that affect their resources, their capacity to mobilize them, and their opportunity to participate in public discourse.

And let's not forget that social control does kill persons. Carlo Giuliani is not the only one. Global activist networks now bring the news too often that a human rights lawyer or a labor leader has been assassinated in the Global South. And Global North alterglobalization activists have been killed abroad. A U.S. woman and two British activists were killed by Israeli forces in Palestine, and U.S. activists were killed by government agents in 2006 and 2008 in Mexico. Activists are uncomfortable expressing outrage at assassinations of Global North activists; an expectation of safety seems like an expression of imperialist/white-skin privilege.

But the relative safety of Northern witnesses abroad is a matter of global power relations—the very power relations that the alterglobalization movement confronts with its solidarity. Something has changed when Israel and México feel comfortable assassinating the rebellious visionary children of their powerful political allies. These assassinations are an assault on the movements of international solidarity. The deaths are called mistakes or are blamed on paramilitaries, but the message is clear: the governments are united against those who oppose their global plans and will collaborate in trivializing political murders of pacifists and journalists. Some assassinations are aimed, others are incidental, but the message is clear. Democratic nations will kill activists. You are by no means safe to express yourself.

6

Antirepression

Resisting the Social Control of Dissent

San Francisco police have repeatedly frustrated protesters by using spatial control tactics, including holding pens, and mass arrests. Preparing another antiwar protest in 2008, rather than announcing a single location or march route, protest organizers released a large list of potential targets for protest. Dissenters subscribed to a Twitter.com feed to receive text messages identifying targets and gathering times, some simultaneous. Meanwhile, activist DJs on a pirate radio station provided information about police massing and action and relayed reports from protesters in the streets. Why did activists feel that such an elaborate infrastructure was necessary to express their dissent? Clearly, they wanted to escape spatial channeling, but why is this so important?

We believe that activist responses to social control contain profound insights into its meaning and significance. This chapter describes antirepression, the tactics activists use to protect themselves from the social control of dissent. We have organized our analysis of antirepression work to match our three approaches to social control, by looking at space, political economy, and violence.

Resisting Spatial Control

We have identified five antirepression tactics that resist spatial control: confronting the zones with blockades or invasions, marching disobediently, organizing in decentralized affinity groups, disturbing police control through observation, and distributing spatially aggregated information about the protest territory.

Breaching the Zones, Blockading Back

Protesters fight back against spatial control with their own spatial tactics. The fundamental spatial project of summits is to exclude all but elites from the conversation and decision making about the global economy. Since this exclusion is not only symbolic of the issue but is the actual issue, it can be challenged in the most direct manner by attempting to get into the meeting site, showing the world just how difficult it is to participate by generating mass-media images of police keeping people out.

In the Tute Bianche tactic, a group stays close together while wearing personal body armor made of household products such as cardboard, foam, rubber, and empty plastic water bottles.[1] Over the armor, many dissenters wear white painter's coveralls and life preservers, resulting in a comic, bulky look. They carry collective shielding such as massive rafts made of balloons, old inner tubes, or plexiglass. Invoking a medieval army (in a humorous way), they ponderously approach the police lines, stop and announce their intention as citizens to pass "with arms up" peacefully through the police lines to attend the meetings. Then they push slowly against the police, producing comic mayhem. This way, they protect their bodies against police violence and also stage theatrical (and often successful) attempts to push through police lines while getting clubbed. After several spectacular interventions using this tactic in Italy (followed by its near-total disappearance after the clashes at Genoa 2001 G8), protesters applied this tactic in various other countries and at many other summits, mainly in Europe.[2]

Protesters also organize to refuse the exclusion more assertively. There are two striking examples. At Québec City 2001 FTAA, a large march arrived (after a very long walk) at the fence, promptly breached it, and walked in to the Red Zone. Unfortunately, most marchers were not expecting or prepared for this turn of events and didn't seize the opportunity, so the few who did were shortly rebuffed by police. At Cancún 2003 WTO, where protesters (organized by the very well-prepared South Korean delegation) collectively tugged down the fence with big ropes, protesters did not pass the fence. They stayed where they were and left the torn-down fence as a message.

Protesters at Seattle 1999 WTO used a different spatial and symbolic strategy: if ordinary people wouldn't be allowed to enter the meetings, then they proposed that no one should be able to go in. Protesters blockaded the flow of delegates into the meeting by blocking intersections, using a variety of creative methods. Since the successful blockades in Seattle, similar (and more or less successful) attempts have been staged at all subsequent summit protests. When global summitry shifted to remote rural venues, protesters applied more decentralized blockades, such as at Évian 2003 G8 and Heiligendamm 2007 G8.

Marching Tactics and Organizing Crowds

Various marching tactics are used to evade spatial control during street actions. In Europe, linking arms is a frequently used tactic for protecting the space of a demonstration and preventing police intrusion or snatch arrests. Alternatively, marches have been intentionally split into several parts to circumvent police lines in order to occupy a certain space. At Prague 2000 IMF/WB, a unified march broke into three color-coded marches using different routes (and tactics!) to reach the conference center. Similarly, at Heilingendamm 2007 G8, after starting as one march, protesters split up into five pre-established (and color-coded) "fingers" each time they encountered a police line. In this way, they forced the police to stretch their lines until they were so thin that protesters could "trickle" through them. The advice given by the BlockG8 coalition organizing the mass blockades to the protesters was: "Don't aim for the cops, aim for the gaps in between them." Later, on the street where the sitting blockades were to be staged, all the "fingers" came together again.

A few months after Heiligendamm 2007 G8, a demonstration was organized in Hamburg to protest security politics and the repression of dissent. In response to the kettle tactic that had been used by police, the call to action for this demonstration asked participants to attempt to remain outside the police encirclement by constantly being on move, "out of control." (The response of the authorities was a ban on walking on the sidewalk during this specific assembly.)

Affinity Groups

Affinity groups are a tactic inspired by the organization of the anarchist resistance in the Spanish civil war. Since the 1970s, this tactic has been used for organizing mass direct actions. Affinity groups are the organizational unit of a mass direct action. They provide security for individuals, enable quick communication and decision making, and try to be self-sufficient, providing their own food and medical supplies. Affinity groups determine their own contribution to the action (within the general action guidelines) and have a high degree of autonomy during the action. Many new action forms that have flourished around summit protests have adapted this organizational model, such as samba bands, pink and silver blocs, and the Clandestine Insurgent Rebel Clown Army. The last is an action form that tactically exploits the figure of a clown, which confuses the police and others. A large Clown Army confronted by a police line can quickly fall apart into many affinity groups ("gaggles"), each doing its own thing. The ensuing chaos frequently spoils police attempts to maintain spatial control and creates space for other protesters.

Affinity groups enable dissenters to maintain spatial mobility by operating in functional units that can pursue their own goals and functions, at times independent of each other. Activists can disperse after a confrontation without becoming impotent, because each affinity group stays together and continues decentralized disruptive actions.

Counterobservation

Activists and sympathetic legal workers have developed a grassroots culture and method of watching and documenting police behavior. Like the efforts of volunteer medics and independent journalists, legal observation (also known in the United States as CopWatch) has become a paraprofessional volunteer role taken on by people who want to support protest and dissent. Law students, legal workers, and lawyers provide this service out of a concern for political rights. At summit mobilizations, they watch for police and protester interactions, move in close to the action, record its sequence, and attempt to record identifying information of arresting officers, violent officers, and commanders on scene. Their presence disrupts the flow of police officers' violence and efforts at control.

Legal observers serve several layered functions. First, they gather evidence that may be useful in the defense of protesters who are arrested and must face charges. Second, they compile data longitudinally, and these data may form the basis of police accountability campaigns or litigation against a specific police agency. Sometimes the presence of observers discourages police misbehavior. However, observers do not serve as negotiators during conflicts, remaining instead in their role of observers. This way, legal observing becomes a form of counterobservation with significant spatial effects. When legal observers are present, protest spaces are less often so isolated by police that they can assert total control. Police often try to hinder the work of observers, photographers, videographers, and even journalists. At Heiligendamm 2007 G8, police severely limited the work of the observers by not letting them get close to a person being arrested, by keeping them away from a corralled demonstration, and even by forbidding one to record what he observed.

Legal observation skills are transmitted beyond legal workers to a wider group of activists through popular education, spreading virally through grassroots networks. People trained at workshops associated with summit protests may then do observation spontaneously whenever they see signs of police misbehavior. At home they feel empowered to keep an eye on local police, watching for harassment of youth, people of color, immigrants, and other vulnerable groups and to train and encourage others to spontaneously watch and document policing. Some even set up formal groups with patrol schedules or volunteer to observe at social events where police harassment is anticipated. Armed with recording devices, knowledge of the law, and official markings, watchers patrol or post observers on call. These practices disrupt police power to impose their will arbitrarily on events they may be hostile to, such as hip hop parties.

A more popular but less formal form of observation can be undertaken by a broad range of people, including but not limited to official observers. People can watch for signs that a fellow protester is in fact an undercover police officer. If they have evidence that someone is in fact an imposter, they can take photos or videos of the person, preferably including evidence of their undercover status (strange communications equipment, possession of weapons, video of the person getting into a police car or going behind police lines). This material can be distributed through independent media to warn activists and is sometimes relevant to litigation.

Communication Infrastructure

Resisting spatial control requires adequate information about (shifting) spatial possibilities. Pirate communication is an important tactic for re-enabling the circulation of information and therefore the tactical flow of protesters. Pirate communication is organized through a combination of trusted face-to-face communication and use of technology, including radios, walkie-talkies, cell phones, and the Internet.

A common element of communication during summit protests is a newswire run on a website (usually an IMC, part of the Independent Media Center network) set up to provide news and information about the protest. The newswire summarizes reports from protesters in the streets (e.g., "Independence Plaza is still occupied. DJs have arrived. People are dancing"; "Commerce Ave. and Rivers St.: arrests now taking place at north side of intersection."). Protesters in the streets can subscribe to the ticker and receive this information on their cell phones. Twitter technology and pirate radio are new ways to distribute this information.

At Prague 2000 IMF/WB, the Centrum coordination center enabled the flow of communication among the various marches trying to get close to the summit's venue. The physical space of the Centrum was a hotel room, whose location was secret from all but its few staff. This communication hub was fed by a team of cyclists who provided status reports by radio. Placards were used to diffuse messages about the situation at the different marches. In the early afternoon, for example, protesters of the Tute Bianche march stuck on the Nussle bridge were informed that the pink and silver march had reached the conference center and could use some reinforcement. The Centrum was not a command center but, rather, one part of a decentralized network. It compiled and disseminated information to action groups so that they could decide where to put their energies as the situation across the city unfolded. In addition, the various marches encircling the conference center also organized their own internal communication structures. Although info-houses like the Centrum are commonly used in protests, the FBI made the first successful raid on one of these facilities during Pittsburgh 2009 G20. The workers in the info-house were charged with "hindering prosecution" because they were providing information on movements of police (via Twitter). However, the state's attempt to criminalize use of Twitter was unsuccessful, and the charges were dropped.[3]

At Heiligendamm 2007 G8, the circulation of information about spatial control was organized through a horizontal network of on-the-ground information centers located in the action camps and in the region around the conference venue. Again, these information points pooled incoming information and distributed it to people passing by and calling.

The Political Economy of Solidarity

Organizing solidarity against the legal consequences of social control is a costly endeavor. To meet the financial burden, social movements create collective structures for sharing the costs of legal prosecution. The German "Rote Hilfe" (or Red Help) is a long-standing collective structure that supports activists who find themselves in political litigation. Functioning as a fund, this organization pools the financial contributions of supporters and redistributes them. In Europe, one successful ad hoc tactic for raising money (often for specific cases or mobilizations) is the promotion of solidarity concerts or parties. To help defray the costs incurred by protesters facing trials after major summit protests, such events have been organized in many cities all over Europe. Besides raising money, solidarity concerts spread awareness and knowledge about legal defense.

At Heiligendamm 2007 G8, Rote Hilfe was an important resource for activists. Equally important was the money raised by the campsite working group and contributed to the antirepression team, which not only supported activists needing legal defense but also encouraged activists to file complaints against police and other authorities, leading to trials.

Legal costs can start even before the protests take place. For example, during a march at Heiligendamm 2007 G8, authorities issued a general ban order for the entire area around the meeting location. Activists planned a Star March, starting in different points and coming together in the middle, which directly challenged the legality of the prohibition. However, the activists' lawyer explained that the expenses involved in the case could be four times the estimated €5,000 cost if each part of the Star March had to be defended separately. Despite being a grassroots network without steady financial structures, the Star March coalition decided to push the case to the Constitutional Court of Germany, a financially demanding and lengthy process.

While some street activists are involved in the various forms of legal work described below, most of the workers are sympathizers who take action in these projects because they wish to defend citizens' political rights. They do not accept the necessity of suspending rights for summit meetings and give their time and energy to protect the most expansive practices of political rights.

Legal Teams

Activist legal teams are part of the summit mobilization framework commonly found in Europe and North America. The action framework includes various protest sectors. Major permitted marches are organized by unions, peace groups, and other large organizations or coalitions. These groups negotiate with the police and often even provide their own internal policing through a "marshal" system that attempts to keep participants on the negotiated course. Meanwhile, the direct-action sector (which may participate in the permitted marches but often also mounts other actions before and after the permitted marches) is organized through a working-group system, which usually includes a headquarters space for distributing information, holding meetings, creating art, and storing supplies; a housing-assistance group; an independent media facility (chapters of www.Indymedia.org); public relations strategists and spokespeople; a school that provides training in nonviolent protest; clinics and medics; a kitchen; a communications team; and action scenario teams. Activist legal teams are part of this structure, one of several autonomous but coordinated action "working groups" that provide infrastructure specific to the protest. Attached to and staffed by the direct-action sector, these working groups see themselves as in service to all protest sectors, including the nondirect-action protest sectors. Media, medical, and legal groups are likely to be used by protesters from all the sectors.

The majority of workers in the legal team are nonlawyers. However, the team must include a few lawyers who are responsible for the tasks requiring credentials, such as filing injunctions, visiting arrestees in detention, and appearing in court. The majority of the work can be done by nonprofessionals, who in the process gain skills and knowledge as "legal workers." The work they do includes teaching Know Your Rights trainings and preparing materials; mapping the participating police agencies and jails; tracking arrestees through the jail system; communicating legal information at activist meetings (interpreting proclamations, summarizing statistics, and reporting on the status of arrestees); issuing press releases; compiling data; and staffing a hotline to record reports, field questions, and provide information to arrestees, their families, and supporters. Experienced protest legal workers train volunteer lawyers in preferred techniques for advising and representing political arrestees, which differ from normal criminal defense strategies.

In advance of a summit mobilization, the legal team announces a hotline phone number and encourages all activists to write this number on their skin daily in indelible ink. (Nevertheless, many of those attending permitted events may not know about this phone number.) The legal team answers calls at this number twenty-four hours a day for the week surrounding the actions. The legal team provides support to all participants and arrestees (who may include nonactivist passersby, journalists, and participants from different protest groups). Given the mayhem that accompanies protest arrests, the activist legal team is often the best first responder, since other lawyers are unprepared for the peculiarities of protest detention systems. In Europe, a number of left-wing lawyers associations (such as the German "Republikanischer Anwaltsverein," which participated in Heiligendamm 2007 G8) are working to establish a permanent European Legal Team to secure a continuity of experience and to avoid having to build a new organization for each mobilization.

Support for arrestees includes vigilantly tracking every arrestee through various facilities, ascertaining conditions for release, visiting arrestees in jail to check on their conditions, communicating each arrestee's status to his or her supporters to assist in securing the arrestee's release, documenting any unusual conditions, archiving evidence, negotiating with city officials regarding arrestees, mounting legal interventions regarding specific cases (e.g., foreign nationals, youths, injured people, those held in solitary confinement, arrestees who need medication), and even arranging to post bond or sign for people who do not have anyone else to do it for them. The legal team is expected to provide reliable information to the public relations team, the independent media, the action scenario team, and Convergence (via nightly meetings) on various subjects, including the number of arrestees, their locations, conditions for release, needed logistical support for released arrestees (e.g., food, transportation, medical care, housing), and the most important political demands being made (such as demands that groups of arrestees be transferred from dangerous facilities, although usually the demand is simply "Release all arrestees now").

After all arrestees are released from detention, the legal team moves on to two phases of postaction work: criminal defense and preparation for civil suits. To mount a criminal defense, the team establishes communication with arrestees, tracks information regarding court dates and charges, recruits volunteer lawyers for court appearances, and organizes an evidence archive for use by the defense team. In addition, the legal team can help develop a strategy for the defenses, organize the arrestees in collective defenses (sometimes conjoining individual cases), and train volunteer lawyers in defense strategies (e.g., maintain solidarity with other arrestees to the maximum extent, and keep the political dimensions of the arrest and prosecution at the forefront of the case). The legal team may also engage in press work.

To prepare for civil suits, the legal team archives reports of harassment and excessive use of force by the police, along with testimony about the conditions and treatment to which arrestees were subject while in detention. This material may be used as part of civil inquiry processes, as well as in the preparation of multiple lawsuits against the city on behalf of various groups of protesters or others violated as part of the social control of protest. One of the most extensive archives, despite the material destroyed by police during the Diaz raids, is the work of "Supporto Legale," a legal support team founded to help protesters at Genoa 2001 G8.[4]

Activists trained as legal workers in political contexts have gone on to use their skills for other solidarity work, such as assisting prisoners in filing appeals (e.g., Up against the Law Legal Collective, Chicago, which is now inactive), supporting homeless people in fighting tickets (as in Toronto), and advocating for the release of detained immigrants.

Street Legal

In addition to serving as legal observers, lawyers and legal workers familiar with the relevant law sometimes provide legal services in the street during protests. There are several types of street legal work. A person, known in the United States as a "police liaison" and in Europe as a "police spokesperson," may serve as a communication device between protesters and the police commander on scene. Liaisons do not negotiate, although they may communicate offers from one side to the other. By identifying and introducing themselves to the commander on duty early on in the action, they may be able to maintain access to that person once things heat up (when access to the police line is often restricted). Decisions are taken by protesters via the use of consensus decision-making procedures, and the police liaison communicates those decisions to commanding officers. This person does not need legal training or credentials, as they are not interpreting the law, just communicating.

A second type of street legal is a lawyer who stations himself or herself at a location where police action, including raids, seems imminent. This person does not represent any protesters but acts alone proactively to defend protesters and spaces by invoking the law. Lawyers who take on this role identify themselves as lawyers and aggressively inform officers and their commanders about illegal acts they are committing or threatening to commit. This person may travel with a legal observer or assistant who has a video camera and other equipment to document any incidents. These lawyers may later head civil suits against the police regarding violations they have witnessed.

The third type of street legal acts as a liaison between the legal team and the top-ranking officials in charge of police operations. This relationship may be established by lawyers on the legal team days or weeks ahead of the action. Again, this liaison has no authority to negotiate on behalf of activists. What the person can do, since he or she has direct contact with police command structures, is to get clear information on changing situations, such as closure of formerly permitted protest areas, imposition of curfews, and locations of arrestees. The liaison can then communicate this information to activist media and organizing spaces. The police are not obligated to provide information to this person and are unlikely to give accurate information on street tactics they plan to use (e.g., mass arrest, tear gas), but they often will provide information on what they have declared to be illegal and about the location of prisoners. It is notable that persons working in all three street legal roles are not immune from arrest or police brutality. For example, volunteers in all three roles, along with legal observers, were arrested at Miami 2003 FTAA.

Political Litigation

There are two kinds of litigation, criminal defense (discussed earlier) and proactive civil litigation against government agencies. There are roughly two types of proactive civil litigation. Individuals and groups of similarly affected individuals may seek damages in connection with injuries inflicted by police either in the streets or in custody. Social movement organizations may organize class-action suits alleging violations of civil rights, including the establishment of exclusion zones, police use of weapons, mass arrests, raids, and other forms of social control. Although both types of lawsuits are useful for raising the costs of and bringing media attention to social control and police misbehavior, class-action suits are more likely to seek sanctions against police operations regarding dissent.

Steven Barkan summarizes the literature on proactive civil litigation by social movements in general. He finds the literature split on the efficacy of such attempts to "regulate business behavior . . . prevent immoral behavior . . . effect desegregation . . . stop construction of nuclear power plants . . . [and] end the [Vietnam] war."[5] Even when litigation is successful, court orders issued in connection with social justice concerns are not necessarily enforced. In his 1990 study of environmental justice struggles, Robert Bullard found that, while neither litigation nor any other single tactic appeared to be effective, a combination of tactics, including litigation, was often successful in securing closure or shrinkage of toxic facilities.[6] Legal victories that establish "claims of right" confer entitlement, and this, according to Barkan, can strengthen movements.[7] Barkan identifies four lines of inquiry with regard to both defense and proactive litigation: "At what stage of social movements are they likely to [devote resources to] litigate?"; "To what extent do various aspect of the legal system affect decisions by social movements to turn to the civil and criminal courts?"; "What is the influence of the press on the frequency of civil disobedience and on decisions to conduct a political defense?"; and "What circumstances lead to decisions by government officials to use the courts as a means of social control?"

Proactive litigation focuses on protecting activism and activists against a creeping affront on their expressive rights and against illicit police practices. Efforts to guarantee protections of expression and association are not as numerous as cases alleging violations of those protections, but there are a variety of efforts under way. We will mention here only a few that are closely associated with the alterglobalization movement, although there are many other relevant and important activities in which many alterglobalization activists are involved, such as the more than one hundred local resolutions suppressing local enforcement of the Patriot Act in the United States and lawsuits regarding 9/11-related detentions and war crimes.

- After Seattle 1999 WTO, Trial Lawyers for Public Justice failed in its challenge to the legality of the no-protest zone but won a settlement from the city for 155 protesters arrested outside the no-protest zone with no probable cause.[8]
- In 2002, the ACLU, joined by a popular movement, challenged the Denver police department and mayor to release files being kept on 3,200 Colorado activists and 208 organizations, among which were the pacifist Quaker American Friends Service Committee, some nuns, and many activists whose only crime was participation in entirely lawful protest activity. The activists dubbed the files "spy files" and, once they were released by court order in 2003, the ACLU organized people to request their files. After this success, the ACLU, on December 2, 2004, "launched a nationwide effort to expose and limit FBI spying on people and groups simply for speaking out or practicing their faith." The initial step of the campaign

was the filing of Freedom of Information Act (FOIA) requests in ten states and in the District of Columbia in an effort to demonstrate that "FBI and local police—working through so-called Joint Terrorism Task Forces (JTTFs)—are spying on environmental, antiwar, political, and faith-based groups." The FOIA requests seek two kinds of information: (1) the actual FBI files of groups and individuals targeted for their political views or their religion; (2) information about how the structure and policies of the JTTFs are encouraging rampant and unwarranted spying.[9] But by 2010 few of the FOIA requests have been answered and the requests for information as to the number of FBI agents assigned to JTTFs and for budgetary information were denied.

- Savvy media work around the revelation that a group called Fresno Peace had been infiltrated led California's attorney general, Bill Lockyer, to mandate that the state's law enforcement agencies "follow the California State Constitution, which prevents them from infiltrating groups that are not under investigation for criminal activity."[10]

- The Partnership for Civil Justice has ongoing litigation in Washington, D.C., regarding infiltration, long-term undercover spying, mass arrests, mass intelligence-gathering operations on protesters, the use of Civil Disturbance Units, checkpoints, odious permission requirements for persons who planned to protest the second inauguration as president of George W. Bush in 2004, and agents provocateurs. They have succeeded in gaining settlements for individuals, as well as policy changes; for example, police may no longer engage in the "illegal practice of rounding up and arresting demonstrators for 'parading without a permit' without notice and opportunity to leave." The D.C. city council has adopted a bill that prohibits use of riot gear and encirclement of First Amendment–protected assemblies without establishment of probable cause, requires display of nameplates and badges, and mandates the release of First Amendment assembly arrestees within four hours.[11]

- After an egregious attack on antiwar demonstrators in 2003, the ACLU of Northern California, the National Lawyers Guild, and a team of prominent civil rights attorneys successfully pressured the Oakland Police Department to end the use of crowd control weapons against demonstrators.[12]

* Individual and group lawsuits related to policing and incarceration at Miami 2003 FTAA have resulted in payment of $1.05 million to claimants. But these suits have addressed only personal damages, not policy that governs the policing of protest.

* Three female activists charged with "failure to disperse" at Miami 2003 FTAA were strip-searched while in jail. In preparing their lawsuit against Miami-Dade County, they found that strip searches of women arrestees facing charges for nonviolent behavior (e.g., prostitution, loitering, traffic offenses) were standard policy. The policy has been changed, and a $6.25 million settlement was distributed to women violated during a five-year period.[13]

* The New York City Civil Liberties Union successfully pressured the city to destroy the fingerprint records of people arrested during New York City 2004 RNC and won the release of police documents regarding undercover infiltration of groups across the nation in advance of the protest.

* The Partnership for Civil Justice brought litigation against the City of New York on behalf of two social movement organizations to protect the groups' access to Central Park. They argued that, by denying permits, including one for a planned protest against the RNC in 2004, the city was essentially privatizing the park, restricting its use to corporate events, and denying the right to public mass demonstrations. The ruling provided both a settlement to the plaintiffs of $50,000 (plus payment of legal fees) and a court order that the park must remain available for First Amendment activity, with research and planning undertaken to ensure that the park would not sustain permanent damage.[14]

* There are two major lawsuits regarding Genoa 2001 G8. The first concerns the violent raid on the Diaz School.[15] The verdict on this lawsuit was reached in November 2008. Thirteen of twenty-nine police defendants were convicted, but none of the commanding officers. As Italy has no law against torture, the victims of the Diaz raid are trying to take the case to the European Court of Human Rights. The second case, the Bolzaneto trial, involved forty-five police, jail staff, and doctors accused by a group of three hundred victims of "misuse of authority, constraint, abuse, intimidation and falsification of evidence."[16] The plaintiffs were granted compensation ranging from €2,500 to €15,000. Only fifteen of the accused were convicted, and the maximum sentence given was five years,

eight months, but the person who received this sentence was a commanding officer, the chief of security of the jail. The defendants appealed, but their convictions were upheld.

Despite the occasional successes won by proactive political litigation, there are thousands of citizens whose rights have been violated and who remain unrepresented. After ten years, Seattle has been challenged on only a few of the many illegalities perpetrated at Seattle 1999 WTO. Fewer than fifty of the thousands of activists violated at Miami 2003 FTAA have been represented in suits against the state, and only a handful of the state's illegal actions have yet been challenged. Fewer than four hundred of the protesters at Genoa 2001 G8 have been represented in court, and only those with the most severe injuries. Those who had their attempt to express themselves violated but who received minor injuries have not been represented at all. Organizing these suits requires a team of dedicated lawyers, capital to cover the costs until the case is completed, and sustained vigilance at the courts. The immediate and tragic result of inadequate prosecution is that police, commanders, and cities can violate the law with relative impunity. They know that they will get away with most of the illegal activities they undertake. Moreover, thanks to the new practice of taking out insurance policies to cover the costs of litigation and settlement, the police and officials are under even less pressure to conform to the law. In the long term, it means that the law is undermined by the practices of the police; de facto social control of dissent increasingly diverges from the law.

One final observation regarding this litigation: its social organization is very different from that of previous efforts to combat social control. As described earlier, many antirepression practices have empowering, self-diffusing, highly participatory, and synthetic qualities. Because of its centralization and its dependence on experts, civil litigation tends not replicate these qualities. While all other phases of antirepression involve the participation of diverse actors and constant communication regarding both strategy and operations, civil suits are strategized and implemented in isolation. While radical democracy and egalitarianism are fiercely enforced in every other aspect and process of the movement, the civil litigation process involves "trusting the experts" (and trusting the state's judicial apparatus), a concept that global justice activists abhor in every other moment of action. This change happens in part because generally the litigators are the same lawyers who participated in the legal team, perhaps in the streets, and in the criminal defense of the activists. They have proved themselves and are the subject of great respect and gratitude. But the other factor is that (with a few exceptions) activists have not made proactive litigation into a participatory process.

Perhaps the lawyers are concerned that winning requires an expert strategy, or perhaps the task of training volunteer legal workers for this kind of case seems unwieldy. As a result, litigation does not benefit from activist resources such as volunteers (so important to the legal team and criminal defense phases), savvy activist media teams, and solidarity actions. Despite the historical recognition that the success of social justice lawsuits is closely related to the persistence of social movement mobilization, political litigation teams often do not manage to publicize the news of the cases through activist networks, with the result that activists don't even know the status of the cases. Moreover, the legal strategy may not be coordinated with the broader social movement strategy. Without a culture and a method of participation, activists are unable to collectively define their procedural or substantive demands, so the lawyers are left to act autonomously. This is not to criticize the few and extraordinarily dedicated lawyers who bring these suits. But, given that such litigation is one of the few methods of compelling state accountability for the effects of social control, its limitations are striking.

Surviving Political Violence

In addition to protecting space, activists have developed tactics for protecting their bodies, minds, psyches, and culture from the violence we discussed in chapter 5.

Know Your Rights, Know Our Past, Know Your Enemy

The most basic aspect of antirepression is a grassroots viral education program to teach people their rights as dissenters. Education takes the form of workshops, pamphlets, Internet resources, video clips, pocket-size cards, and stickers covering issues such as speech and expression, interactions with police, rights in custody, and recommended behavior such as remaining silent.

Know Your Rights educational materials are customized for particular political events, in which case they address local or event-specific laws; they have also been developed by political activists for solidarity work with immigrants, youth, sex workers, and other groups.[17] This empowering information flows beyond specific political contexts, empowering learners and turning them into spontaneous educators.

A special form of Know Your Rights education in the United States relates to preparation for appearing before grand juries. Witnesses called before grand juries don't have the rights that criminal defendants have; for example, they can be jailed for refusing to testify. Since the proceedings are secret and there is no judge, it is easy to use witnesses to sow fear throughout a community. This is why the Grand Jury Resistance Project and other groups recommend refusing rather than cooperating with grand jury subpoenas. They provide community training to help people prepare to deal with grand juries.[18]

In addition to educating people about their rights, this form of resisting social control is also about sharing antirepression experiences and histories. Grounded and situated knowledge is often the most useful way to push tactical innovation. All the reports, magazines, and mailing-list discussions that take place before, after, and between protest events are an important part of building a collective tactical memory.[19]

Solidarity

Political arrestees are often subject to exaggerated detention, unusual conditions, excessive charges, and targeted abuse based on the political dimension of their criminalization. These conditions can be addressed as they are happening and also later in court through various forms of collective action. The legal strategies for addressing the poor or illegal conditions to which people are subjected are called solidarity, and they begin at the moment of arrest. Solidarity is one more subject of trainings and grassroots viral education offered in the weeks and days prior to a summit mobilization. Viral training in solidarity principles and tactics even takes place in arrest vehicles and continues in jail.

Activists have developed a set of tactics that enable arrestees to disrupt the jail in order to protect endangered compatriots, demand better conditions, and pressure for collective release and/or minimal charges. When hundreds of people are in jail, the impact of these tactics can be significant. They include refusing to be identifiable (this requires that people not carry any form of identification), refusing to identify their citizenship (in solidarity with noncitizens), refusing to cooperate with processing procedures, singing, chanting, dancing, stripping, going limp, clinging together, and staging hunger strikes. These tactics have been successful in winning concessions such as return of prescription medicine to arrestees, return of isolated prisoners to the larger group, and collective reduction of charges. Jail solidarity works in conjunction with ongoing negotiation between city officials and lawyers from the legal team, solidarity vigils by activists outside the jail, press conferences, and phone campaigns (often generating encouraging and disruptive noise).

When jail solidarity is not feasible or is unsuccessful in reducing charges, arrestees may use court solidarity to address their criminal charges. Court solidarity includes tactics that may be disruptive but that, more important, help arrestees strategize collectively and keep public discourse focused on the political content of activists' court appearances and trials. Court solidarity tactics include mass appearances in court (including sympathetic nonarrestees); signs and costumes that draw attention to violations of free speech; petitions for combined charges/cases, trials, and sentences; demands for full trials, speedy trials, or jury trials (if many people request full court proceedings, it pressures the prosecuting attorney to dismiss charges in order not to clog up the court system and impose onerous workloads on staff); introduction of political content in the court proceedings; and press conferences and other media work that draws attention to the trials and sentences.

A focal point of solidarity is always the subset of arrestees charged with severe crimes. The resistance of a larger group facing less serious charges helps maintain a spotlight on the political nature of the serious charges and criminalization facing the smaller group, in an effort to delegitimize those charges. Arrestee networks can develop strategies and share experiences to minimize the number of convictions. The arrestee network after Philadelphia 2000 RNC was particularly strong and democratic.

The normal strategy for criminal defense seeks to minimize the defendant's risk by accepting reduced charges, pleading guilty, seeking dismissal on the basis of technicalities, and distinguishing individuals in order to separate them from alleged group criminality. The defense of prosecuted political activists generally takes a different strategy, maintaining a collective dimension to defense (individuals are being targeted because of their participation in collective action), keeping the politics in the forefront of the defense, and extending court proceedings to the maximum (asserting prosecuted dissenters' innocence and insisting on the recognition of charged activity as protected expression), while discouraging the prosecution of activists by increasing the costs and burden of such prosecutions on the police and courts.

Collective organizing of arrestees and access to movement lawyers enables large groups of arrestees to reject states' attempts to negotiate guilty pleas to minor charges. In this way, the state is prevented from minimizing the burden on the courts while still criminalizing protest. Insisting on court proceedings for charged dissenters is more likely to yield acquittal and to maximize exposure of the state's undemocratic attempt to constrain dissent. Following Heiligendamm 2007 G8, the strength of the legal team available to the protesters reduced the risk run by charged protesters in rejecting the state's proposal of a small fine; instead, they went through a real trial and were acquitted. The state was thus thwarted in its bid to establish criminal records for the protesters.

Trauma Groups

Trauma groups are part of the established repertoire of strategies for resisting the social control of dissent. Along with many of the other working groups organized around a summit mobilization, healers and psychologists offer space and services to assist activists to recover from trauma. The healing or trauma center may operate during the days of action and may continue for months afterward. People with strengths in various methods of healing may join this working group and focus their energy on caring for fellow activists after their experiences of social control in the street and/or in jail.

In Europe, a well-known trauma group was started after the experience of a group of protesters who attempted to block a bridge in order to prevent the Évian 2003 G8 delegations from reaching the summit venue. The blockade consisted of a rope across the bridge, with two activists (experienced climbers) hanging from either end of the rope. The group had installed a careful security and warning system, and traffic was stopped instantly. It did not take long for the police to arrive. The police did not try to communicate with the activists but immediately started to clear the road and to push the activists to the sides. More police arrived soon; there were German, Swiss, and French police and military present. As soon as the road was more or less cleared, they lifted the rope and let cars pass underneath. The police commander was clearly aware of the climbers hanging on the two ends of the rope. Another policeman was caught on film as he looked down the bridge to check the rope construction. A little bit later, the same police officer walked to the rope and cut it. Martin Shaw fell twenty meters into the stony bed of the shallow Aubonne River. He survived but sustained serious injuries. On the other end of the rope, Gesine Wenzel avoided a similar fate because activists on the bridge managed to catch her rope. Many of the participants in this action subsequently started the healing group to deal collectively with their traumatic experiences of police brutality and violence.

Security Culture

Security culture refers to practices commonly used in the alterglobalization movement, practices that allow activists to take precautionary actions to minimize police infiltration and surveillance. These tactics demonstrate that activists already know that law enforcement will infiltrate the movement, often using "state security" and the threat posed by acts of terrorism as an excuse. Activists' practices may include keeping some information private, organizing in smaller groups, and avoiding the use of technologies that are easily infiltrated. Overall, these practices serve as a double-edged sword; while they provides some protection from overzealous law enforcement, they also tend to disrupt organizing activities and other important aspects of movement culture, such as the development of trust and outreach. Sometimes security culture is practiced at an unhealthy level, usually induced by a heavy dose of paranoia. Most damaging is the difficulty it creates for including newer members in the group.

For example, during preparatory meetings for Heilingendamm 2007 G8, we experienced a familiar security culture ritual. A few minutes after the start of the meeting, one person asked whether cell phones should be switched off, a common practice that everyone at the meeting knew. Nevertheless, several people had not turned off their phones, so there was a bit of fumbling around for the phones. This ritualized moment was prolonged by a short discussion about whether it was necessary as well to take out the batteries in the cell phones. Activists are aware that police use cell phones not only to intercept phone conversations but also to tap real-life meetings. While switching off cell phones prevents such a possibility, the batteries still send signals, which means that intelligence services can potentially trace who is present at a given meeting. Many activists, therefore, prefer to take out the battery during meetings or, for even greater security, to leave their cell phones at home. Being aware of the danger of interception, activists have developed a security culture. In this case, the ritual is relatively benign. But, as discussed in chapter 5, security culture can easily become excessive, undermining the trust and discourse necessary to build a social movement.

Protecting Bodies

Activists are innovative in finding ways to protect their bodies during street actions.[20] Street actions are the moments when the bodies of protesters are most exposed to physical harm, and the high numbers of injured protesters at several summit protests testifies to the urgency of taking such precautions. The protective structures developed by activists also include tactics used to protect bodies before and after actions, as well.

The most spectacular form of protecting bodies in the streets is the tactic of the Italian White Overalls/Tute Bianche, described earlier in this chapter. Two long-standing tactics used by protesters are the practices of wearing masks and of wearing black clothes. Both serve to make individual bodies unidentifiable and protect protesters against the widespread surveillance techniques used by authorities. The rather arbitrary term "Black Bloc" is used to describe protesters who dress in black. The term was created by a German court as part of an attempt to prosecute activists for being part of a criminal association. Besides inhibiting identification, the practice of wearing black clothes and masks (certainly when marching in a tight bloc) creates a threatening image. At the same time, such a bloc can serve to protect other, less militant protesters, as was seen at Washington, D.C., 2000 IMF/WB. The tactic of resisting identification and forming a tight bloc is often reinforced by holding banners on each side of the demonstrating group. Gas masks (when not prohibited by a temporary ordinance; they are also illegal in Germany, where they are viewed as a "passive armament") are also worn as protection against tear gas and pepper spray attacks. An alternative protection against tear gas is a vinegar-soaked cloth.

Most countries have a structure of action medics who offer their services during big protest events. Moreover, they offer trainings at the Convergence Centers or action camps in order to spread basic knowledge about how to deal with the specific effects of police weapons and how to help wounded people. Ideally, during actions, each affinity group would include at least one person with this training. People trained to provide medical services at mass protests have also served in other emergencies. Some of the most effective emergency medical personnel in New Orleans following Hurricane Katrina were the medics network developed in the U.S. alterglobalization movement.

Another more precautionary method of protecting individual bodies from police violence is de-arresting (retrieving a person who has just been placed under arrest). De-arresting is often carried out by organized affinity groups in spontaneous response to the arrest of an individual. However, the refined police tactics of snatch squads, whereby several riot police insulate the arrest team, make it more difficult for activists to implement this tactic effectively.

Besides their organizational and spatial function, protest camps and Convergence Centers also fulfill an important function in protecting protesters' bodies. Offering a safe space for retreat, they provide a place where activists can rest, regenerate, sleep, and eat. The skills and infrastructure of activist (mobile) food kitchens are crucial for the daily life of such camps. In Europe, most countries have one or several such groups with the materials and skills to cook for up to several thousand people. It comes as no surprise that police tried to bar such a mobile food kitchen from entering France prior to Strasbourg 2009 NATO. Police argued that hundreds of kitchen knives would constitute illegal armaments and that kitchen towels could serve to mask the Black Bloc.

Camps also provide a medical clinic, which is important because activists do not feel safe visiting (and in the United States cannot afford to visit) a hospital for help with injuries caused by police violence. Cancun 2003 WTO was a rare occasion in which state medical services insisted upon providing healthcare to activists while refusing to cooperate with police agencies. Activist medics provide prompt, free, and knowledgeable care for injuries from police weapons (and accidents).

Since police attacks on Convergence Centers and camps have happened several times, activists have developed more careful security systems for guarding, protecting, and defending these spaces. Another innovation in the organization of the camps is the creation of chill-out spaces, In Europe, these chill-out spaces are often called "out-of-action" tents. They are especially important for activists staying for a long time at the camp to perform a lot of organizing tasks and for protesters who have had traumatic experiences. Creating a relaxed atmosphere for relaxing from the daily pressure at a protest camp is an important step in countering the frequent phenomenon of burn-out.

Remaining Out of Order

Activists want to remain out of order. We understand that effective dissent must be potent, loud, well placed, expansive, and free. Activists and our sympathizers know we need access to political rights in their fullness, and more. We need the psychic space to nurture creativity, courage, and connection. We need to experience our own actions as crucial to the political scene and therefore worth all the effort and risk. To dissent we must first stay visible. Spatially channeled, held at a distance, and marginalized, activists innovate tactics for invading, blockading, and seeping in. We dissolve on one side of a boundary and re-form on the other. We use creative combinations of high- and low-tech communications, large and small mobilizations. We present ourselves in every possible symbolic language, from armies to tug-of-war teams to dancers. We are committed to reterritorializing the political landscape with our rights and our refusals, enforcing democracy in the war zone that has imposed itself on this neighborhood, that village, those fields. Disrupting the presumption of control, only our insistent presence indicates that something is very, very wrong.

Summits have huge budgets at their disposal to normalize their presumptive "leadership" and to criminalize unwelcoming citizens. Activists defend our rights and lives with volunteer lawyers, training legal workers on the fly, answering the phone all night. The political economy of social control is a bill that someone will pay later. The political economy of dissent is encamped in a borrowed school or stadium, voluntaristic, participatory, stuck in another long meeting, due back at work on Tuesday, bringing home memorabilia in the form of legal skills that will change communities. Lay medics learn to care for the wounds caused by "less lethal" weapons. Lay legal workers learn the relevant laws, the court system, to provide counsel and evidence. The ragtag legal collectives of the activist scene compile the data: they can prove the political integrity of the unarmed activists and the illegal brutality of the police.

As we have shown, political violence takes many forms, affecting trust as well as bodies, daily lives as well as mass mobilizations, self-concepts as well as criminal records. All of these violences must be avoided if possible and, if necessary, healed. Activists develop technologies of education, solidarity, communal institutions, and culture to thwart and recover from these violences. How to build continuous solidarity structures that can respond to the effects of social control measures in the daily life of people who may not yet even have considered participating in protest is less clear. Just as social control extends beyond those present, so must solidarity beyond the protest event can only advance the struggle against the pervasive and preemptive effects of social control.

Democracy Out of Order

*There is only one good democracy, the one that represses
the catastrophes of democratic civilization.*

—Jacques Rancière[1]

This is a book we wish we did not have to write. You might prefer not to have read it. At stake in our subject is democracy itself. For those who see the liberal democratic state as a medium of peaceful and progressive social change, that promise is in deep trouble. To protect democracy, we must confine it because too much democracy is dangerous. Thus, we witness the reduction of democratic liberties in the name of the preservation of democracy itself. Defending democracy from democracy is becoming an indelicate matter, as pointed out so lucidly by Jacques Rancière, who concludes that democracy is (and has been) the enemy of the elite, an object of "hatred" among that class. To those unfazed by such a discovery, those who believe that the liberal state manufactures consent in the interests of capitalism, this book confirms the consolidation of that project.

We began our investigation with two observations. First, the concept of "policing" is inadequate to describe the temporality, spatiality, complexity, and diversity of social control tactics we witnessed. Second, "protest" is the wrong unit of analysis. We surmised that the impressive apparatuses of control were impacting a much broader public—dissenters. Their unit of organization is the social movement.

Exploring the literature on social control and dissent, we found that the legitimacy of social control is based in the idea that it is both neutral and positive for social cohesion. This perspective led for some period to a narrowing of the field to deviance and criminal deterrence. Marxist criminologists questioned the construction of criminality in the context of capitalism. Most helpfully, social theorists, along with critical scholars of media and education, have postulated that control is exercised through the production of norms, so that people discipline themselves and do not experience coercion. With a few notable exceptions, social movement scholars have focused on the policing of protest as the locus of social control, leaving aside analysis of the impacts of political criminalization on would-be dissenters. Dissent is generally envisioned as based on the legal right of individuals to free speech. But dissent—particularly dissent ultimately linked to social change—is produced in a landscape of activities that are collective. This collectivity is part of social movements. While assemblies and associations have some legal protections, social movements do not.

Seeking to better describe the landscape of social control in the era of globalization, we began with geography, territory, and space. Our analysis in chapter 2 demonstrates that the social control of space is not about preventing dissent completely but rather about channeling and controlling the form of protest. Many observers expect the state to engage in some degree of social control of protest—to make sure that it doesn't "get out of hand." But these observers may not have fully appreciated the historic role of dissent in democracy. Skeptics might ask, "So what if the state moves the protest around? Aren't people still expressing themselves?" Channeling dissent to reduce its social impact ultimately diminishes the quality of democracy.

Channeling predesigns the spaces of possible confrontations, setting the stage for some forms of dissent, while reducing the possibility of others. Social movements scholars have concluded definitively that the effective expression of dissent is a function of its *disruptive capacity*. Without the opportunity to be disruptive, dissent is impotent, decorative, and unable to effect the political contention that is its aim, and right, in a democratic society. Disruption, in turn, relies on access to the unexpected. This means that dissenters must have the right to disrupt spatial routines, to dislodge the normal happenstance of everyday life to create opportunities for fellow citizens to pause, think, reflect, and act. When the state channels a protest through permits and established routes or incapacitates movement, dissent becomes predictable and governable. Denying protest the capacity to be unexpected in space and/or time deprives dissent of its disruptive capacity, thereby canceling its contentious participation in the political arena.

The territories defined by security fences are only one aspect of such preemptive rearrangement of space. A second aspect is spatial operations, such as intruding into activist headquarters and preparatory meetings or incapacitating the creation of Convergence Centers or protest camps. By depriving activists of materials, artworks, and the capacity to organize, the state again channels their forms of expression.

Preemption is not only precaution or prevention of effective contention but also the criminalization of dissent. Security territory clearly demarcates a space inhabited by legitimate authority and a space occupied by illegitimate assault. In these spaces, the protester is no longer a participant in democracy but a violent offender, a ferocious unknown, who must be fenced, channeled, and guarded. The explicit and implicit implications are clear to those who might consider expressing themselves: today, you are already a criminal.

Next, we turned to the political economy of social control in the era of globalization. As we show in chapter 3, summit security budgets are huge. In addition to the official expenditures bankrolled at a federal level, extensive direct and indirect costs are (contentiously) imposed on localities and regions. Moreover, summit security has become an industry, with permanent security think tanks, departments of the European Union, and collaborative agencies. More striking yet is the scope of the multiagency international networks, which attend to each successive event. These networks comprise the military, immigration and border control agencies, intelligence services, and other civil agencies of several countries. The low-intensity operations performed by a mix of military and civil agencies are advised by international experts; while the local police agency might be a new one each time, these agencies are increasingly advised by a formally networked agglomerate of security organizations, which provide an accumulation of experience that otherwise could not take place. This is the global control of dissent.

The institutionalization of this extensive mobilization for social control makes the threat ever more real and ever more "Other." We must read this mobilization as communicating in no uncertain terms that dissent is not part of us; dissent is an Other that we must defend against. Dissent is not a normal part of history, political process, and daily life but a new and extraordinary threat that governments have to be ready for.

The architecture of Othering (or "security") is very expensive. It is becoming increasingly more costly to police global governance events, which are now routinely the most expensive police operations in host nations' history. The expenditure and networked control of a summit protest has no precursor in normal policing operations; summits mobilize extraparliamentary national budgets and international expert advisement. The willingness to spend increasingly larger sums of money is comparable to the discourse and practices of war, for which costs steadily increase but must be borne. But recent wars have been accompanied by extensive public debate about morality, strategy, and expense. In comparison, security operations for global governance summits are mostly taken for granted. The budgeting for security at global governance events looks like the budgeting for war, but there is no political objective for the military operation, and never a victor. The search for a comparison is elusive and informative.

The abrupt, jarring, and intense militarization of space for brief periods, followed by an equally abrupt and surreal return to "normality," could be described as the creation of what Giorgio Agamben calls a *state of exception*—a legal event in which the sovereign power dispenses with the rule of law, purportedly in order to preserve the rule of law. For example, the state calls for martial law so that the rule of law can survive an external or internal threat. Agamben argues that the state of exception, overused, becomes the permanent rule.[2] States of exception are constructed around civil flashpoints (or "emergencies"), such as riots, in which laws are suspended in order to impose "calm." But domestic riot control does not generally involve long-term investigations and prosecution of "organizers," border controls, security geography, and appellations of "terrorism." So "state of exception" is not an entirely adequate comparison.

Another possible comparison is counterinsurgency. Counterinsurgency involves a long time scale, a focus on individuals and groups, and expenditure of extensive and focused government resources. It involves domestic militarization, ongoing campaigns against insurgent groups that far outlast the flashpoint event (low-intensity operations), and the suspension of rights as in a "state of emergency." Most striking in this comparison are the European and U.S. efforts regarding individuals associated with the alterglobalization movement (who have been treated as counterinsurgents) and the organized state programs to identify, isolate, criminalize, prosecute (with punishments up to twenty-year sentences), and assault them (with extrajudicial force).

While imperfect, these comparisons are revealing. Protest events are subject to a physical and budgetary environment comparable to that for war. Protests are now routinely defined as necessitating a "state of exception." Activism relating to global governance is being dealt with not as protest, the right to which is guaranteed in every modern democracy, but as counterinsurgency. It is important, however, that this not be the official story. National elites are not at war with their own people but with the domestic Other (and his confederates from nearby countries). Thus, the discourse of terrorism is the public face of elites' mobilization for domestic counterinsurgency.

In preparing the material for chapter 4, which describes the legal machinations and police operations that take place immediately proximate to global governance events, we found our data-organizing schemes perpetually tangled in their own web. When we tried to analyze what we knew best and most personally, we were unable to clearly distinguish policing itself from public relations, surveillance from event policing, and policing from prosecution. Most frustrating, we had great difficulty distinguishing those public order tactics from psychological operations. Recognizing that this tangle pointed to knowledge we had yet to articulate, we turned to a more inductive and experiential analysis. The themes that emerged to structure chapter 5 were about marginalization, preemption, permeation, and impacts on political consciousness, collectivities, discourse, and movement culture. We recognized that *every* policing tactic has psychological impacts and that these impacts are in fact its most powerful. We recognized, finally, that security perimeters, massive budget outlays, personnel mobilization in the tens of thousands, use of new weapons, and the rest of the police tactics discussed in chapter 4 have the unmistakable effect of discouraging participation in the social spaces that nurture dissent and thus constitute, singly and together, political violence against the population as a whole.

As we demonstrate in the chapters on geography and policing, social control of protest is taking the form of preemptive criminalization. Such criminalization is now familiar in a world where teenage activities like painting graffiti and skateboarding have been criminalized. When we analyze the criminalization of protest and the use of counterinsurgency tactics, we must conclude that the crime is insurrection. But this "crime" is a right asserted at the foundations of democracy. So, policing and prosecuting it do, indeed, constitute political repression, rather than public order policing.

We conclude that the control of dissent has become a project in itself, which might resemble war but is not quite the same. While this may indeed not be a new practice, it makes sense that there is a newly organized form of violence for these internal wars. Counterinsurgency will look different in an era of the "rule of law" and manufactured consent.

This form of violence is organized to operate against dissent at the psychic level, not only through criminalization and the threat of force but also through othering, marginalization and trivialization.

Chapter 6 describes "antirepression" activism. This work has a solitary responsibility, which is to assemble sober and precise information about the points of impact between dissenters and the state. Antirepression activism avoids ideology and hyperbole in the interest of presenting incontrovertible data to the press and in court. This stark focus, accompanied by severe frugality, affords a unique view on social control.

We showed that antirepression work produces key analyses about how social control functions. This is possible because antirepression collects a particular kind of data through time and space and can therefore analyze the police operation in total and compare it with other operations. For instance, the Miami 2003 FTAA legal defense team was able to assemble data to demonstrate that the police operation had shifted from a security to a terror operation. The legal team at Genoa 2001 G8 was able to determine that the assault on the *Disobeddienti* march to the red zone was a preplanned police attack, rather than a public order operation. Moreover, antirepression work eventually gains precise information about victims, which, among other things, provides the decisive finding that they are neither terrorists nor violent insurrectionaries and, moreover, that (except for some passersby) they qualify as dissenters.

Social movements, to be effective, require two kinds of space that we think are particularly important sites for studying social control. First, they require diverse, secure, and informal social space for exploration to nurture collective intellectual and creative development. This is the space would-be dissenters enter to find solidarity, education, encouragement, and collaboration as they look for ways to express themselves. Our chapter on political violence shows the destruction of this space. Social movements also require access to public space where they can effect disruptive challenges to the existing system. Our chapter on geography shows the preemptive foreclosure of this public space.

Critical criminologists have long questioned the political motivations for criminalization. Our chapter on policing shows the creeping criminalization of dissent through laws, police behavior, surveillance, and prosecution. Our chapter on political economy shows that the expenditures on controlling alterglobalization can be compared to those for low-intensity warfare and civil war counterinsurgency. Yet our chapter on activist forms of legal defense (antirepression work) shows how this work has documented that the victims of social control are indeed dissenters, not violent insurrectionists. We must conclude that dissent is being treated as insurrection and that political violence is now directed against the foundation of democracy.

Tragically, social control of dissent has been litigated only around harm to individuals and formal organizations. We believe that the most important sociolegal project is to gain legal standing for social movements as a class so that the interests of innumerable affinity groups of dissenters may be litigated.

Until then, it's cameras, lemons, and fast sneakers.

Appendix A

Summits Directly Observed by Authors

- Seattle November 1999 World Trade Organization (WTO)
- Washington, D.C., April 2000 International Monetary Fund/World Bank (IMF/WB)
- Los Angeles August 2000 Democratic National Committee (DNC)
- Cincinnati November 2000 TABD (Trans Atlantic Business Dialogue)
- Prague September 2000 IMF/WB
- Québec City April 2001 Free Trade Area of the Americas (FTAA)
- Genoa July 2001 G8
- Washington, D.C., September 2001 Antiwar protest
- Göteborg June 2001 EU
- New York City February 2002 WEF
- Washington, D.C., April 2003 IMF/WB
- Denver May 2002 International Chamber of Commerce (ICC)
- Sacramento June 2003 U.S. Department of Agriculture preparatory meeting for WTO
- Évian June 2003 G8
- Cancún September 2003 WTO (Biotech)
- Miami November 2003 FTAA
- San Francisco February 2004 Antiwar protest
- Gleneagles July 2005 G8
- Heiligendamm July 2007 G8
- Strasbourg April 2009 NATO

Appendix B

Of Stones and Flowers[1]

This is an electronic mail dialogue between John Holloway and Vittorio Sergi, both of whom are involved in the alterglobaliza-tion movement. The dialogue was initiated following the Hei-ligendamm 2007 G8 summit. We include the entire correspon-dence here because it demonstrates the complex perspectives on violence in the alterglobalization movement. It is reproduced with permission of both authors. Nothing has been removed. Elipses, where they appear, were used in the original text.

"'Of stones and flowers," a dialogue between John Holloway and Vittorio Sergi around the events in Rostock on June 2, 2007.

Dear Vittorio,

The events at the end of the anti-G8 march in Rostock on Saturday 2 June, when there was an outbreak of prolonged and violent fighting between some of the demonstrators (the so-called "black block") and the police, disturbed and challenged me. I felt critical of the violence of the black block, but also felt the need to discuss and understand. I think a lot of people on the march felt the same way—critical but wanting to talk and understand rather than condemn (there were, of course, others who sim-ply condemned the action, but that is not my position).

I wanted to discuss with you in particular because I know you were in the middle of the battle and because I have a very great respect for you and I think we can discuss honestly and without disqualifications. The aim for me is not to win an argument, not to come to an agreement, but to understand.

(1) Let me explain the way I experienced the march:

My friends and I did not have a pre-established place of affiliation on the march. We walked along the march before it started, looking for an attractive place to insert ourselves. We walked past the large block of people (generally young, mostly men) dressed in black, many with hoods and many with their faces masked. We inserted ourselves finally near the front of the march, just behind the samba group with their drums and their dancing. From our perspective, the march was very big, colourful and fun. There was a massive, but at that stage inactive, police presence at the side of the road. We were particularly impressed by the clowns and the way in which they went up to the squadrons of police and made fun of them, imitating them, blowing bubbles at them, dancing around their cars and so on.

When the march reached its end-point, the harbour, I felt it had been a successful, enjoyable and colourful march. The "black block" arrived shortly afterwards and a friend I was with remarked that it looked as if they were ready for a fight. A minute later the fighting broke out, with columns of heavily-armoured police rushing back and forth and lots of young people dressed in black throwing stones at them. This was the first I saw of the violence which would dominate both the reports in the media and many of the discussions in Rostock over the next few days.

(2) I think there are three main reasons why I found the violence disturbing.

Firstly, I felt that it was the unfolding of a two-sided, predictable ritual. There were two sides prepared for battle, two sides who knew that, once the preamble of the march was completed, there would be open, violent conflict, in which the majority of people present on the march would be mere spectators. What was disturbing was the predictability and the symmetry of the conflict. In this there was a sharp contrast with the clowns who confronted the police in an unpredictable and absolutely asymmetrical way: in terms of sexuality, movement, dress, behaviour, solemnity and so on, the clowns were the opposite of the police, whereas the black block, in terms of uniform, sexual composition, disposition to violence, solemnity were very like the police.

Secondly, I was disturbed by the macho tone of the black block. Although there were some women and perhaps some older people, the block was dominated by young men, and the atmosphere generated was of the sort often associated with large gatherings of young men: aggressive, boastful, insensitive to the feelings of those who surrounded them.

Thirdly, the action was divisive. It seemed to me to go against the wishes of the great majority of those present, and caused considerable resentment among many. The participants in the action seemed to dismiss the feelings of the other demonstrators as irrelevant. I had the feeling that the other demonstrators were in some way being labeled as reformist or non-revolutionary. In other words, the action was identitarian, imposing a label upon others and dismissing their feelings as unimportant. An anti-identitarian approach would recognise other people as being self-contradictory and try to find a way of stirring the contradictions within them.

A very different and more sympathetic reading of the action would be to say that that was precisely the aim of the violence: to appeal to the hatred of the police and to move people to action. Someone in one of the discussions compared throwing stones at the police to occupying a house: in both cases you help people to overcome their fear of authority. This argument I can understand, but I think it is probably not true, in the sense that I think the action probably did not have this effect. I think the clowns' mockery of the police was probably far more effective in demystifying state authority.

Perhaps I am saying that in any action, the question of its resonance is very important: not that the action should be judged simply by its resonance, but that its capacity to resonate with the rebelliousness that exists in repressed form in most people is of very great importance. Not only that but that resonance is a question of asymmetry. That which we want to stir inside people is their anti-capitalism, and the only way in which we can do that is through actions that are anti-capitalist in their form, actions that propose ways of behaving and ways of relating that are quite unlike those of capitalism. The resonance of asymmetry seems to me the key to thinking about forms of anti-capitalist action.

(3) In explaining why I feel disturbed and challenged by the events of 2 June, I do not simply condemn the violence. It is clear that the violence used by the demonstrators was virtually nothing compared with the violence exercised every day by capital against us. I accept too that there may be circumstances in which the use of violent methods strengthens the movement against capital. But this is the problem: the action in this case seemed to be separated from any consideration of its effect on the movement as a whole. I may well be wrong about this and I may be quite unfair in much that I have said, but then I would be glad if you could explain it to me (and to anyone else who may read this).

Best,
John

Caro John,

Your letter, in which you express your criticism towards the violent clashes of the 2nd of June in Rostock, seemed to me an excellent opportunity to begin an honest and necessary discussion. I will try to answer all your major questions. My reply is not motivated by the abstract need to bring forward an apology of violence or of the "black block," but by the urgency to explain, as a participant myself, the reasons, problems and state of an open process of rebellion.

The march of June 2nd had, in all its aspects, a ritual and predictable character. The fact that it would take place before the beginning of the summit cast a shadow on the following days, when more radical groups would confront a long week of actions without the coverage of a great event during the days of the summit. The march also constituted an effort to represent a united movement, despite its differences. This aspect is closely linked to the customary dynamics of summits and counter summits which has, for the past ten years at least, constituted one of the main public expressions of anti-capitalist movements around the world.

On the other hand, due to the precedents in Germany and the rest of Europe, the march of June 2nd had a different air to it; there was energy and hope for a new drive for social movements: that also explains the large number and strong militant spirit of the participants. All organized political subjects, from the clowns you mention to ATTAC and the "black block" itself, wished to be represented and have their space of representation on the big stage. And so did the police, actually . . . it had announced the biggest security operation of its history, with a contingent of 17,000, and it couldn't fail. . . .

The so-called black block was created as a large group of affinities, made up by various smaller groups which varied as to composition and geographical origin. The etiquette (black clothes, covered faces) should not fool anyone as to the diversity of subjects present.

The Dissent! group took up the role of a "hub," that is, a centre of connection and distribution of information amongst groups which were more inclined towards direct action and did not consider it convenient to participate in the Block G8 alliance, which due to its broad and plural character included, amongst others, important reformist subjects such as ATTAC and the German section of the European Left party, known today as "Die Linke."

Thus, the block included anarchist groups from many different places (Poland, Germany, Denmark, Holland, England, United States, Greece,

Catalunya), as well as autonomous groups from Italy, Sweden, France, Euskadi, Switzerland and Germany, amongst others.

Also, many anti-fascist groups which in Germany do not have a sole organization but are largely influenced by the Antifascistiche Linke Berlin (part of the Interventionist Left, i.e., also of the Block G8 coalition) joined the Block from the bus bearing the slogan "Make Capitalism History."

The block thus included 3,000 to 5,000 people who defied the ban on covering their faces and carrying sticks and other instruments of self-defence in the marches. The common intention of the participants in the block was to directly attack the private property of banks and corporations, as well as the police. There were also discussions as to measuring the amount of force which could be employed according to the response of the rest of the march; almost the majority agreed on acting in a way which would not harm it.

So I do not believe that this choice was in total contrast with the spirit and intentions of the rest of the march. Maybe of one part, but then again there is always a great deal of differences in this kind of international marches. However, throughout these years it has been established that all forms of protest should have the right of "citizenship," in the boundaries of respect for others. Also, the block did not wish to stay in the background or fringes of the march for a political reason. Radical forms of direct action are also a part of the movement and militant groups involved in that kind of action, or simply those who support it or individually participate in it, respect other forms of struggle; there would be no sense in separating them.

The tactics of the block was an escalation of actions which would lead to a direct confrontation once having reached the harbour, where most police forces were concentrated.

It is true that, as you mention, the block also aimed at motivating and involving the rest of the march in a resistance against the police and in attacking corporations and their façades. Indeed, that did happen when the police, frustrated at not being able to defend itself from the beginning, attacked the entire march as well as the people watching the concert. Those present reacted in many ways when that happened, from throwing stones to creating chains and advancing with their hands in the air, managing to contain the offensive of the police, despite the armoured cars and water tanks.

It is true that the block was made up mostly of young people and the fact that there were not so many women as men is an aspect of a differentiated participation in actions and initiatives; however, that is something that occurs in many communities and organizations and depends on a broader problem surrounding the forms and languages of political action. Nonetheless, I was surprised by the number of women participating in the clashes, by much larger than what could have been observed in Italy.

You also consider the majority of young radicals as a lack of comprehension towards other forms of life and ages. On the contrary, I consider it to be a starting point, as well as a necessary form of construction of a common movement which, as always, begins amongst the young, due to the urgency, rage and passion with which the negation of the existing is exercised, "the negation of the negation" in practice.

Turning our gaze towards México, Oaxaca for example, we observe a very different composition in the barricades, but that is due to a political and social "popular" form that exists only in few occasions and places in Europe. The division between young generations and the rest is deeper and relates to complex causes which also bear political implications; however, this issue cannot be solved in one march.

Against those who speak of a depressed and apathetic generation, I felt, on the contrary, a lot of positive energy and passion in this contingent. Many different ways of living and a lot of decisiveness and will for conspiring and cooperating altogether in order to achieve a radical social change.

Action, in the case of a march, is not simply symbolic; it seeks direct effectiveness. It has shown, for example, that the police is not invincible when put up against a multitude that seizes the initiative and cooperates. It has also shown that the struggle against an economic, social and military system cannot limit itself to events or public moments of representation (and mediation), but that it rather overflows and takes the initiative, it can mark the time, space and form of a confrontation that can also be called class struggle, that it does not have to restrain itself to defending the few collective riches that still remain in hands of the people.

For this reason, I attach the document which resulted from the discussion between various groups that participated in the confrontation march of June 2nd and has been put up on the Dissent! website.

Plan B has started already: join to the battle of joy
4 June 2007—international brigades
There are certain moments when it seems appropriate, without it ever being a matter of calculation, to address everybody in a manner as simple and direct as possible. One of these moments has arrived.

We want to speak briefly about what happened on the 2nd of June in the city of Rostock during the demonstration against the G8. We speak, of course, from a partisan position, but one forged of multiple voices which at certain moments manage to become singular. One of these moments has arrived.

This 2nd of June, thousands of people didn't wait for the ritual which we have so often been subjected to in this movement to play itself out: mobilizations, demonstrations, less than symbolic actions, conferences crowned with pat conclusions long ago prepared by some obscure functionary. Nor did they accept donning the worn out postures of those who pretend to be concerned with the state of the world and abandon themselves to a pious compassion for the most misfortunate.

These thousands, on the contrary, did not content themselves with reacting or resisting, but took the initiative, consciously attacking the places where, day after day, capitalist exploitation and the material effectiveness of the global civil war are extended. The G8 is not only the expression of the domination of capital over the world, a theatre of dubious quality where the leaders put onto the stage another ritual, one that serves to codify their rule over the lives of subjects. The G8 is the symbol of the suffering inflicted daily on millions of people. That we should be reproached for our violence when it is they who have their hands full of blood!

In the end what happened was very simple: free beings decided to collectively and practically oppose the symbols of capitalism and the baleful face of the state incarnated by all the police of the world. The assemblies and long speeches, if they are not followed by irruptions in the streets of our metropolis, produce only suspicion and resignation.

We want to also recall another truth in relation to the combatants in the battle of Rostock: they are women and men originating from every corner of the world and have no need of an identity card to recognize each other, constitute gangs, and experiment new forms of life. We are the nationless who seek to destroy the frontiers—as much material as symbolic—which separate our lives, thought and bodies. We are made of multiple singularities who desire to join in order to create the conditions of a more ecstatic life. We come from everywhere, it is why we are everywhere. Those who affirm the contrary are brazen-faced liars.

There is another truth: under every black mask was a smile, in every stone thrown against the common enemy there was joy, in every body revolting against oppression there was desire. We don't harbor sad passions and resentments, if that had been the case we wouldn't have fought and resisted for so long. Thus don't be deceived, look at those with whom you are connected, or whom you love; perhaps you will find one of these bodies, one of these smiles, one of these hands engaged in the struggle. Joyful passions placed in common and joined to the assault on command—such is the secret of the battles waged in the heart of the asymmetrical conflict which opposes us to the sadness of the weapons and bodies of power. Individually we are nothing, together we are a power. Together we are a commune: the commune of Rostock.

We all arrived here with a personal and collective history, a history of struggle and battle waged in every corner of the earth. We don't want this event to be perceived as a simple continuation of the old cycle of struggle which, since September the 11th, has known so many disappointments. We believe on the contrary that the 2nd of June was the signal of a powerful and determined rupture with this phase of defeat and that this battle inaugurates new offensives. That this breach permits us to flee together to the other side of the mirror, the side of freedom.

And now comrades, we block the flows . . .

Long live the commune of Rostock and Reddelich!

International Brigades

June 2nd must also be judged in a broader time frame. During the following days, the same people that encouraged the clashes were involved in constructing and participating in many self-managed camp activities: from the kitchen to the collective bars, workshops, alternative media, parties, political and artistic workshops, the multitude (yes, mostly young . . .) returned to its everyday positive forms of action.

The massive blockades of the 6th, 7th and 8th were in benefit of the variety of forms of struggle and action; none was more determinant than the others. Dissent!, as well as Block G8 and non-organized groups and individuals joined the marches and blockades, other forms of swarms. . . . Everyone, from the most radical pacifists to the toughest anarchist groups, cooperated in order to avoid a violent escalation of the conflict and to make blockades effective.

That leads us to the conclusion that in the minds of most of the participants in the June 2nd march, the black block is but a transitory form, a swarm, and not the "army of the movement." It also adopts an aesthetic form that is closely linked to the influences of the "Autonomen" German movement of the 80s, as well as to the Anglo-Saxon anarchist movement, especially active in the environmental struggle. It is, thus, a transitory form, a kind of intelligent mob with a long history in radical dissent in Europe and the United States. The donning of black clothes and covered faces is of a practical utility in times of generalized video control. It also reflects the resonance of powerful symbols of rebellion such as the balaclava. From the Zapatistas of 1994 to Carlo Giuliani in Genoa in 2001, the rebels cover their faces in order to be seen.

The clashes of June 2nd and the following days urgently pose the question as to how to react against the repressive apparatus. Pacifism and its ethics cannot be an alibi for impotence, or worst, as in the case of ATTAC, for the collaboration with the repressive military apparatus. However, there have been consistent pacifists, whom I have seen receive blows and gas discharges in the face for trying to break the police lines or resist in a blockade, on the ground with dogs and truncheons biting their skin. Nonetheless, we must work together in a wider and more coordinated sense in order to be able to defend autonomous spaces, in the countryside as well as the cities, defend strikes, road and train blockades, marches and meetings, in a growing state of siege and militarization, in México as well as in Europe.

That is why I do not believe that the clowns that you so admire are an efficient response to these matters either. They have a very positive role in confusing and delegitimate the authority and aggressiveness of the police, but we cannot all become clowns, neither will we always be able to stop tanks with flowers. We need everyone, we cannot disqualify anyone in this movement and uneven power relation.

By the way, we will always love flowers, but the days of putting flowers in gun barrels have gone by. The images of military helicopters flying above the heads of thousands of unarmed protesters, launching police assault troops, gas charges, water tanks and horses against the defenceless crowd speak of the madness and dangerousness of the police apparatus in our days. That is not insignificant. Put up against this phenomenon, most radical groups do not respond with militarization; on the contrary, there is a conscience and a rejection of symmetrical violence, of hierarchic organization and authority. However, this does not mean there is not a search for forms of power, for ways of changing power relations through asymmetrical forms of resistance and attack.

I hope I have answered a few questions and maybe cleared some doubts. However, everything is under an open process of discussion and creation; that is the positive aspect of today's movement. Rostock was a partial, but encouraging victory. We continue to walk and discuss!

Saludos,
Vittorio

Caro Vittorio,
We agree on much, but not on all. The question of the composition of the "black block" (or perhaps "black non-block") is not so important—although I do remain suspicious of any group composed largely of young men, and I would be even more suspicious of one composed largely of old men. And I agree that it is important to see the march in the context of the week's actions, where the atmosphere was certainly a very good one of respectful unity-in-diversity. I also agree that violence is not the central issue: my argument is not a pacifist one. And yet the whole thing of the stone-throwing keeps worrying me.

Let me emphasise again that I respect those who throw stones at the police. But for me respect cannot mean just a side-by-side co-existence: it means saying "we are comrades, that is why we must discuss our differences and doubts openly." That is what these notes are about.

We are at war. Let's start from there. The last twenty years or so (and especially the last five years) have seen a great intensification of capitalist violence against humanity. We can see this as the Fourth World War (as the Zapatistas put it) or as the war of all states against all people (as Eloína and I put it in an article a few years ago). The question then is how we should fight this war.

The notion of war is perhaps unfortunate, because it usually suggests asymmetry: one army fights another army, and there is not much difference between the organisation (the social relations) of the two sides. Generally, it does not matter very much which side wins: either way, the war and the militarization which accompany it signify a defeat for humanity, for the sort of social relations that we want to construct. It is generally the more numerous, better equipped, more cleverly aggressive side that wins.

There are two problems about thinking of the struggle for a new world in these symmetrical terms. Firstly, we would probably lose: there is no way we can match the military power of the capitalist states. And secondly, and even more important: symmetrical organisation means that we are reproducing the social relations that we are struggling against.

The question then is how we think about fighting this war asymmetrically. The enormous strength of the flowers in the guns and of the clowns confronting the police is that they emphasise this asymmetry. They say clearly "our strength is that we are not like you and that we shall never be like you."

You suggest that clowns and flowers may be important but that it is not enough. You say "we must work together in a wider and more coordinated sense in order to be able to defend autonomous spaces, in the countryside as well as the cities, defend strikes, road and train blockades, marches and meetings, in a growing state of siege and militarization, in México as well as in Europe. That is why I do not believe that the clowns that you so admire are an efficient response to these matters either." But what does "defence" mean? It does not mean "defence" in any absolute sense. The armed force of the state could overcome stone-throwers just as easily as it could overcome flower-carriers or clowns. Defence really has to be understood as dissuasion. How do we dissuade the state from exercising the full force of its armed power? Is stone-throwing more effective in this respect than flower-carrying? Probably not, because the dissuasive effect is not a question of physical strength but of resonances: of the resonances that the participants succeed in stirring throughout society. It is above all these resonances that impose limits on state action: the degree to which the resonances make the state afraid of the social reaction that might follow from a violent repression. Thinking in terms of resonances and reactions, we must ask: is it easier for the state to violently repress a group of stone-throwers or a group of flower-carriers? Violent repression is possible in both cases, but I think it is probably easier for the state in the case of stone-throwers.

Take the Zapatistas, for example. How do we explain the ability of the Zapatistas to resist (so far) a violent repression by the state? Not so much in terms of "defence" but in terms of dissuasion. The Zapatistas have dissuaded the state from violent repression by being armed for self-defence, but above all by their communiqués which have resonated so strongly through the world. Maybe we should see the Zapatistas as armed clowns: by being armed but always acting in a way that emphasised their asymmetrical relation with the state. Their flight, with marimba and all, when the army attacked on 9 February 1995, is an outstanding example of that. Perhaps the greatest strength of the Zapatistas is that they have always understood war as a question of aesthetics, of theatre. The obvious contrast in México is with the EPR, which is a classical armed organisation and has never succeeded (or perhaps tried) in stirring the sort of resonances that would act as a defence against a state.

Which is more radical, the EZLN or the EPR? For me, without doubt, the EZLN, because they are constantly re-thinking the struggle, above all because they are far more asymmetrical in their relation to the state. But I can see that for some people, groups like the EPR may appear more radical, because they appear to represent a more direct and violent confrontation with the state.

The state, in its fight against us, constantly tries to weaken the social resonances of our movement, in part by pushing us more towards direct, symmetrical confrontation with it. If they succeed in doing that, then open repression becomes politically more easy for them. That is my worry: not a moral condemnation of stone-throwing, but that what appears to be more radical is in fact less radical and weakens the struggle against capital.

If we think of the issue in terms of the Fourth World War and how we fight that war, then I would suggest as a principle of the effectiveness of struggle that our struggle must be asymmetrical to that of capital. Asymmetry (the clear manifestation that we are not like them and will never be like them) is crucial to the strength of anti-capitalist resonances. There should be room for people who throw stones, but there must also be room for people who say that stone- throwing is not a very effective way of fighting (and of course that guns would be an even less effective way).

Saludos,

John

Caro John,

By a strange coincidence, I write these lines while returning to Italy from México. I had to return for personal reasons, today, when a new confrontation is feared in the town of Oaxaca, where I was last week, when thousands of people who wished to celebrate the popular festivity of Guelaguetza were violently repressed by the police and the army, resulting in many men and women imprisoned and injured.

The reality of violence, of its menace and its use against the nonconformists, is presented over and over again as the reality of oppression, of inequality, of exploitation. That is, as a social relation.

And also as a form of organization, of military and militarized groups and apparatus, such as the army and the police. The history of these people is filled with this violence, its memory, in America as well as in Europe, records a long chain of violations, injustices, unpunished crime perpetrated by these organizations, whose reason of existence lies in the defence of the State and capital.

Now, our discussion has led us to some important points, on which I still disagree with you: I agree with your approach on asymmetry. It is of great importance and an obvious significance in relation to the current situation. Parting from the inequality of power in the current social power relations, it is reasonable to think that no radical change will be accomplished in a symmetrical revolution, in a sort of topsy-turvy world, but rather through a diagonal change, a tearing, thousands of ruptures. This perspective obviously affects political practices and, therefore, practices of confrontation with the established powers. However, I believe it does not exclude open confrontation.

I see the need for blending various forms of action in this asymmetrical confrontation, in the same way that the forms of breaking the relation of violent domination which imposes relations of exploitation depend greatly on cultural differences and different historical heritages. For example, the same practice of participating in a demonstration is very different in Germany, against the G8, or in Oaxaca, this morning, in order to boycott the Guelaguetza of the authoritarian PRI government, in the same way that participating in a pacific march in Pakistan, Guinea Conakry or Colombia can mean risking one's life. Thus, according to the context, the violence used by the people for their defence is of different forms and natures than the ones used by those in power, it has different political aims, it responds to different criteria, to that of the defence of dignity and not of the imposition of an abstract order and legality.

Obviously, aspects of symmetry and forms of coordination are also present. When we think of an asymmetrical confrontation with power we cannot ignore the issue of organization. Our action must be spontaneous and creative, but it must also be coordinated and organized along with others, so as to consider three fundamental aspects of the development of all revolutionary politics: time, space and, as Machiavelli pointed out, opportunity. Referring to a violent confrontation with the state forces, you say: "Firstly, we would probably lose: there is no way we can match the military power of the capitalist states. And secondly, and even more important: symmetrical organisation means that we are reproducing the social relations that we are struggling against."

I do not agree. Given that we are going through the "Fourth World War" and that the violence of power is not simple defensive, i.e., it is not presented as a police officer safeguarding a bank, but rather as a thief who enters our house in order to steal, we must consider defence as necessary and pledge our commitment to the possibility that asymmetrical forms of confrontation could also put the military power of capitalist states in a difficult position.

If we think that it is not possible, that it is not possible to put an end to the oppression of the armed groups of the state, then symmetrical confrontation for gaining power (and control over the repressive bodies) would once again be the only tragic options for us, who are underneath.

My second comment is on your mention of the EZLN. I agree with your observation about the theatrical and ritual sense of this army of indigenous peasants. From their point of view, I have even heard the militaries being called "brothers." The Zapatistas do not dehumanize the enemy, they try to conserve its human face and, to this moment, they have managed to avoid fratricide war with the paramilitary groups despite their numerous crimes. Their form of political struggle has been, without doubt, peculiar and the fact that the conflict in the South East of México has not ended in carnage, as happened ten years ago in Guatemala, is without a shred of doubt something positive that partly depends on the EZLN itself. However, we must consider that the EZLN had, and still has, a disposition to war. In this sense, I do not believe this organization should be considered more or less radical than the EPR, for example. To this day, the latter has a modus operandi which is much closer to forms of the past, more openly confrontational and focused on the enemy army; however, despite its clear Marxist-Leninist political positioning, it would adopt markedly asymmetrical forms of guerrilla warfare if that were to lead to a tactical advantage. We could rather say that, from our point of view, the EZLN had the capacity to adapt and innovate its forms of political action, and its experience of "asymmetrical" struggle is a good base for thinking about possible forms of revolutionary political struggle in the near future.

Despite our differences, I agree with your concern about the need to turn asymmetrical struggle into a virtue of the anti-capitalist movement, to express our rejection towards the system in a negative, non-dialectical way.

Taking "Fourth World War" seriously amounts to admitting that there is a system of violence set up against us. Therefore, our strategy of confrontation cannot be accused of triggering the repression; maybe it can supply media elements for its justification, but then again we know that the latter can occur without the need for an effective excuse.

You say: "It is above all these resonances that impose limits on state action: the degree to which the resonances make the state afraid of the social reaction that might follow a violent repression." The resonances of our action can indeed put a limit, dissuade the State, and there will be, no doubt, marches and actions where it will be better to throw flowers instead of stones. However, as the recent history of the people of Oaxaca shows, there are moments when it becomes clear that violence comes from above, against our flowers and our dancing.

We began our discussion in the protests against the G8 in Germany and ended up in the streets of Oaxaca, without a conclusion, it would seem. . . . We know there is an ongoing confrontation, made up by different simultaneous confrontations, and that the security machinery of all States is being militarized and organized against the "internal enemy."

However, we also know that our victory, from a revolutionary perspective, has to commit to the defeat of war and of the enemy at the same time. It would be meaningless to win a war and lose dignity.

How this is possible, we can only found out in practice. Ciudad de México—Madrid, 23 de julio de 2007.

Caro Vittorio,
You are right, of course, that we are talking not just of Rostock but of many different situations in the world that require different responses.

Thinking of México, there is one image that keeps on coming to my mind in the last few days: the famous photo of the Zapatista women literally pushing back big armed soldiers who were trying to invade their village. This photo has been very widely circulated all over the world and has undoubtedly had an enormous political impact. For me it illustrates the force of asymmetry, but it could be argued that it also creates a romantic, unreal image of the conflict in Chiapas. Perhaps one way to close the dialogue (for the moment) would be to leave that image as a question.

Ciao,
John

Appendix C

Suggestions for Future Research

We believe that the new landscape of social control of dissent that we have articulated should be explored through the matrix shown in Table 4, which encourages a combination of analytic categories from social movements with ours for social control.

TABLE 4.

Social Movements	Social Control		
	Geography	Political Economy	Political Violence
Resources			
Political Opportunities			
Framing			
Cultures of Resistance			

Political violence, particularly psychological operations, constrains the ability of the movement to make its own frame. Laws affecting activists, particularly ongoing prosecutions, as we've described, affect movement cultures because they affect everyday lives. As states exert social control through the geography of cities and public space and manage a geography of global governance itself, they deny and create political opportunities, not only for street fights but also on a symbolic and discursive level. Criminalization steals the frame from dissenters, who must struggle to retain their personal, organizational, and political focus. Prosecution and surveillance invade the everyday life of activists and organizations, disrupting their capacity to build and maintain cultures of resistance.

We hope that this book inspires as many questions as it answers and thereby contributes to vigorous investigation of social control and an equally vigorous protection of dissent. Some of the research agendas we would like to see further developed are:

+ The quantitative extent of discouragement of dissenters
+ The long-term effects on local police of temporary militarization and intense "Othering" of citizens
+ The extent and content of critical intragovernmental discourse on security budgets
+ The extent of linkage between domestic and regional dissent-management institutions and terrorism-management institutions
+ The international cooperation of intelligence services and their role in criminalizing dissenters
+ An assessment of how far nationalisms counter the tendency to globalize security operations
+ The interrelation of social control and cooptation mechanisms in channeling dissent

Notes

CHAPTER 1

1. Ben Trott, "Gleneagles, Activism and Ordinary Rebelliousness," in Shut Them Down! The G8, Gleneagles 2005 and the Movement of Movements, ed. David Harvie et al. (Dissent! and Autonomedia, 2005), 213–33, http://shutthemdown.org/details.html.

2. Morris Janowitz, "Sociological Theory and Social Control," American Journal of Sociology 81, no. 1 (July 1975): 82–108.

3. George Herbert Mead, "The Genesis of the Self and Social Control," International Journal of Ethics 35, no. 3 (April 1925): 251–77.

4. George Vincent, "The Province of Sociology," American Journal of Sociology (January 1896): 488.

5. Karl Mannheim and Edward Shils, Man and Society in an Age of Reconstruction: Studies in Modern Social Structure (Routledge and Kegan Paul, 1949).

6. Edward Shils, "The Theory of Mass Society," Diogenes, no. 39 (1962): 45–66.

7. Barrington Moore, "Reflections on Conformity in Industrial Society," in Political Power and Social Theory (Harvard University Press, n.d.).

8. Janowitz, "Sociological Theory and Social Control."

9. Noam Chomsky, Necessary Illusions: Thought Control in Democratic Societies (Pluto Press, 1989); Edward S. Herman and Noam Chomsky, Manufacturing Consent: The Political Economy of the Mass Media (Pantheon, 2002); Robert W. McChesney, The Problem of the Media: U.S. Communication Politics in the Twenty-First (Monthly Review Press, 2004); Sut Jhally, Advertising and the End of the World, Media Education Foundation, 1997, http://www.mediaed.org/cgi-bin/commerce.cgi?preadd=action&key=101.

10. Jack P. Gibbs, "Social Control, Deterrence, and Perspectives on Social Order," Social Forces 56, no. 2 (December 1977): 408–23.

11. Jack P. Gibbs, Social Control: Views from the Social Sciences (Sage, 1982); Jack P. Gibbs, Control: Sociology's Central Notion (University of Illinois Press, 1989).

12. Dorothy E. Chunn and Shelley A. M. Gavigan, "Social Control: Analytical Tool or Analytical Quagmire?," Contemporary Crises 12, no. 2 (1988): 107–24.

13. Robert F. Meier and Weldon T. Johnson, "Deterrence as Social Control: The Legal and Extralegal Production of Conformity," American Sociological Review 42, no. 2 (April 1977): 292–304.

14. Richard Quinney, Critique of Legal Order: Crime Control in Capitalist Society (Transaction, 1974); Peter B. Kraska, "Criminal Justice Theory: Toward Legitimacy

and an Infrastructure," Justice Quarterly 23, no. 2 (2006): 167–85; Paddy Hillyard et al., "Leaving a 'Stain upon the Silence': Contemporary Criminology and the Politics of Dissent," British Journal of Criminology 44, no. 3 (May 2004): 369–90.

15. P. A. J. Waddington, Policing Citizens: Authority and Rights (Routledge, 1999), 64.

16. Nicos Ar Poulantzas, Political Power and Social Classes (Humanities Press, 1973).

17. György Lukács, History and Class Consciousness, trans. Rodney Livingstone (Merlin Press, 1923); Antonio Gramsci, Prison Notebooks (International, 1929); Max Horkheimer and Theodor W. Adorno, Dialectic of Enlightenment: Philosophical Fragments (Stanford University Press, 1944); Theodor W. Adorno, Aesthetic Theory (Routledge, 1970); Theodor W. Adorno, Negative Dialectics (Routledge, 1966); Herbert Marcuse, One-Dimensional Man: Studies in the Ideology of Advanced Industrial Society (Beacon Press, 1964); Herbert Marcuse, "Repressive Tolerance," in A Critique of Pure Tolerance, ed. Robert Paul Wolff, Berkeley Commune, and Herbert Marcuse (Beacon Press, 1965); Louis Althusser, "Ideology and Ideological State Apparatuses, first published in La Pensée, 1970," in Lenin and Philosophy and Other Essays, trans. Ben Brewster (Monthly Review Press, 2002), 272.

18. Paul E. Willis, Learning to Labor: How Working Class Kids Get Working Class Jobs (Columbia University Press, 1981); Jay MacLeod, Ain't No Makin' It: Aspirations and Attainment in a Low-Income Neighborhood (Westview Press, 1987).

19. Chomsky, Necessary Illusions; Herman and Chomsky, Manufacturing Consent; Michael Parenti, Inventing Reality (Palgrave Macmillan, 1986); McChesney, The Problem of the Media.

20. Jürgen Habermas, The Theory of Communicative Action, trans. Thomas McCarthy (Beacon Press, 1981).

21. Judith Butler, Gender Trouble: Feminism and the Subversion of Identity (Routledge, 1990); Annamarie Jagose, Queer Theory (Otago University Press, 1997).

22. Erich Goode, Deviant Behavior (Prentice-Hall, 1984).

23. Michel Foucault et al., Technologies of the Self (University of Massachusetts Press, 1988); Michel Foucault, The History of Sexuality (Vintage, 1988).

24. Charles Tilly, From Mobilization to Revolution (McGraw-Hill, 1978).

25. Frances Fox Piven and Richard A. Cloward, Poor People's Movements: Why They Succeed, How They Fail (Vintage, 1977).

26. David P. Waddington, Karen Jones, and C. Critcher, Flashpoints: Studies in Public Disorder (Routledge, 1989); David P. Waddington, Contemporary Issues in Public Disorder (Routledge, 1992).

27. Pamela Oliver, "How Does Repression Work?" 2002, http://www.ssc.wisc.edu/~oliver/PROTESTS/PROTESTS.HTM. She excludes the cooptation seen as important by Piven and Cloward.

28. John Wilson, "Social Protest and Social Control," Social Problems 24, no. 4 (April 1977): 470, 475.

29. Pamela Oliver, "Repression and Crime Control: Why Social Movements Scholars Should Pay Attention to Mass Incarceration as a Form of Repression," Mobilization 13, no. 1 (February 2008).

30. Ibid.

31. Ibid., 185.

32. Robert Weissman, "First Amendment Follies: Expanding Corporate Speech Rights," Multinational Monitor, May 1998, http://www.multinationalmonitor.org/mm1998/051998/weissman.html.

33. Ronald J. Krotoszynski Jr., "Dissent, Free Speech, and the Continuing Search for the 'Central Meaning' of the First Amendment. Review of The Dissent of the Governed: A Meditation on Law, Religion, and Loyalty. By Stephen L. Carter. Cambridge: Harvard University Press. 1998. Dissent, Injustice, and the Meanings of America. By Steven H. Shiffrin. Princeton: Princeton University Press. 1999," Michigan Law Review 98, no. 6 (2000): 1613–77.

34. Jean L. Cohen and Andrew Arato, Civil Society and Political Theory (MIT Press, 1992).

35. Cass R. Sunstein, Why Societies Need Dissent (Harvard University Press, 2003).

36. William A. Gamson, Power and Discontent (Dorsey Press, 1968).

37. David C. Schwartz, Political Alienation and Political Behavior (Aldine Transaction, 1973).

38. Stephen C. Craig and Michael A. Maggiotto, "Political Discontent and Political Action," Journal of Politics 43, no. 2 (May 1981): 514–22.

39. Henry A. Giroux, "When Hope Is Subversive," Tikkun, 2004.

40. Sunstein, Why Societies Need Dissent.

41. Bryan S. Turner, "The Erosion of Citizenship," British Journal of Sociology 52, no. 2 (June 2001): 189–209.

42. John Gaventa, Power and Powerlessness: Quiescence and Rebellion in an Appalachian Valley (University of Illinois Press, 1980).

43. Kusper v. Pontikes, 414 U.S. 51, 56 (1973).

44. Archon Fung, "Associations and Democracy: Between Theories, Hopes, and Realities," Annual Review of Sociology 29 (August 2003): 515–39.

45. For a nice summary of the major options and what is at stake in them, see Nick Crossley, Making Sense of Social Movements (Open University Press, 2002).

46. Sidney Tarrow, Power in Movement: Social Movements and Contentious Politics (Cambridge University Press, 1998).

47. Ron Eyerman and Andrew Jamison, Social Movements: A Cognitive Approach (Pennsylvania State University Press, 1991).

48. Richard Flacks, Making History: The American Left and the American Mind (Columbia University Press, 1988); Paul Gilroy, The Black Atlantic: Modernity and Double Consciousness (Verso, 1993); Carlos Muñoz, Youth, Identity, Power: The Chicano Movement (Verso, 1989); Ann Bookman, Women and the Politics of Empowerment (Temple University Press, 1988). The collective behavior tradition (Smelser 1962), which initially shared Weber's concerns about dangerous crowds, continues in the form of political consciousness studies, which focus on explaining the psychology of activists. Recent North American explorations of political consciousness include Gloria Anzaldúa, Making Face, Making Soul: Haciendo Caras : Creative and Critical Perspectives by Feminists of Color (Aunt Lute Foundation Books, 1990).

49. Mayer N. Zald and Roberta Ash, "Social Movement Organizations: Growth, Decay and Change," Social Forces 44, no. 3 (1966): 327–41.

50. John D. McCarthy and Mayer N. Zald, "Resource Mobilization and Social Movements: A Partial Theory," American Journal of Sociology 82, no. 6 (May 1977): 1212–41.

51. Peter K. Eisinger, "The Conditions of Protest Behavior in American Cities," American Political Science Review 67, no. 1 (March 1973): 11–28; David S. Meyer and Debra C. Minkoff, "Conceptualizing Political Opportunity," Social Forces 82, no. 4 (June 2004): 1457–92.

52. David A. Snow et al., "Frame Alignment Processes, Micromobilization, and Movement Participation," American Sociological Review 51, no. 4 (August 1986): 464–81; Robert D. Benford and David A. Snow, "Framing Processes and Social Movements: An Overview and Assessment," November 28, 2003, http://arjournals. annualreviews.org/doi/abs/10.1146/annurev.soc.26.1.611.

53. Eyerman and Jamison, Social Movements, in the later case summarizing Rucht 1988.

54. Pamela E. Oliver and Hank Johnston, "What a Good Idea! Ideologies and Frames in Social Movement Research," Mobilization 5, no. 1 (2000): 37–54.

55. Marcuse, "Repressive Tolerance," 817–58.

56. Alain Touraine, The Voice and the Eye: An Analysis of Social Movements (Cambridge University Press, 1981).

57. Alberto Melucci, Nomads of the Present: Social Movements and Individual Needs in Contemporary Society (Hutchinson, 1989); Alessandro Pizzorno, "Political Exchange and Collective Identity in Industrial Conflict," in The Resurgence of Class Conflict in Western Europe since 1968, ed. Colin Crouch and Alessandro Pizzorno, vol. 2 (Macmillan, n.d.), 277–98.

58. Eyerman and Jamison, Social Movements.

59. Susan Bibler Coutin, The Culture of Protest: Religious Activism and the U.S. Sanctuary Movement (Westview Press, 1993); Hank Johnston and Bert Klandermans, eds., Social Movements and Culture (Routledge, 1995); James M. Jasper, The Art of Moral Protest: Culture, Biography, and Creativity in Social Movements (University of Chicago Press, 1999); George McKay, DiY Culture: Party and Protest in Nineties Britain (Verso, 1998); Francesca Polletta, "Culture and Its Discontents: Recent Theorizing on the Cultural Dimensions of Protest," Sociological Inquiry 67, no. 4 (fall 1997): 431–50; Richard Gabriel Fox and Orin Starn, Between Resistance and Revolution: Cultural Politics and Social Protest (Rutgers University Press, 1997); Sonia E. Alvarez, Evelina Dagnino, and Arturo Escobar, Cultures of Politics, Politics of Cultures: Re-visioning Latin American (Westview Press, 1998); Lawrence Grossberg, Cary Nelson, and Paula Treichler, Cultural Studies, 1st ed. (Routledge, 1991).

60. Melucci, Nomads of the Present.

61. Ulrich Beck, "World Risk Society as Cosmopolitan Society?: Ecological Questions in a Framework of Manufactured Uncertainties," Theory, Culture and Society 13, no. 4 (1996): 1–32; Anthony Giddens, Modernity and Self-Identity: Self and Society in the Late Modern Age (Stanford University Press, 1991); Michele Micheletti, Political Virtue and Shopping: Individuals, Consumerism, and Collective Action (Palgrave Macmillan, 2003).

62. Butler, Gender Trouble: Feminism and the Subversion of Identity.

63. Deborah B. Gould, "Passionate Political Processes: Bringing Emotions Back into the Study of Social Movements," in Rethinking Social Movements: Structure, Meaning, and Emotion, ed. Jeff Goodwin and James M. Jasper (Rowman and Littlefield, 2003), 307.

64. Melucci, *Nomads of the Present*, 26, 11.

65. Ibid.

66. Tarrow, Power in Movement.

67. Eyerman and Jamison, Social Movements; Frances Fox Piven, Challenging Authority: How Ordinary People Change America (Rowman and Littlefield, 2006).

68. Sanjeev Khagram, James V. Riker, and Kathryn Sikkink, Restructuring World Politics: Transnational Social Movements, Networks, and (University of Minnesota Press, 2002).

69. William F. Fisher and Thomas Ponniah, Another World Is Possible: Popular Alternatives to Globalization at the World Social Forum (Zed Books, 2003).

70. Notes from Nowhere, We Are Everywhere: The Irresistible Rise of Global Anticapitalism (Verso, 2003).

71. Michael Hardt and Antonio Negri, Multitude: War and Democracy in the Age of Empire (Penguin, 2004).

72. Étienne de la Boétie, The Politics of Obedience: The Discourse of Voluntary Servitude, trans. Harry Kurz (1552; Black Rose Books).

73. Henry David Thoreau, The Variorum Civil Disobedience (Resistance to Civil Government) (Twayne, 1849).

74. Voltairine de Cleyre, Direct Action (Mother Earth, 1912).

75. David Graeber, "The New Anarchists," New Left Review, no. 13 (2002): 61–73; Saskia Poldervaart, The Utopian Politics of Feminist Alterglobalisation Groups: The Importance of Everyday Life-politics and Personal Change for Utopian Practices (Amsterdam School for Social Science Research, January 2006), http://www2.fmg. uva.nl/assr/workingpapers/; Barbara Epstein, "Anarchism and the Anti-Globalization Movement," Monthly Review 53, no. 4 (n.d.), http://www.monthlyreview. org/0901epstein.htm.

76. George McKay, DiY Culture: Party and Protest in Nineties Britain (Verso, 1998).

77. Tarrow, *Power in Movement*.

78. George Katsiaficas, The Subversion of Politics: European Autonomous Social Movements and the Decolonization of Everyday Life (AK Press, 1997); Barbara Epstein, Political Protest and Cultural Revolution (University of California Press, 1993).

79. Tim Jordan and Adam Lent, Storming the Millennium: The New Politics of Change (Lawrence and Wishart, 1999).

80. Max Weber, "The Types of Legitimate Authority," in Economy and Society: An Outline of Interpretive Sociology (University of California Press, 1925), 2.

81. Giorgio Agamben, Homo Sacer: Sovereign Power and Bare Life (Stanford University Press, 1998).

82. James C. Scott, Domination and the Arts of Resistance: Hidden Transcripts (Yale University Press, 1990).

83. Frantz Fanon, The Wretched of the Earth (Grove Press, 1965).

84. Michel Foucault, Discipline and Punish: The Birth of the Prison (Vintage, 1975); Gilles Deleuze and Félix Guattari, A Thousand Plateaus: Capitalism and Schizophrenia (Continuum International, 2004); Agamben, Homo Sacer; Michael Hardt and Antonio Negri, Empire (Harvard University Press, 2000); Michael Hardt and Antonio Negri, Multitude: War and Democracy in the Age of Empire (Penguin, 2004).

85. Piven and Cloward, Poor People's Movements; Tarrow, Power in Movement.

86. Amory Starr et al., "The Impacts of State Surveillance on Political Assembly and Association: A Socio-Legal Analysis," Qualitative Sociology 31, no. 3 (2008): 251–70.

87. For a broader discussion of the innovations in protesters' repertoires see Christian Scholl, "Desiring Disruption. The Two Sides of a Barricade during Summit Protests in Europe," Ph.D. dissertation, University of Amsterdam.

88. Ernesto Laclau and Chantal Mouffe, Hegemony and Socialist Strategy: Towards a Radical Democratic Politics (London: Verso, 1985).

CHAPTER 2

1. John Walton and David Seddon, Free Markets and Food Riots: The Politics of Global Adjustment (Blackwell, 1994).

2. Walden Bello and Stephanie Rosenfeld, Dragons in Distress: Asia's Miracle Economies in Crisis (Penguin, 1992); Davison L. Budhoo, Enough Is Enough: Dear Mr. Camdessus—Open Letter of Resignation to the Managing Director of the International Monetary Fund (New Horizons Press, 1990); Kevin Danaher, Fifty Years Is Enough: The Case against the World Bank and the International Monetary Fund (South End Press, 1994).

3. Henri Lefebvre, The Production of Space (Wiley-Blackwell, 1991).

4. David Harvey, Spaces of Hope (University of California Press, 2000); David Harvey, Spaces of Capital: Towards a Critical Geography (Routledge, 2001).

5. Edward W. Soja, Seeking Spatial Justice (University of Minnesota Press, 2010).

6. See Randall Amster, Lost in Space: The Criminalization, Globalization, and Urban Ecology of Homelessness (LFB Scholarly Publishing, 2008).

7. Charles Tilly, "Contention over Space and Place," Mobilization 8, no. 2 (June 2003): 221–25.

8. Doreen B. Massey, "Politics and Space/Time," New Left Review, no. 196 (1992): 65–84.

9. Luis A. Fernandez, Policing Dissent: Social Control and the Anti-globalization Movement (Rutgers University Press, 2008).

10. John A. Agnew, Geopolitics: Re-visioning World Politics (Routledge, 1998).

11. Gilles Deleuze and Félix Guattari, A Thousand Plateaus: Capitalism and Schizophrenia (Continuum International, 2004).

12. See the work of the following authors for a discussion on the decentralized character of the movement: Kevin McDonald, "From Solidarity to Fluidarity: Social Movements beyond 'Collective Identity'—The Case of Globalization Conflicts," Social Movement Studies: Journal of Social, Cultural and Political Protest 1, no. 2 (2002): 109; David Graeber, "The New Anarchists," New Left Review, no. 13 (2002): 61–73.

13. Deleuze and Guattari, A Thousand Plateaus.

14. At the time, this fenced-in protest perimeter was considered large, but shortly after these types of perimeters would grow to encompass much larger areas.

15. States News Service, "Public Announcement by the U.S. Department of State: G8 Summit in Alberta Creates Potential for Disruptions," June 17, 2002.

16. Michel Foucault, Discipline and Punish: The Birth of the Prison (Vintage, 1975).

17. City of Miami Police Department (2004). FTAA: After Action Review, 2004.

18. Donatella della Porta and Herbert Reiter, eds., Policing Protest: The Control of Mass Demonstrations in Western Democracies (University of Minnesota Press, 1998).

19. Because the exact legal definition of the difference between detention and arrest differs across countries, we conflate the numbers here.

20. Josee Legault, "We Need a G20 Probe: Arrest Record Shows Police Were out of Control in Toronto," The Gazette, July 9, 2010, http://scholar.google.com/schol ar?hl=en&q=++Legault%2C+Josee+We+need+a+G20+probe&btnG=Search&as_ sdt=2000&as_ylo=&as_vis=0.

21. Peter B. Kraska and Victor E. Kappeler, "Militarizing American Police: The Rise and Normalization of Paramilitary Units," Social Problems 44 (1997): 1.

22. Peter B. Kraska, Militarizing the American Criminal Justice System: The Changing Roles of the Armed Forces and the Police (UPNE, 2001).

23. Peter B. Kraska, "Militarization and Policing—Its Relevance to 21st Century Police," Policing 1, no. 4 (2007): 501–13.

24. Avery F. Gordon, Ghostly Matters: Haunting and the Sociological Imagination (University of Minnesota Press, 1997).

25. Foucault, Discipline and Punish.

26. Michel Foucault, Michel Senellart, and François Ewald, Security, Territory, Population: Lectures at the Collège de France, 1977–78 (Palgrave Macmillan, 2007).

27. Patrick F. Gillham and John A. Noakes, "More Than a March in a Circle: Transgressive Protests and the Limits of Negotiated Management," Mobilization 12, no. 4 (December 2007): 341–57.

CHAPTER 3

1. House of Commons, G8: Gleneagles Summit Costs, 2005, http://www.publica-tions.parliament.uk/pa/ld200506/ldhansrd/vo050706/text/50706-03.htm.

2. For example, private security guards were hired for the 2010 G8/G10 meeting in Toronto, as this newspaper story chronicles: "Private Security Firm Hired for G8/G20 Summits," Ottowa Citizen, May 31, 2010, http://www.ottawacitizen.com/news/Private+security+firm+hired+summits/3093558/story.html.

3. Office of the Parliamentary Budget Officer, Assessment of Planned Security Costs for the 2010 G8 and G20 Summits. Ottawa, Canada, June 23, 2010, http://www2.parl.gc.ca/sites/pbo-dpb/documents/SummitSecurity.pdf.

4. Mary Vallis, "G20: Security Cameras Installed on Nearly Every Corner of Downtown Toronto," National Post, June 3, 2010, http://news.nationalpost.com/2010/06/03/g20-security-cameras-installed-on-nearly-every-corner-of-downtown-toronto/#ixzzotgTRNfLa.

5. "DHS Helps Local Police Buy Military-style Sonic Devices," Washington Times, October 1, 2009, http://www.washingtontimes.com/news/2009/oct/01/police-buy-sonic-device-to-subdue-unruly-crowds/print/.

6. We have found only a single, as yet unpublished, scholarly report: John Kirton, Jenilee Guebert, and Shamir Tanna, G8 and G20 Summit Costs, unpublished report, G8/G20 Research Groups, Munk School for Global Affairs, University of Toronto, 2010, http://www.g8.utoronto.ca/evaluations/factsheet/factsheet_costs.html.

7. "G8 Information Centre," n.d., http://www.g8.utoronto.ca/; "G8 Research Group," n.d., http://g8live.org/.

8. The expenditures cited are documented in Luis A. Fernandez, Policing Dissent: Social Control and the Anti-globalization Movement (Rutgers University Press, 2008).

9. In 2010, the G8 and the G20 met simultaneously.

10. Kirton, Guebert, and Shamir Tanna, G8 and G20 Summit Costs.

11. Patrick Gillham and Gary T. Marx, "Complexity and Irony in Policing and Protesting: The World Trade Organization Seattle," Social Justice 27, no. 2 (n.d.): 212–36.

12. Office of the Parliamentary Budget Officer, Assessment of Planned Security Costs for the 2010 G8 and G20 Summits.

13. In total, fourteen of these Tornados were used for the security operations in Heiligendamm. The Ministry of Defense, however, claimed that these flight hours would be counted as official training hours, which have to be completed by the soldiers in training.

14. Landtag Mecklenburg-Vorpommern, "Antwort der Landesregierung Mecklenburg-Vorpommern auf die Kleine Anfrage der Abgeordneten Birgit Schwebs, Fraktion Die Linke," Drucksache 5, no. 2411 (March 31, 2009).

15. Fernandez, Policing Dissent.

16. Rudolf Stumberger, "Molli, Macht und Meer: Der G8-Gipfel als Höhepunkt von Politik-Inszenierung," Telepolis, May 26, 2007, http://www.heise.de/tp/r4/artikel/25/25332/1.html.

17. Landtag Mecklenburg-Vorpommern, "Antwort der Landesregierung Mecklenburg-Vorpommern auf die Kleine Anfrage der Abgeordneten Birgit Schwebs, Fraktion Die Linke."

18. Landtag Mecklenburg-Vorpommern, "Antwort der Landesregierung auf die Große Anfrage der Fraktion der NPD," Drucksache 5, no. 1160 (December 20, 2007).

19. Landtag Mecklenburg-Vorpommern, "Antwort der Landesregierung auf die Kleine des Abgeordneten Udo Pastörs, Fraktion der NPD," Drucksache 5, no. 1811 (February 10, 2008).

20. Gipfelsoli, "28.7.2007 Heiligendamm—Genua," July 28, 2007, http://gipfelsoli.org/Repression/Heiligendamm_2007/Texte_davor/3843.html.

21. Von Manuela Pfohl, "G8-Gipfel-Bilanz: Meck-Pom muss für Gipfelschäden zahlen," STERN.DE, August 28, 2007, http://www.stern.de/politik/deutschland/g8-gipfel-bilanz-meck-pom-muss-fuer-gipfelschaeden-zahlen-596306.html.

22. An estimated one-third of the shop windows in the wealthy shopping district of Geneva were broken during the summit protests.

23. Andreas Beckmann, "Central Europe Review—A Bubble Burst: The IMF-World Bank meetings in Prague," Central Europe Review 2, no. 31 (September 18, 2000), http://www.ce-review.org/00/31/beckmann31.html.

24. House of Commons, UK, G8: Gleneagles Summit Costs.

25. Elliott Lianne, "G20 Fake Lake Revealed," June 23, 2010.

26. Paul Marsden, What Price a Global Future?, 2001, http://globalization.icaap.org/content/v1.1/paulmarsden.html.

27. Anneke Halbroth, "Hätten sie das nicht woanders machen können?," April 20, 2007, http://www.stadtgespraeche-rostock.de/046/0229/.

28. D. A. Fahrenthold, "D.C. Police Struggle to Staff IMF Protests; Outside Agencies Hesitate," Washington Post, August 27, 2002.

29. Ibid.

30. "Nach Krawallen beruhigt sich Lage in Genf-hohe Sachschäden," February 6, 2003, http://www.nadir.org/nadir/initiativ/agp/free/evian/2003/0602nachkrawallen.htm.

31. Initially, France had promised to cover two-thirds of the costs of the protest.

32. Michael Howie, "MoD Accuses Police of Keeping G8 Cash Needed for Frontline Troops," news.scotsman.com, April 9, 2008, http://news.scotsman.com/uk/MoD-accuses-police-of-keeping.3960688.jp.

33. Interestingly, the Ministry of Defense pretended that the actual wars going on in Iraq and Afghanistan would impose budgetary restrictions on homeland support.

34. Bill Jacobs and Brian Ferguson, "Blair Refuses to Help Meet Cost of G8 Summit," news.scotsman.com, March 9, 2005, http://news.scotsman.com/edinburgh/Blair-refuses-to-help-meet.2609125.jp.

35. Ibid.

36. Interestingly, the rise in the estimated costs was justified by citing security protocols related to the alleged danger of international terrorism, protocols that were beyond the influence of the provincial government. Landtag Mecklenburg-Vorpommern, "Beschlussempfehlung und Bericht des Finanzausschusses (4. Ausschuss) zu dem Gesetzentwurf der Landesregierung," Drucksache 5, no. 100 (May 12, 2006).

37. Deutscher Bundestag, "Antwort der Bundesregierung auf die Kleine Anfrage der Fraktion Die Linke," Drucksache 16, no. 6090 (2007).

38. K. M. Mathur, Challenges to Police, Human Rights and National Security (Gyan Books, 2003).

39. From an interview with a member of the planning team, first published in Fernandez, Policing Dissent.

CHAPTER 4

1. Jennifer Earl, "Tanks, Tear Gas, and Taxes: Toward a Theory of Movement Repression," Sociological Theory 21, no. 1 (January 1, 2003): 44–68.

2. Ibid.

3. John Wilson, "Social Protest and Social Control," Social Problems 24, no. 4 (April 1977): 470, 475.

4. Donatella della Porta and Herbert Reiter, eds., *Policing Protest: The Control of Mass Demonstrations in Western Democracies* (University of Minnesota Press, 1998).

5. P. A. J. Waddington, "Policing Public Order and Political Contention," in A Handbook of Policing, ed. Tim Newburn (Willan Publishing, 2003), 928.

6. Earl, "Tanks, Tear Gas, and Taxes."

7. Wilson, "Social Protest and Social Control," 470, 475.

8. Jennifer Earl, "'You Can Beat the Rap, but You Can't Beat the Ride': Bringing Arrests Back into Research on Repression," Research in Social Movements, Conflicts and Change 26 (2005): 101–39.

9. Gary T. Marx, "Civil Disorders and the Agents of Social Control," Journal of Social Issues 26, no. 1 (winter 1970): 19–57.

10. Pamela Oliver, "How Does Repression Work?" 2002, http://www.ssc.wisc.edu/~oliver/PROTESTS/PROTESTS.HTM. She excludes the cooptation seen as important by Piven and Cloward.

11. Karl-Dieter Opp and Wolfgang Roehl, "Repression, Micromobilization, and Political Protest," Social Forces 69, no. 2 (December 1990): 521–47.

12. Della Porta and Reiter, Policing Protest, 30–31.

13. Donatella della Porta, Abby Peterson, and Herbert Reiter, eds., The Policing of Transnational Protest (Ashgate, 2006), 3.

14. Ibid., 5–6.

15. Ibid., 33.

16. Ibid., 5.

17. Raid of the Hvitfeldtska School, Göteborg 2001 EU.

18. Abby Peterson, "Policing Contentious Politics at Transnational Summits: Darth Vader or the Keystone Cops?," in The Policing of Transnational Protest, ed. Donatella della Porta, Abby Peterson, and Herbert Reiter (Ashgate, 2006), 60–63.

19. FTAA meetings in November 2003 in Miami, Florida.

20. Della Porta, Peterson, and Reiter, The Policing of Transnational Protest, 16.

21. Ibid., 29. Also see Paul de Armond, "Netwar in the Emerald City: WTO Protest Strategy and Tactics," in Networks and Netwars: The Future of Terror, Crime, and Militancy, ed. John Arquilla and David Ronfeldt (Rand, 2001), http://www.rand.org/pubs/monograph_reports/MR1382/.

22. Della Porta, Peterson, and Reiter, The Policing of Transnational Protest, 27; Mike King and David Waddington, "The Policing of Transnational Protest in Canada," in The Policing of Transnational Protest, ed. Donatella Della Porta, Abby Peterson, and Herbert Reiter (Ashgate, 2006), 75–96.

23. Della Porta, Peterson, and Reiter, *The Policing of Transnational Protest*, 33.

24. John Noakes and Patrick F. Gillham, "Aspects of the 'New Penology' in the Police Response to Major Political Protests in the United States, 1999-2000," in The Policing of Transnational Protest, ed. Donatella della Porta, Abby Peterson, and Herbert Reiter (Ashgate, 2006), 97–116.

25. Judy Rebick, "It Won't End in Québec City," rabble.ca, April 26, 2001, http://www.rabble.ca/columnists/it-wont-end-in-Québec-city; For example, regarding the

Québec City 2001 FTAA meeting, see Judy Rebick, "Policing the People in Québec," rabble.ca, April 22, 2001, http://www.rabble.ca/news/policing-people-Québec; Naomi Klein, "The Bonding Properties of Tear Gas," Naomi Klein, April 25, 2001, http://www.naomiklein.org/articles/2001/04/.

26. Heidi Boghosian, The Assault on Free Speech, Public Assembly, and Dissent: A National Lawyers Guild Report on Government Violations of First Amendment Rights in the United States (North River Press, 2004), www.nlg.org/resources/DissentBookWeb.pdf; New York Civil Liberties Union, Rights and Wrongs at the RNC: A Special Report about Police and Protest at the Republican National Convention (New York Civil Liberties Union, 2005), www.nyclu.org/pdfs/rnc_report_083005.pdf.

27. Frances Fox Piven and Richard A. Cloward, Poor People's Movements: Why They Succeed, How They Fail (Vintage, 1977).

28. RNCNotWelcomCollective, http://slingshot.tao.ca/displaybi.php?0082020, "Face Masks" Slingshot Issue #082.

29. Piven and Cloward, Poor People's Movements.

30. David Cunningham, There's Something Happening Here: The New Left, the Klan, and the FBI (University of California Press, 2004), 6.

31. Ibid., 185.

32. Ibid., 6.

33. Ibid., 180–214.

34. T'Okup, "Nestlegate ist Kein inzelfall: Eine Weitere securitas-angestellte als spitzelin entlarvt!," 2008.

35. John Clyde Stauber and Sheldon Rampton, Toxic Sludge Is Good for You (Common Courage Press, 1995).

36. Jules Boykoff, The Suppression of Dissent: How the State and Mass Media Squelch US American Social Movements (Routledge, 2006); Cunningham, There's Something Happening Here; Christian Davenport, "Understanding Covert Repressive Action: The Case of the U.S. Government against the Republic of New Africa," Journal of Conflict Resolution 49, no. 1 (February 2005): 120–40; Helena Flam, Mosaic of Fear: Poland and East Germany before 1989, East European Monographs, Boulder (Columbia University Press, 1998); Robert Justin Goldstein, Political Repression in Modern America (Schenkman, 1978); Marx, "Civil Disorders and the Agents of Social Control"; Gary T. Marx, "Thoughts on a Neglected Category of Social Movement Participant: The Agent Provocateur and the Informant," American Journal of Sociology 80, no. 2 (September 1974): 402–42; Gary T. Marx, "External Efforts to Damage or Facilitate Social Movements," in The Dynamics of Social Movements: Resource Mobilization, Social Control, and Tactics, ed. Mayer N. Zald and John David McCarthy, Frontiers of Sociology Symposium, Vanderbilt University (University Press of America, 1979), 94–125; Gary T. Marx, Undercover: Police Surveillance in America (University of California Press, 1988).

37. Christian Davenport, "Killing the Afro: State Repression, Social Movement Decline and the Death of Black Power," 2006, http://www.bsos.umd.edu/gvpt/davenport/killing%20the%20afro%20041006.pdf; Hank Johnston, "Talking the Walk: Speech Acts and Resistance in Authoritarian Regimes," in Repression and Mobilization, ed. Christian Davenport, Hank Johnston, and Carol McClurg Mueller (University of Minnesota Press, 2005), 108–137; Gilda Zwerman, Patricia Steinhoff, and

Donatella della Porta, "Disappearing Social Movements: Clandestinity in the Cycle of New Left Protest in the U.S., Japan, Germany, and Italy," Mobilization 5, no. 1 (2000): 85–104.

38. Donatella della Porta, Social Movements, Political Violence, and the State: A Comparative Analysis (Cambridge University Press, 1995).

39. Marx, "Civil Disorders and the Agents of Social Control"; Marx, "Thoughts on a Neglected Category of Social Movement Participant"; Marx, "The Dynamics of Social Movements"; Marx, Undercover; Gary T. Marx, "Under-the-Covers Undercover Investigations: Some Reflections on the State's Use of Sex and Deception in Law Enforcement," Criminal Justice Ethics 11, no. 1 (1992): 13–24; Flam, Mosaic of Fear; Ward Churchill and Jim VanderWall, The COINTELPRO Papers: Documents from the FBI's Secret Wars against Dissent (South End Press, 1990); Frank J. Donner, The Age of Surveillance: The Aims and Methods of America's Political Intelligence System (Vintage, 1980); Frank J. Donner, Protectors of Privilege: Red Squads and Police Repression in Urban America (University of California Press, 1990); Bud Schultz and Ruth Schultz, It Did Happen Here: Recollections of Political Repression in America (University of California Press, 1989); Bud Schultz and Ruth Schultz, The Price of Dissent: Testimonies to Political Repression in America (University of California Press, 2001); Richard Gid Powers, Secrecy and Power: Life of J.Edgar Hoover (Free Press, 1987); Cunningham, There's Something Happening Here; Davenport, "Understanding Covert Repressive Action"; Davenport, "Killing the Afro: State Repression, Social Movement Decline and the Death of Black Power," http://www.bsos.umd.edu/gvpt/davenport/killing%20the%20afro%20041006.pdf; Boykoff, The Suppression of Dissent.

40. Donner, Protectors of Privilege.

41. Della Porta and Reiter, Policing Protest.

42. At http://annalist.noblogs.org/static/library.

43. Cliff Pearson, "Released Dallas Activist Recounts Jail Abuses," Philadelphia Independent Media Center, August 4, 2000, http://www.phillyimc.org/en/node/33582.

44. At http://rnc8.org.

45. At www.leiu.org.

46. Chip Berlet, "The Law Enforcement Intelligence Unit," in The Hunt for Red Menace (Political Research Associates, 2003), http://www.publiceye.org/huntred/Hunt_For_Red_Menace-07.html.

47. New York Civil Liberties Union/American Civil Liberties Union, "Police Trampled Civil Rights during Republican National Convention, NYCLU Charges," October 7, 2004, http://www.aclu.org/free-speech/police-trampled-civil-rights-during-republican-national-convention-nyclu-charges.

48. Erin Starr, "Little Guantanamo and the Republican Convention" (e-mail widely circulated on the Internet), 2004, http://www.mail-archive.com/laamn@yahoogroups.com/msg00022.html; Drew Poe, "Pier 57: The LMDC / RNC Connection," nyc.indymedia.org, November 17, 2004, http://nyc.indymedia.org/feature/display/132549/index.php.

49. Adam Porter, "It Was Like This Before . . . 75–79," in On Fire: The Battle of Genoa and the Anti-capitalist Movement (One-Off Press, 2001), 77.

50. Anonymous, "Being Busy," in On Fire: The Battle of Genoa and the Anti-capitalist Movement (One-Off Press, 2001), 49.

51. Please see Appendix B for an extensive discussion of this concept.

52. John Hughes, "Life during Wartime," in On Fire: The Battle of Genoa and the Anti-capitalist Movement (One-Off Press, 2001), 26.

53. Allison Kilkenny, "Police Use Painful New Weapon on G20 Protesters," AlterNet, September 28, 2009, http://www.truthout.org/092909D.

54. Colin Clark, "Marines Fund Non-Lethal Heat Ray," www.defensetech. org, October 9, 2008, http://www.defensetech.org/archives/004461.html; David A. Fulghum, "High Power Microwave Nearly Operational," Aviation Week, October 9, 2008, http://www.aviationweek.com/aw/generic/story_channel. jsp?channel=defense&id=news/MICR10098.xml; Tom Burghardt, "Curbing Social Protest in America: Microwave 'Non-lethal' Weapons to Be Used for "Crowd Control," www.GlobalResearch.ca, October 14, 2008, http://www.globalresearch.ca/index. php?context=va&aid=10564.

55. Jazz, "Life during Wartime," in On Fire: The Battle of Genoa and the Anti-capitalist Movement (One-Off Press, 2001), 88.

56. Amnesty International, USA: Less than Lethal?, December 16, 2008, http:// www.amnesty.org/en/for-media/press-releases/usa-safety-tasers-questioned-death-toll-hits-334-mark-20081216.

57. U.S. Department of Justice, Office of Justice Programs, National Institute of Justice, "The Effectiveness and Safety of Pepper Spray (Research for Practice)," April 2003, http://74.125.95.132/search?q=cache:rm5xsZVHst4J:www.ncjrs.gov/pdffiles1/ nij/195739.pdf+safety+of+pepper+spray&hl=en&ct=clnk&cd=1&gl=us&client=firef ox-a.

58. For a summary of medical literature, see "Are Tasers Safe?," Center for Investigative Reporting, December 1, 2008, http://centerforinvestigativereporting.org/ articles/aretaserssafe.

59. Michael Bond, "Could Non-lethal Weapons Increase Conflict?," New Scientist, September 17, 2008, http://www.newscientist.com/article/ mg19926745.700-could-nonlethal-weapons-increase-conflict.html; David Hambling, "U.S. Police Could Get 'Pain Beam' Weapons," New Scientist, December 24, 2008, http://www.newscientist.com/article/dn16339-us-police-could-get-pain-beam-weapons.html.

60. See http://www.less-lethal.org.

61. "Coverage from Gothenburg EU Summit Protests," www.indymedia.org.uk, June 17, 2001, https://www.indymedia.org.uk/en/2003/09/277946.html.

62. Isaac D. Balbus, The Dialectics of Legal Repression: Black Rebels before the American Criminal Courts (Russell Sage, 1973).

63. Media G8way Gipfelsoli Infogroup, "G8 Genoa: State Prosecution Demands 225 Years of Jail Sentences," Gipfelsoli, October 29, 2007, https://gipfelsoli.org/Home/ Heiligendamm_2007/MediaG8way_Heiligendamm/english/4366.html.

64. Supportolegale, "In Any Case, No Regret," press release, 2007, http://www. supportolegale.org/?q=node/1271.

65. http://en.wikipedia.org/wiki/Gothenburg_Riots#Statistics.

66. Chris Steller, "Minnesota Independent: News. Politics. Media. Judge to RNC8: See You Next Year," Minnesota Independent, December 17, 2008, http://minnesotain-dependent.com/20527/judge-to-rnc8-see-you-next-year And see http://www.rnc8.org.

67. Keith Coffman, "Nuns Sentenced to Prison for Colorado Nuclear Protest," www.commondreams.org, July 26, 2003, http://www.commondreams.org/head-lines03/0726-01.htm.

68. See http://www.freefreenow.org. Luers is due to be released early in December 2009.

69. See http://shac7.com.

70. See http://www.freesherman.org.

71. Wolfram Metzger, "Repression in Germany: Editor of Venezuelan Book Incarcerated for Terrorism," www.venezuelanalaysis.com, November 17, 2007, http://einstellung.so36.net/en/ps/630.

72. Greenpeace USA, "Bush vs. Greenpeace Overview," May 10, 2004, http://www.greenpeace.org/usa/news/bush-vs-greenpeace-overview.

73. Rick Anderson, "Delta's Down with It: The Justice Department and the Elite Delta Force Pushed for Seattle Crackdown against WTO Protesters," Seattle Weekly, December 22, 1999, http://www.seattleweekly.com/1999-12-22/news/delta-s-down-with-it/.

74. Marius Heuser, "Germany: Huge Security Operation Exposed in Wake of G8 Summit," World Socialist website, June 21, 2007, http://www.tni.org/detail_page.phtml?act_id=17014.

CHAPTER 5

1. "[a]ctors who experience and contest the system's contradictory requirements do not do so all their lives and do not belong to a single social category" (p. 61).

2. Albert Melucci, Nomads of the Present: Social Movements and Individual Needs in Contemporary Society (Hutchinson, 1989), 60.

3. Ibid., 173.

4. After asking this question, the interviewer turned off the tape recorder and/or left the room so that participants could coordinate their tallies so as not to count anyone twice.

5. Richard Flacks, Making History: The American Left and the American Mind (Columbia UniversityPress, 1988).

6. John Hughes, "Life during Wartime," in On Fire: The Battle of Genoa and the Anti-capitalist Movement (One-Off Press, 2001), 25. In Europe, lemon is the favored low-tech chemical barrier against tear gas. In North America, vinegar is used, instead. In both cases, those attacked wet a cloth with the liquid and place it over their nose and mouth.

7. Amory Starr et al., "The Impacts of State Surveillance on Political Assembly and Association A Socio-Legal Analysis," Qualitative Sociology 31, no. 3 (2008): 251–70.

8. George Katsiaficas, The Subversion of Politics: European Autonomous Social Movements and the the Decolonization of Everyday Life (AK Press, 1997).

9. Alberto Melucci, Challenging Codes: Collective Action in the Information Age (Cambridge University Press, 1996), 70–71.

10. Jules Boykoff, *The Suppression of Dissent: How the State and Mass Media Squelch USAmerican Social Movements* (Routledge, 2006); David Cunningham, *There's Something Happening Here: The New Left, the Klan, and FBI* (University of California Press, 2004); Christian Davenport, "Understanding Covert Repressive Action: The Case of the U.S. Government against the Republic of New Africa," *Journal of Conflict Resolution* 49, no. 1 (February 2005): 120–40; Gary T. Marx, "Civil Disorders and the Agents of Social Control," *Journal of Social Issues* 26, no. 1 (Winter 1970): 19–57; Gary T. Marx, "Thoughts on a Neglected Category of Social Movement Participant: The Agent Provocateur and the Informant," *American Journal of Sociology* 80, no. 2 (September 1974): 402–42; Gary T. Marx, "Under-the-Covers Undercover Investigations: Some Reflections on the State's Use of Sex and Deception in Law Enforcement," *Criminal Justice Ethics* 11, no. 1 (1992): 13–24; Helena Flam, *Mosaic of Fear: Poland and East Germany before 1989*, East European Monographs, Boulder (Columbia University Press, 1998).

11. Critical Mass is an international tactic in which a group of bicyclists travel city streets together to defend rights of bicycles, oppose automobilism, and have fun. Acting on the concept "We aren't blocking traffic, we are traffic," participants directly challenge traffic policy. In several U.S. cities, Critical Mass has been criminalized and riders arrested, and so on; see http://www.critical-mass.org/.

12. The reduction of anonymity is clearly present in community policing, as indicated by its association with Neighborhood Watch programs. These programs use the vigilance of neighborhood residents to reduce the anonymity of any "outsider" entering the neighborhood.

13. Michel Foucault, *Discipline and Punish: The Birth of the Prison* (Vintage Books, 1975), 237.

14. Barry Glassner, *The Culture of Fear* (Basic Books, 2000).

15. Francesca Polletta, *Freedom Is an Endless Meeting: Democracy in American Social Movements* (University of Chicago Press, 2002).

16. Marianne Maeckelbergh, *The Will of the Many: How the Alterglobalisation Movement Is Changing the Face of Democracy* (Pluto Press, 2009).

17. Mark Irving Lichbach, *The Rebel's Dilemma* (Ann Arbor: University of Michigan Press, 1995); Robert W. White, "From Peaceful Protest to Guerrilla War: Micromobilization of the Provisional Irish Republican Army," *American Journal of Sociology* 94, no. 6 (May 1989): 1277–1302; Sidney Tarrow, *Power in Movement: Social Movements and Contentious Politics* (Cambridge: Cambridge University Press, 1998); Gilda Zwerman and Patricia Steinhoff, "When Activists Ask for Trouble: and the New Left Cycle of Resistance in the United States and Japan," in *Repression and Mobilization*, ed. Christian Davenport, Hank Johnston, and Carol McClurg Mueller (University of Minnesota Press, 2005), 85–107.

18. Christian Davenport, "Killing the Afro: State Repression, Social Movement Decline and the Death of Black Power," http://www.bsos.umd.edu/gvpt/davenport/killing%20the%20afro%20041006.pdf; Hank Johnston, "Talking the Walk: Speech Acts and Resistance in Authoritarian Regimes," in *Repression and Mobilization*, ed. Christian Davenport, Hank Johnston, and Carol McClurg Mueller (University of

Minnesota Press, 2005), 108–37; Gilda Zwerman, Patricia Steinhoff, and Donatella della Porta, "Disappearing Social Movements: Clandestinity in the Cycle of New Left Protest in the U.S., Japan, Germany, and Italy," Mobilization 5, no. 1 (2000): 85–104.

19. Melucci, Challenging Codes, 386.

20. Donatella della Porta, Social Movements, Political Violence, and the State: A Comparative Analysis (Cambridge University Press, 1995).

21. Luis Corradi, Patricia Weiss Fagen, Manuel Antonio Garretón Merino, and Manuel Antonio Garretón, *Fear at the Edge: State Terror and Resistance in Latin America* (University of California Press, 1992); Cynthia Kepley Mahmoud, ed., *The Ethnography of Political Violence* (University of Pennsylvania Press, 1997); Antonius C.G.M. Robbens, *Political Violence and Trauma in Argentina* (University of Pennsylvania, 2005).

22. Donatella della Porta and Herbert Reiter, eds., Policing Protest: The Control of Mass Demonstrations in Western Democracies (University of Minnesota Press, 1998).

23. Black Bloc is a tactic in which a group of protesters wear black clothing, black boots, and black ski masks, bandanas, or motorcycle helmets to cover their face. The tactics, which originally developed in Germany in 1980s, is intended to prevent identification of the protesters.

CHAPTER 6

1. For a material description of the equipment used, see Sarin, "Bodyhammer: Tactics and Self-defence for the Modern Protester," http://www.wombles.org.uk/article2008041819.php.

2. The tactic of Tute Bianche is influenced by the struggle and methods of the Zapatistas in Chiapas, México: expressing fierceness that avoids violence, radicalism that does not seek to take the state, politics beyond ideologies, and face for the invisible. Politically, Tute Bianche blocs are generally aligned with immigration rights, prisoners, marginalized radicals (including communists and anarchists), and "everyone else made invisible by the free market"(Giorgio, a member of Ya Basta from Rome, quoted in *The Guardian*, July 19, 2001. Like other tactics, Tute Bianche is not a standing organization with members. Persons from many groups participate in the Tute Bianche tactic on demos.

3. Ed Pilkington, "New York Man Accused of Using Twitter to Direct Protesters during G20 Summit," The Guardian, October 4, 2009, http://www.guardian.co.uk/world/2009/oct/04/man-arrested-twitter-g20-us.

4. Several films have been made on the basis of these archives: *Difesa Legitima* (2005), *OP Genova 2001* (Genoa Social Forum), *L'Ordine Publicco durante il G8* (2007), *Genoa. Il Libro Bianco*.

5. Steven E. Barkan, "Political Trials and Resource Mobilization: Towards an Understanding of Social Movement Litigation," Social Forces 58, no. 3 (1980): 946–47.

6. Robert D. Bullard, *Dumping in Dixie: Race, Class, and Environmental Quality* (Westview Press, 1990).

7. Barkan, "Political Trials and Resource Mobilization," 948.

8. *Hickey v. City of Seattle*, 236 FRD 659, 660 (WD Wash. 2006).

9. American Civil Liberties Union, "FBI Spy Files," April 25, 2005, http://www.aclu.org/national-security/fbi-spy-files.

10. Mike Rhodes, "Local Law Enforcement Violates the State Constitution," Indybay.org, April 6, 2005, http://www.indybay.org/newsitems/2005/04/06/17317531.php.

11. Washington, D.C., City Council, "First Amendment Rights and Police Standards Act of 2004, Bill 15-968," 2004, http://dcwatch.com/archives/council15/15-968.htm.

12. ACLU of Northern California, "In Landmark Agreement, Oakland Prohibits Less Lethal Weapons for Crowd Control," November 9, 2004, http://www.aclunc.org/news/press_releases/in_landmark_agreement,_oakland_prohibits_less_lethal_weapons_for_crowd_control.shtml.

13. Noaki Schwartz and Trenton Daniel, "Lawsuit on Strip Searches Settled," Miami Herald, April 18, 2005, http://www.brennancenter.org/content/elert/lawsuit_on_strip_searches_settled/.

14. U.S. District Court for the Southern District of New York, *National Council of Arab Americans and the A.N.S.W.E.R. Coalition v. The City of New York City et al.*, 04-CV-6602 (WHP), www.justiceonline.org.

15. For a description of this event, see Nick Davies, "The Bloody Battle of Genoa," The Guardian, July 17, 2008, http://www.guardian.co.uk/world/2008/jul/17/italy.g8.

16. Media G8way Gipfelsoli Infogroup, "G8 Genoa: Police Receive Low Sentences," Gipfelsoli, July 15, 2008, http://gipfelsoli.org/Home/Genua_2001/Genoa_2001_english/5384.html.

17. For an example, see http://www.midnightspecial.net/comic.

18. See www.grandjuryresistance.org.

19. A lot of activist discussion texts emerging in the context of summit protests are collected on the website www.gipfelsoli.org and www.infoshop.org.

20. For a detailed account of the epistemology of the use of bodies during summit protests in Europe see Christian Scholl, "Desiring Disruption. The Two Sides of a Barricade during Summit Protests in Europe," Ph.D. dissertation, University of Amsterdam.

CHAPTER 7

1. Jacques Rancière, Hatred of Democracy (Verso, 2006), 4.

2. Giorgio Agamben, State of Exception (University of Chicago Press, 2005).

APPENDIX B

1. This material previously appeared in *Gipfelsoli* (http://gipfelsoli.org/Home/Heiligendamm_2007/G8_2007_english/G8_2007_Texts/4087.html) and is reprinted here with permission from John Holloway and Vittorio Sergi.

Bibliography

ACLU of Northern California. "In Landmark Agreement, Oakland Prohibits Less Lethal Weapons for Crowd Control." November 9, 2004. http://www.aclunc.org/news/press_releases/in_landmark_agreement,_oakland_prohibits_less_lethal_weapons_for_crowd_control.shtml.

Adorno, Theodor W. *Aesthetic Theory*. Routledge, 1970.

———. *Negative Dialectics*. Routledge, 1966.

Agamben, Giorgio. *State of Exception*. University of Chicago Press, 2005.

———. *Homo Sacer: Sovereign Power and Bare Life*. Stanford University Press, 1998.

Agnew, John A. *Geopolitics: Re-visioning World Politics*. Routledge, 1998.

Althusser, Louis. "Ideology and Ideological State Apparatuses," first published in *La Pensée*, 1970." In *Lenin and Philosophy and Other Essays*. Translated by Ben Brewster, 272. Monthly Review Press, 2002.

Alvarez, Sonia E., Evelina Dagnino, and Arturo Escobar. *Cultures of Politics, Politics of Cultures: Re-visioning Latin American*. Westview Press, 1998.

American Civil Liberties Union. "FBI Spy Files." April 25, 2005. http://www.aclu.org/national-security/fbi-spy-files.

Amnesty International. *USA: Less Than Lethal?* December 16, 2008. http://www.amnesty.org/en/for-media/press-releases/usa-safety-tasers-questioned-death-toll-hits-334-mark-20081216.

Amster, Randall. *Lost in Space: The Criminalization, Globalization, and Urban Ecology of Homelessness*. LFB Scholarly Publishing, 2008.

Anderson, Rick. "Delta's Down with It: The Justice Department and the Elite Delta Force Pushed for Seattle Crackdown against WTO Protesters." *Seattle Weekly*, December 22, 1999. http://www.seattleweekly.com/1999-12-22/news/delta-s-down-with-it/.

Anonymous. "Being Busy." In *On Fire: The Battle of Genoa and the Anti-capitalist Movement*, 41–54. Tucson, AZ: One-Off Press, 2001.

Anzaldúa, Gloria. *Making Face, Making Soul: Haciendo Caras: Creative and Critical Perspectives by Feminists of Color*. Aunt Lute Foundation Books, 1990.

"Are Tasers Safe?" *Center for Investigative Reporting*, December 1, 2008. http://centerforinvestigativereporting.org/articles/aretaserssafe.

de Armond, Paul de. "Netwar in the Emerald City: WTO Protest Strategy and Tactics." In *Networks and Netwars: The Future of Terror, Crime, and Militancy*. Edited by John Arquilla and David Ronfeldt. Rand, 2001. http://www.rand.org/pubs/monograph_reports/MR1382/.

Balbus, Isaac D. *The Dialectics of Legal Repression: Black Rebels before the American Criminal Courts*. Russell Sage, 1973.

Barkan, Steven E. "Political Trials and Resource Mobilization: Towards an Under-standing of Social Movement Litigation." *Social Forces* 58, no. 3 (1980): 944–61.

Beck, Ulrich. "World Risk Society as Cosmopolitan Society?: Ecological Questions in a Framework of Manufactured Uncertainties." *Theory, Culture, and Society* 13, no. 4 (1996): 1–32.

Beckmann, Andreas. "Central Europe Review—A Bubble Burst: The IMF-World Bank Meetings in Prague." *Central Europe Review* 2, no. 31 (September 18, 2000). http://www.ce-review.org/00/31/beckmann31.html.

Bello, Walden, and Stephanie Rosenfeld. *Dragons in Distress: Asia's Miracle Economies in Crisis*. Penguin Books, 1992.

Benford, Robert D., and David A. Snow. "Framing Processes and Social Movements: An Overview and Assessment." November 28, 2003. http://arjournals.annualreviews.org/doi/abs/10.1146/annurev.soc.26.1.611.

Berlet, Chip. "The Law Enforcement Intelligence Unit." In *The Hunt for Red Menace*. Cambridge, MA: Political Research Associates, 2003. http://www.publiceye.org/huntred/Hunt_For_Red_Menace-07.html.

Boghosian, Heidi. *The Assault on Free Speech, Public Assembly, and Dissent: A National Lawyers Guild Report on Government Violations of First Amendment Rights in the United States*. North River Press, 2004. www.nlg.org/resources/DissentBookWeb.pdf.

Bond, Michael. "Could Non-lethal Weapons Increase Conflict?" *New Scientist*, September 17, 2008. http://www.newscientist.com/article/mg19926745.700-could-nonlethal-weapons-increase-conflict.html.

Bookman, Ann. *Women and the Politics of Empowerment*. Temple University Press, 1988.

Boykoff, Jules. *The Suppression of Dissent: How the State and Mass Media Squelch USAmerican Social Movements*. New York: Routledge, 2006.

Budhoo, Davison L. *Enough Is Enough: Dear Mr. Camdessus—Open Letter of Resignation to the Managing Director of the International Monetary Fund*. New Horizons Press, 1990.

Burghardt, Tom. "Curbing Social Protest in America: Microwave "Non-lethal" Weapons to Be Used for "Crowd Control." *www.GlobalResearch.ca*, October 14, 2008. http://www.globalresearch.ca/index.php?context=va&aid=10564.

Butler, Judith. *Gender Trouble: Feminism and the Subversion of Identity*. Routledge, 1990.

Chomsky, Noam. *Necessary Illusions: Thought Control in Democratic Societies*. Pluto Press, 1989.

Chunn, Dorothy E., and Shelley A. M. Gavigan. "Social Control: Analytical Tool or Analytical Quagmire?." *Contemporary Crises* 12, no. 2 (1988): 107–24.

Churchill, Ward, and Jim VanderWall. *The COINTELPRO Papers: Documents from the FBI's Secret Wars against Dissent*. South End Press, 1990.

City of Miami Police Department (2004). *FTAA: After action review*, 2004.

Clark, Colin. "Marines Fund Non-Lethal Heat Ray." *www.defensetech.org*, October 9, 2008. http://www.defensetech.org/archives/004461.html.

Cleyre, Voltairine De. *Direct Action*. Mother Earth Publishing Association, 1912.

Coffman, Keith. "Nuns Sentenced to Prison for Colorado Nuclear Protest." *www. commondreams.org*, July 26, 2003. http://www.commondreams.org/head-lines03/0726-01.htm.

Cohen, Jean L., and Andrew Arato. *Civil Society and Political Theory*. MIT Press, 1992.

Coutin, Susan Bibler. The Culture of Protest: Religious Activism and the U.S. Sanctuary Movement. Westview Press, 1993.

"Coverage from Gothenburg EU Summit Protests." *www.indymedia.org.uk*, June 17, 2001. https://www.indymedia.org.uk/en/2003/09/277946.html.

Crossley, Nick. *Making Sense of Social Movements*. Open University Press, 2002.

Cunningham, David. *There's Something Happening Here: The New Left, the Klan, and FBI*. University of California Press, 2004.

Danaher, Kevin. *Fifty Years Is Enough: The Case against the World Bank and the International Monetary Fund*. South End Press, 1994.

Davenport, Christian. "Killing the Afro: State Repression, Social Movement Decline and the Death of Black Power," 2006. http://www.bsos.umd.edu/gvpt/davenport/killing%20the%20afro%20041006.pdf.

———. "Understanding Covert Repressive Action: The Case of the U.S. Government against the Republic of New Africa." *Journal of Conflict Resolution* 49, no. 1 (February 2005): 120–40.

Davies, Nick. "The Bloody Battle of Genoa." *The Guardian*, July 17, 2008. http://www.guardian.co.uk/world/2008/jul/17/italy.g8.

De la Boétie, Étienne. *The Politics of Obedience: The Discourse of Voluntary Servitude*. Translated by Harry Kurz. Black Rose Books, 1552.

Deleuze, Gilles, and Félix Guattari. *A Thousand Plateaus: Capitalism and Schizophrenia*. Continuum International, 2004.

Della Porta, Donatella. *Social Movements, Political Violence, and the State: A Comparative Analysis*.Cambridge University Press, 1995.

Della Porta, Donatella, and Herbert Reiter, eds. *Policing Protest: The Control of Mass Demonstrations in Western Democracies*. University of Minnesota Press, 1998.

Della Porta, Donatella, Abby Peterson, and Herbert Reiter, eds. *The Policing of Transnational Protest*. Ashgate, 2006.

Deutscher Bundestag. "Antwort der Bundesregierung auf die Kleine Anfrage der Fraktion Die Linke." *Drucksache* 16, no. 6090 (2007).

"DHS Helps Local Police Buy Military-style Sonic Devices." *Washington Times*, October 1, 2009.

Donner, Frank J. *Protectors of Privilege: Red Squads and Police Repression in Urban America*. University of California Press, 1990.

———. *The Age of Surveillance: The Aims and Methods of America's Political Intelligence System*. Vintage, 1980.

Earl, Jennifer. "'You Can Beat the Rap, but You Can't Beat the Ride:' Bringing Arrests Back into Research on Repression." *Research in Social Movements, Conflicts and Change* 26 (2005): 101–39.

———. "Tanks, Tear Gas, and Taxes: Toward a Theory of Movement Repression." *Sociological Theory* 21, no. 1 (January 1, 2003): 44–68.

Eisinger, Peter K. "The Conditions of Protest Behavior in American Cities." *American Political Science Review* 67, no. 1 (March 1973): 11–28.

Epstein, Barbara. "Anarchism and the Anti-Globalization Movement." *Monthly Review* 53, no. 4 (n.d.).

———. *Political Protest and Cultural Revolution*. University of California Press, 1993.

Eyerman, Ron, and Andrew Jamison. *Social Movements: A Cognitive Approach*. Penn State Press, 1991.

Fahrenthold, D. A. "D.C. Police Struggle to Staff IMF Protests; Outside Agencies Hesitate." *Washington Post*, August 27, 2002.

Fanon, Frantz. *The Wretched of the Earth*. Grove Press, 1965.

Fernandez, Luis A. *Policing Dissent: Social Control and the Anti-globalization Movement*. New Brunswick, NJ: Rutgers University Press, 2008.

Fisher, William F., and Thomas Ponniah. *Another World Is Possible: Popular Alternatives to Globalization at the World Social Forum*. Zed Books, 2003.

Flacks, Richard. *Making History: The American Left and the American Mind*. Columbia University Press, 1988.

Flam, Helena. *Mosaic of Fear: Poland and East Germany before 1989*. East European Monographs, Boulder. Columbia University Press, 1998.

Foucault, Michel. *Discipline and Punish: The Birth of the Prison.* Vintage, 1975.

———. *The History of Sexuality*. Vintage, 1988.

Foucault, Michel, Luther H. Martin, Huck Gutman, and Patrick H. Hutton. *Technologies of the Self*. University of Massachusetts Press, 1988.

Foucault, Michel, Michel Senellart, and François Ewald. *Security, Territory, Population: Lectures at the Collège de France, 1977-78*. Palgrave Macmillan, 2007.

Fox, Richard Gabriel, and Orin Starn. *Between Resistance and Revolution: Cultural Politics and Social Protest*. Rutgers University Press, 1997.

Fulghum, David A. "High Power Microwave Nearly Operational." *Aviation Week*, October 9, 2008. http://www.aviationweek.com/aw/generic/story_channel.jsp?channel=defense&id=news/MICR10098.xml.

Fung, Archon. "Associations and Democracy: Between Theories, Hopes, and Realities." *Annual Review of Sociology* 29 (August 2003): 515–39.

"G8 Information Centre," n.d. http://www.g8.utoronto.ca/.

"G8 Research Group," n.d. http://g8live.org/.

Gamson, William A. *Power and Discontent*. Dorsey Press, 1968.

Gaventa, John. Power and Powerlessness: Quiescence and Rebellion in an Appalachian Valley. University of Illinois Press, 1980.

Gibbs, Jack P. *Control: Sociology's Central Notion*. University of Illinois Press, 1989.

———. *Social Control: Views from the Social Sciences*. Sage, 1982.

———. "Social Control, Deterrence, and Perspectives on Social Order." *Social Forces* 56, no. 2 (December 1977): 408–23.

Giddens, Anthony. *Modernity and Self-Identity: Self and Society in the Late Modern Age*. Stanford University Press, 1991.

Gillham, Patrick, and Gary T. Marx. "Complexity and Irony in Policing and Protesting: The World Trade Organization Seattle." *Social Justice* 27, no. 2 (n.d.): 212–36.

Gillham, Patrick F., and John A. Noakes. ""More Than A March in a Circle": Transgressive Protests and the Limits of Negotiated Management." *Mobilization* 12, no. 4 (December 2007): 341—57.

Gilroy, Paul. *The Black Atlantic: Modernity and Double Consciousness.* Verso, 1993.

Gipfelsoli. "28.7.2007 Heiligendamm—Genua." July 28, 2007. http://gipfelsoli.org/ Repression/Heiligendamm_2007/Texte_davor/3843.html.

Giroux, Henry A.. "When Hope Is Subversive." *Tikkun*, 2004.

Glassner, Barry. *The Culture of Fear.* Basic Books, 2000.

Goldstein, Robert Justin. *Political Repression in Modern America.* Schenkman, 1978.

Goode, Erich. *Deviant Behavior.* Prentice-Hall, 1984.

Gordon, Avery F. *Ghostly Matters: Haunting and the Sociological Imagination.* University of Minnesota Press, 1997.

Gould, Deborah B. "Passionate Political Processes: Bringing Emotions Back into the Study of Social Movements." In *Rethinking Social Movements: Structure, Meaning, and Emotion* . Edited by Jeff Goodwin and James M. Jasper, 307. Rowman and Littlefield, 2003.

Graeber, David. "The New Anarchists." *New Left Review*, no. 13 (2002): 61–73.

Gramsci, Antonio. *Prison Notebooks.* International Publishers, 1929.

Greenpeace USA. "Bush vs. Greenpeace Overview." May 10, 2004. http://www.greenpeace.org/usa/news/bush-vs-greenpeace-overview.

Grossberg, Lawrence, Cary Nelson, and Paula Treichler. *Cultural Studies.* 1st ed. Routledge, 1991.

Habermas, Jürgen. *The Theory of Communicative Action.* Translated by Thomas McCarthy. Beacon Press, 1981.

Halbroth, Anneke. "Hätten sie das nicht woanders machen können?" April 20, 2007. http://www.stadtgespraeche-rostock.de/046/0229/.

Hambling, David. "U.S. Police Could Get 'Pain Beam' Weapons." *New Scientist*, December 24, 2008.

Hardt, Michael, and Antonio Negri. *Multitude: War and Democracy in the Age of Empire.* Penguin, 2004.

———. *Empire.* Harvard University Press, 2000.

Harvey, David. *Spaces of Capital: Towards a Critical Geography.* London: Routledge, 2001.

———. *Spaces of Hope.* University of California Press, 2000.

Herman, Edward S., and Noam Chomsky. Manufacturing Consent: The Political Economy of the Mass Media. Pantheon, 2002.

Heuser, Marius. "Germany: Huge Security Operation Exposed in Wake of G8 Summit." *World Socialist Web Site*, June 21, 2007. http://www.tni.org/detail_page. phtml?act_id=17014.

Hillyard, Paddy, Joe Sim, Steve Tombs, and Dave Whyte. "Leaving a 'Stain upon the Silence': Contemporary Criminology and the Politics of Dissent." *British Journal of Criminology* 44, no. 3 (May 2004): 369–90.

Horkheimer, Max, and Theodor W. Adorno. *Dialectic of Enlightenment: Philosophical Fragments.* Stanford University Press, 1944.

House of Commons. *G8: Gleneagles Summit Costs.* 2005. http://www.publications. parliament.uk/pa/ld200506/ldhansrd/vo050706/text/50706-03.htm.

Howie, Michael. "MoD Accuses Police of Keeping G8 Cash Needed for Front-line Troops." *NEWS.scotsman.com,* April 9, 2008. http://news.scotsman.com/uk/MoD-accuses-police-of-keeping.3960688.jp.

Hughes, John. "Life during Wartime." In *On Fire: The Battle of Genoa and the Anti-capitalist Movement,* 23–29. One-Off Press, 2001.

Jacobs, Bill, and Brian Ferguson. "Blair Refuses to Help Meet Cost of G8 Summit." *news.scotsman.com,* March 9, 2005. http://news.scotsman.com/edinburgh/Blair-refuses-to-help-meet.2609125.jp.

Jagose, Annamarie. *Queer Theory.* Otago University Press, 1997.

Janowitz, Morris. "Sociological Theory and Social Control." *American Journal of Sociology* 81, no. 1 (July 1975): 82–108.

Jasper, James M. *The Art of Moral Protest: Culture, Biography, and Creativity in Social Movements.* Chicago: University of Chicago Press, 1999.

Jazz. "Life during Wartime." In *On Fire: The Battle of Genoa and the Anti-capitalist Movement,* 80-99. One-Off Press, 2001.

Jhally, Sut. *Advertising and the End of the World.* Media Education Foundation, 1997. http://www.mediaed.org/

Johnston, Hank. "Talking the Walk: Speech Acts and Resistance in Authoritarian Regimes." In *Repression and Mobilization.* Edited by Christian Davenport, Hank Johnston, and Carol McClurg Mueller, 108–37. University of Minnesota Press, 2005.

Johnston, Hank, and Bert Klandermans, eds. *Social Movements and Culture.* London: Routledge, 1995.

Jordan, Tim, and Adam Lent. *Storming the Millennium: The New Politics of Change.* Lawrence and Wishart, 1999.

Juris, Jeffrey S. *Networking Futures: The Movement Against Corporate Globalization.* Duke University Press, 2008.

Katsiaficas, George. *The Subversion of Politics: European Autonomous Social Movements and the Decolonization of Everyday Life.* AK Press, 1997.

Khagram, Sanjeev, James V. Riker, and Kathryn Sikkink. *Restructuring World Politics: Transnational Social Movements, Networks, and Norms.* University of Minnesota Press, 2002.

Kilkenny, Allison. "Police Use Painful New Weapon on G20 Protesters." *AlterNet,* September 28, 2009. http://www.truthout.org/092909D.

King, Mike, and David Waddington. "The Policing of Transnational Protest in Canada." In *The Policing of Transnational Protest.* Edited by Donatella della Porta, Abby Peterson, and Herbert Reiter, 75–96. Ashgate, 2006.

Kirton, John, Jenilee Guebert, and Shamir Tanna. *G8 and G20 Summit Costs.* Unpublished report, G8-G20 Research Groups, Munk School for Global Affairs, University of Toronto, 2010. http://www.g8.utoronto.ca/evaluations/factsheet/factsheet_costs.html.

Klein, Naomi. "The Bonding Properties of Tear Gas." *Naomi Klein,* April 25, 2001. http://www.naomiklein.org/articles/2001/04/.

Kraska, Peter B. "Militarization and Policing—Its Relevance to 21st Century Police." *Policing* 1, no. 4 (2007): 501–13.

———. "Criminal Justice Theory: Toward Legitimacy and an Infrastructure." *Justice Quarterly* 23, no. 2 (2006): 167–85.

———. *Militarizing the American Criminal Justice System: The Changing Roles of the Armed Forces and the Police.* UPNE, 2001.

Kraska, Peter B., and Victor E. Kappeler. "Militarizing American Police: The Rise and Normalization of Paramilitary Units." *Social Problems* 44 (1997): 1.

Krotoszynski, Jr., Ronald J. "Dissent, Free Speech, and the Continuing Search for the 'Central Meaning' of the First Amendment." Review of *The Dissent of the Governed: A Meditation on Law, Religion, and Loyalty.* By Stephen L. Carter. Harvard University Press. 1998. *Dissent, Injustice, and the Meanings of America.* By Steven H. Shiffrin. Princeton University Press. 1999." *Michigan Law Review* 98, no. 6 (2000): 1613—77.

Kusper v. Pontikes, 414 U.S. 51, 56 (1973).

Laclau, Ernesto, and Chantal Mouffe. *Hegemony and Socialist Strategy: Towards a Radical Democratic Politics.* Verso, 1985.

Landtag Mecklenburg-Vorpommern. "Antwort der Landesregierung Mecklenburg-Vorpommern auf die Kleine Anfrage der Abgeordneten Birgit Schwebs, Fraktion Die Linke." *Drucksache* 5, no. 2411 (March 31, 2009).

———. "Antwort der Landesregierung auf die Kleine des Abgeordneten Udo Pastörs, Fraktion der NPD." *Drucksache* 5, no. 1811 (February 10, 2008).

———. "Antwort der Landesregierung auf die Große Anfrage der Fraktion der NPD." *Drucksache* 5, no. 1160 (December 20, 2007).

———. "Beschlussempfehlung und Bericht des Finanzausschusses (4. Ausschuss) zu dem Gesetzentwurf der Landesregierung." *Drucksache* 5, no. 100 (May 12, 2006).

Lefebvre, Henri. *The Production of Space.* Wiley-Blackwell, 1991.

Legault, Josee. "We Need a G20 Probe: Arrest Record Shows Police Were Out of Control in Toronto." *Gazette*, July 9, 2010.

Lianne, Elliott. "G20 Fake Lake Revealed." June 23, 2010.

Lichbach, Mark Irving. *The Rebel's Dilemma.* University of Michigan Press, 1995.

Lukács, György. *History and Class Consciousness.* Translated by Rodney Livingstone. Merlin Press, 1923.

MacLeod, Jay. *Ain't No Makin' It: Aspirations and Attainment in a Low-Income Neighborhood.* Westview Press, 1987.

Maeckelbergh, Marianne. *The Will of the Many: How the Alterglobalisation Movement Is Changing the Face of Democracy.* Pluto Press, 2009.

Mannheim, Karl, and Edward Shils. *Man and Society in an Age of Reconstruction: Studies in Modern Social Structure.* Routledge and Kegan Paul, 1949.

Marcuse, Herbert. "Repressive Tolerance." In *A Critique of Pure Tolerance.* Edited by Robert Paul Wolff, Berkeley Commune, and Herbert Marcuse. Beacon Press, 1965.

———. *One-Dimensional Man: Studies in the Ideology of Advanced Industrial Society.* Beacon Press, 1964.

Marsden, Paul. *What Price a Global Future?* 2001. http://globalization.icaap.org/content/v1.1/paulmarsden.html.

Marx, Gary T. "Under-The-Covers Undercover Investigations: Some Reflections on the State's Use of Sex and Deception in Law Enforcement." *Criminal Justice Ethics* 11, no. 1 (1992): 13–24.

———. *Undercover: Police Surveillance in America.* University of California Press, 1988.

———. "External Efforts to Damage or Facilitate Social Movements." In *The Dynamics of Social Movements: Resource Mobilization, Social Control, and Tactics.* Edited by Mayer N. Zald and John David McCarthy, 94–125. Frontiers of Sociology Symposium, Vanderbilt University. University Press of America, 1979.

———. "Thoughts on a Neglected Category of Social Movement Participant: The Agent Provocateur and the Informant." *American Journal of Sociology* 80, no. 2 (September 1974): 402–42.

———. "Civil Disorders and the Agents of Social Control." *Journal of Social Issues* 26, no. 1 (winter 1970): 19–57.

Massey, Doreen B. "Politics and Space/Time." *New Left Review*, no. 196 (1992): 65–84.

Mathur, K.M. *Challenges to Police, Human Rights and National Security.* Gyan Books, 2003.

McCarthy, John D., and Mayer N. Zald. "Resource Mobilization and Social Movements: A Partial Theory." *American Journal of Sociology* 82, no. 6 (May 1977): 1212–41.

McChesney, Robert W. *The Problem of the Media: U.S. Communication Politics in the Twenty-First Century.* Monthly Review Press, 2004.

McDonald, Kevin. "From Solidarity to Fluidarity: Social Movements beyond 'Collective Identity'—The Case of Globalization Conflicts." *Social Movement Studies: Journal of Social, Cultural and Political Protest* 1, no. 2 (2002): 109.

McKay, George. *DiY Culture: Party and Protest in Nineties Britain.* Verso, 1998.

Mead, George Herbert. "The Genesis of the Self and Social Control." *International Journal of Ethics* 35, no. 3 (April 1925): 251–77.

Media G8way Gipfelsoli Infogroup. "G8 Genoa: Police Receive Low Sentences." *Gipfelsoli*, July 15, 2008. http://gipfelsoli.org/Home/Genua_2001/Genoa_2001_english/5384.html.

———. "G8 Genoa: State Prosecution Demands 225 Years of Jail Sentences." *Gipfelsoli*, October 29, 2007. https://gipfelsoli.org/Home/Heiligendamm_2007/MediaG-8way_Heiligendamm/english/4366.html.

Meier, Robert F., and Weldon T. Johnson. "Deterrence as Social Control: The Legal and Extralegal Production of Conformity." *American Sociological Review* 42, no. 2 (April 1977): 292–304.

Melucci, Alberto. *Challenging Codes: Collective Action in the Information Age.* Cambridge University Press, 1996.

———. *Nomads of the Present: Social Movements and Individual Needs in Contemporary Society.* Hutchinson, 1989.

Metzger, Wolfram. "Repression in Germany: Editor of Venezuelan Book Incarcerated for Terrorism." *www.venezuelanalaysis.com*, November 17, 2007. http://einstellung.s036.net/en/ps/630.

Meyer, David S., and Debra C. Minkoff. "Conceptualizing Political Opportunity." *Social Forces* 82, no. 4 (June 2004): 1457–92.

Micheletti, Michele. *Political Virtue and Shopping: Individuals, Consumerism, and Collective Action.* Palgrave Macmillan, 2003.

Moore, Barrington. "Reflections on Conformity in Industrial Society." In *Political Power and Social Theory.* Harvard University Press, n.d.

Muñoz, Carlos. *Youth, Identity, Power: The Chicano Movement.* Verso, 1989.

"Nach Krawallen beruhigt sich Lage in Genf - hohe Sachschäden," February 6, 2003. http://www.nadir.org/nadir/initiativ/agp/free/evian/2003/0602nachkrawallen.htm.

New York Civil Liberties Union. *Rights and Wrongs at the RNC: A Special Report about Police and Protest at the Republican National Convention.* New York Civil Liberties Union, 2005. www.nyclu.org/pdfs/rnc_report_083005.pdf.

New York Civil Liberties Union/ACLU. "Police Trampled Civil Rights during Republican National Convention, NYCLU Charges," October 7, 2004. http://www.aclu.org/free-speech/police-trampled-civil-rights-during-republican-national-convention-nyclu-charges.

Noakes, John, and Patrick F. Gillham. "Aspects of the 'New Penology' in the Police Response to Major Political Protests in the United States, 1999–2000." In *The Policing of Transnational Protest.* Edited by Donatella della Porta, Abby Peterson, and Herbert Reiter, 97–116. Ashgate, 2006.

Notes from Nowhere. *We Are Everywhere: The Irresistible Rise of Global Anticapitalism.* Verso, 2003.

Offe, Claus. "New Social Movements: Challenging the Boundaries of Institutional Politics." *Social Research* 52, no. 4 (1985): 817–58.

Office of the Parliamentary Budget Officer. *Assessment of Planned Security Costs for the 2010 G8 and G20 Summits.* Ottawa, Canada, June 23, 2010. http://www2.parl.gc.ca/sites/pbo-dpb/documents/SummitSecurity.pdf.

Oliver, Pamela. "Repression and Crime Control: Why Social Movements Scholars Should Pay Attention to Mass Incarceration as a Form of Repression." *Mobilization* 13, no. 1 (February 2008).

———. "How Does Repression Work?" 2002. http://www.ssc.wisc.edu/~oliver/PROTESTS/PROTESTS.HTM.

Oliver, Pamela E., and Hank Johnston. "What a Good Idea! Ideologies and Frames in Social Movement Research." *Mobilization* 5, no. 1 (2000): 37–54.

Opp, Karl-Dieter, and Wolfgang Roehl. "Repression, Micromobilization, and Political Protest." *Social Forces* 69, no. 2 (December 1990): 521–47.

Parenti, Michael. *Inventing Reality.* Palgrave Macmillan, 1986.

Pearson, Cliff. "Released Dallas Activist Recounts Jail Abuses." *Philadelphia Independent Media Center,* August 4, 2000. http://www.phillyimc.org/en/node/33582.

Peterson, Abby. "Policing Contentious Politics at Transnational Summits: Darth Vader or the Keystone Cops?" In *The Policing of Transnational Protest.* Edited by Donatella della Porta, Abby Peterson, and Herbert Reiter, 43–74. Ashgate, 2006.

Pilkington, Ed. "New York Man Accused of Using Twitter to Direct Protesters during G20 Summit." *The Guardian,* October 4, 2009. http://www.guardian.co.uk/world/2009/oct/04/man-arrested-twitter-g20-us.

Piven, Frances Fox. *Challenging Authority: How Ordinary People Change America.* Rowman and Littlefield, 2006.

Piven, Frances Fox, and Richard A. Cloward. *Poor People's Movements: Why They Succeed, How They Fail.* Vintage, 1977.

Pizzorno, Alessandro. "Political Exchange and Collective Identity in Industrial Conflict." In *The Resurgence of Class Conflict in Western Europe since 1968*. Edited by Colin Crouch and Alessandro Pizzorno, 2: 277–98. Macmillan, n.d.

Poe, Drew. "Pier 57: The LMDC / RNC Connection." *nyc.indymedia.org*, November 17, 2004. http://nyc.indymedia.org/feature/display/132549/index.php.

Poldervaart, Saskia. *The Utopian Politics of Feminist Alterglobalisation Groups: The Importance of Everyday Life—Politics and Personal Change for Utopian Practices*. Amsterdam School for Social Science Research, January 2006. http://www2.fmg.uva.nl/assr/workingpapers/.

Polletta, Francesca. *Freedom Is an Endless Meeting: Democracy in American Social Movements*. University of Chicago Press, 2002.

———. "Culture and Its Discontents: Recent Theorizing on the Cultural Dimensions of Protest." *Sociological Inquiry* 67, no. 4 (fall 1997): 431–50.

Porter, Adam. "It Was Like This Before . . . 75–79." In *On Fire: The Battle of Genoa and the Anti-capitalist Movement*, 75–79. One-Off Press, 2001.

Poulantzas, Nicos Ar. *Political Power and Social Classes*. Humanities Press, 1973.

Powers, Richard Gid. *Secrecy and Power: Life of J.Edgar Hoover*. Free Press, 1987.

"Private Security Firm Hired for G8/G20 Summits." *Ottowa Citizen*, May 31, 2010. http://www.ottawacitizen.com/news/Private+security+firm+hired+summ its/3093558/story.html.

Quinney, Richard. *Critique of Legal Order: Crime Control in Capitalist Society*. Transaction, 1974.

Rancière, Jacques. *Hatred of Democracy*. Verso, 2006.

Rebick, Judy. "It Won't End in Québec City." *rabble.ca*, April 26, 2001. http://www.rabble.ca/columnists/it-wont-end-Québec-city.

———. "Policing the People in Québec." *rabble.ca*, April 22, 2001. http://www.rabble.ca/news/policing-people-Québec.

Rhodes, Mike. "Local Law Enforcement Violates the State Constitution." *Indybay.org*, April 6, 2005. http://www.indybay.org/newsitems/2005/04/06/17317531.php.

Sarin. "Bodyhammer: Tactics and Self-defence for the Modern Protester." http://www.wombles.org.uk/article2008041819.php, n.d .

Scholl, Christian. "Desiring Disruption. The Two Sides of a Barricade during Summit Protests in Europe." Ph.D. dissertation, University of Amsterdam.

Schultz, Bud, and Ruth Schultz. *The Price of Dissent: Testimonies to Political Repression in America*. University of California Press, 2001.

———. *It Did Happen Here: Recollections of Political Repression in America*. University of California Press, 1989.

Schwartz, David C. *Political Alienation and Political Behavior*. Aldine Transaction, 1973.

Schwartz, Noaki, and Trenton Daniel. "Lawsuit on Strip Searches Settled." *Miami Herald*, April 18, 2005. http://www.brennancenter.org/content/elert/lawsuit_on_strip_searches_settled/.

Scott, James C. *Domination and the Arts of Resistance: Hidden Transcripts*. Yale University Press, 1990.

Shils, Edward. "The Theory of Mass Society." *Diogenes*, no. 39 (1962): 45–66.

Snow, David A., E. Burke Rochford Jr., Steven K. Worden, and Robert D. Benford. "Frame Alignment Processes, Micromobilization, and Movement Participation." *American Sociological Review* 51, no. 4 (August 1986): 464–81.

Soja, Edward W. *Seeking Spatial Justice.* University of Minnesota Press, 2010.

Starr, Amory. *Naming the Enemy: Anti-Corporate Movements Confront Globalization.* Zed Books, London, 2000.

———. Global Revolt: *A Guide to Alterglobalization.* Zed Books, London, 2005.

Starr, Amory, Luis Fernandez, Randall Amster, Lesley Wood, and Manuel Caro. "The Impacts of State Surveillance on Political Assembly and Association: A Socio-Legal Analysis." *Qualitative Sociology* 31, no. 3 (2008): 251–70.

Starr, Erin. "Little Guantanamo and the Republican Convention." 2004. http://www.mail-archive.com/laamn@yahoogroups.com/msg00022.html.

States News Service. "Public Announcement by the U.S. Department of State: G8 Summit in Alberta Creates Potential for Disruptions." June 17, 2002.

Stauber, John Clyde, and Sheldon Rampton. *Toxic Sludge Is Good for You.* Common Courage Press, 1995.

Steller, Chris. "Minnesota Independent: News. Politics. Media. Judge to RNC8: See You Next Year." *Minnesota Independent*, December 17, 2008. http://minnesotaindependent.com/20527/judge-to-rnc8-see-you-next-year.

Stumberger, Rudolf. "Molli, Macht und Meer: Der G8-Gipfel als Höhepunkt von Politik-Inszenierung." *Telepolis*, May 26, 2007. http://www.heise.de/tp/r4/artikel/25/25332/1.html.

Stephen C. Craig, and Michael A. Maggiotto. "Political Discontent and Political Action." *Journal of Politics* 43, no. 2 (May 1981): 514–22.

Sunstein, Cass R. *Why Societies Need Dissent.* Harvard University Press, 2003.

supportolegale. "In Any Case, No Regret.." Press release, 2007. http://www.supporto-legale.org/?q=node/1271.

Tarrow, Sidney. *Power in Movement: Social Movements and Contentious Politics.* Cambridge University Press, 1998.

Thoreau, Henry David. *The Variorum Civil Disobedience (Resistance to Civil Government).* Twayne, 1849.

Tilly, Charles. "Contention over Space And Place." *Mobilization* 8, no. 2 (June 2003): 221–25.

———. *From Mobilization to Revolution.* McGraw-Hill, 1978.

T'Okup. "Nstlegate ist Kein inzelfall: Eine Weitere securitas-angestellte als spitze-lin entlarvt!" Lausanne, 2008. http://ch.indymedia.org/media/2008/09//62886.pdf.

Touraine, Alain. *The Voice and the Eye: An Analysis of Social Movements.* Cambridge University Press, 1981.

Trott, Ben. "Gleneagles, Activism and Ordinary Rebelliousness." In *Shut Them Down! The G8, Gleneagles 2005 and the Movement of Movements.* Edited by David Harvie, Keir Milburn, Ben Trott, and David Watts. Dissent! and Autonomedia, 2005. http://shutthemdown.org/details.html.

Turner, Bryan S. "The Erosion of Citizenship." *British Journal of Sociology* 52, no. 2 (June 2001): 189–209.

U.S. Department of Justice, Office of Justice Programs, National Institute of Justice. "The Effectiveness and Safety of Pepper Spray (Research for Practice)," April 2003. http://74.125.95.132/search?q=cache:rm5xsZVHst4J:www.ncjrs.gov/pdffiles1/nij/195739.pdf+safety+of+pepper+spray&hl=en&ct=clnk&cd=1&gl=us&client=firefox-a.

Vallis, Mary. "G20: Security Cameras Installed on Nearly Every Corner of Downtown Toronto." *National Post*, June 3, 2010. http://news.nationalpost.com/2010/06/03/g20-security-cameras-installed-on-nearly-every-corner-of-downtown-toronto/#ixzzotgTRNfLa.

Vincent, George. "The Province of Sociology." *American Journal of Sociology* (January 1896): 488.

Von Manuela Pfohl. "G8-Gipfel-Bilanz: Meck-Pom muss für Gipfelschäden zahlen." *STERN.DE*, August 28, 2007. http://www.stern.de/politik/deutschland/g8-gipfel-bilanz-meck-pom-muss-fuer-gipfelschaeden-zahlen-596306.html.

Waddington, David P. *Contemporary Issues in Public Disorder*. Routledge, 1992.

Waddington, David P., Karen Jones, and C. Critcher. *Flashpoints: Studies in Public Disorder*. Routledge, 1989.

Waddington, P. A. J. "Policing Public Order and Political Contention." In P. A. J. Waddington, "Policing Public Order and Political Contention," in *A Handbook of Policing* . Edited by Tim Newburn, 928. Willan, 2003.

———. *Policing Citizens: Authority and Rights*. Routledge, 1999.

Walton, John, and David Seddon. *Free Markets and Food Riots: The Politics of Global Adjustment*. Blackwell, 1994.

Washington, DC, City Council. "First Amendment Rights and Police Standards Act of 2004, Bill 15-968," 2004. http://dcwatch.com/archives/council15/15-968.htm.

Weber, Max. "The Types of Legitimate Authority." In *Economy and Society: An Outline of Interpretive Sociology*, 2. University of California Press, 1925.

Weissman, Robert. "First Amendment Follies: Expanding Corporate Speech Rights." *Multinational Monitor*, May 1998. http://www.multinationalmonitor.org/mm1998/051998/weissman.html.

White, Robert W. "From Peaceful Protest to Guerrilla War: Micromobilization of the Provisional Irish Republican Army." *American Journal of Sociology* 94, no. 6 (May 1989): 1277–1302.

Willis, Paul E. *Learning to Labor: How Working Class Kids Get Working Class Jobs*. Columbia University Press, 1981.

Wilson, John. "Social Protest and Social Control." *Social Problems* 24, no. 4 (April 1977): 469–81.

Zald, Mayer N., and Roberta Ash. "Social Movement Organizations: Growth, Decay and Change." *Social Forces* 44, no. 3 (1966): 327–41.

Zwerman, Gilda, and Patricia Steinhoff. "When Activists Ask for Trouble: and the New Left Cycle of Resistance in the United States and Japan." In *Repression and Mobilization*. Edited by Christian Davenport, Hank Johnston, and Carol McClurg Mueller, 85–107. University of Minnesota Press, 2005.

Zwerman, Gilda, Patricia Steinhoff, and Donatella della Porta. "Disappearing Social Movements: Clandestinity in the Cycle of New Left Protest in the U.S., Japan, Germany, and Italy." *Mobilization* 5, no. 1 (2000): 85–104.

Index

About the Authors

AMORY STARR is the author of many books, including *Naming the Enemy: Anti-Corporate Movements Confront Globalization* and *Global Revolt: A Guide to Alterglobalization*. She holds a Ph.D. from the University of California, Santa Barbara.

LUIS FERNANDEZ is Assistant Professor in the Department of Criminology and Criminal Justice at Northern Arizona University and the author of *Policing Dissent: Social Control and the Anti-Globalization Movement*.

CHRISTIAN SCHOLL is Lecturer of Political Science at the University of Amsterdam.